FoxTrot Sundaes

Other *FoxTrot* Books by Bill Amend

FoxTrot • Pass the Loot • Black Bart Says Draw • Eight Yards, Down and Out
Bury My Heart at Fun-Fun Mountain • Say Hello to Cactus Flats • May the Force Be with Us, Please
Take Us to Your Mall • The Return of the Lone Iguana • At Least This Place Sells T-Shirts
Come Closer, Roger, There's a Mosquito on Your Nose • Welcome to Jasorassic Park
I'm Flying, Jack . . . I Mean, Roger • Think iFruity • Death by Field Trip
Encyclopedias Brown and White • His Code Name Was The Fox
Your Momma Thinks Square Roots Are Vegetables • Who's Up for Some Bonding?
Am I a Mutant or What! • Orlando Bloom Has Ruined Everything
My Hot Dog Went Out, Can I Have Another? • How Come I'm Always Luigi?
Houston, You Have a Problem • And When She Opened the Closet, All the Clothes Were Polyester
Math, Science, and Unix Underpants

Anthologies

FoxTrot: The Works • FoxTrot *en masse* • Enormously FoxTrot • Wildly FoxTrot
FoxTrot Beyond a Doubt • Camp FoxTrot • Assorted FoxTrot • FoxTrot: Assembled with Care
FoxTrotius Maximus • Jam-Packed FoxTrot • Wrapped-Up FoxTrot

FoxTrot Sundaes

**A FoxTrot Collection
by Bill Amend**

**Andrews McMeel
Publishing, LLC**

Kansas City • Sydney • London

FoxTrot is distributed internationally by Universal Uclick.

FoxTrot Sundaes © 2010 by Bill Amend. All rights reserved. Printed in the United States of America. No part of this book may be used or reproduced in any manner whatsoever without written permission except in the case of reprints in the context of reviews. For information, write Andrews McMeel Publishing, LLC, an Andrews McMeel Universal company, 1130 Walnut Street, Kansas City, Missouri 64106.

10 11 12 13 14 BAM 10 9 8 7 6 5 4 3 2 1

ISBN-13: 978-0-7407-9557-2
ISBN-10: 0-7407-9557-0

Library of Congress Control Number: 2009940858

www.andrewsmcmeel.com
www.foxtrot.com

ATTENTION: SCHOOLS AND BUSINESSES

Andrews McMeel books are available at quantity discounts with bulk purchase for educational, business, or sales promotional use. For information, please write to: Special Sales Department, Andrews McMeel Publishing, LLC, 1130 Walnut Street, Kansas City, Missouri 64106.

To K, M, and W

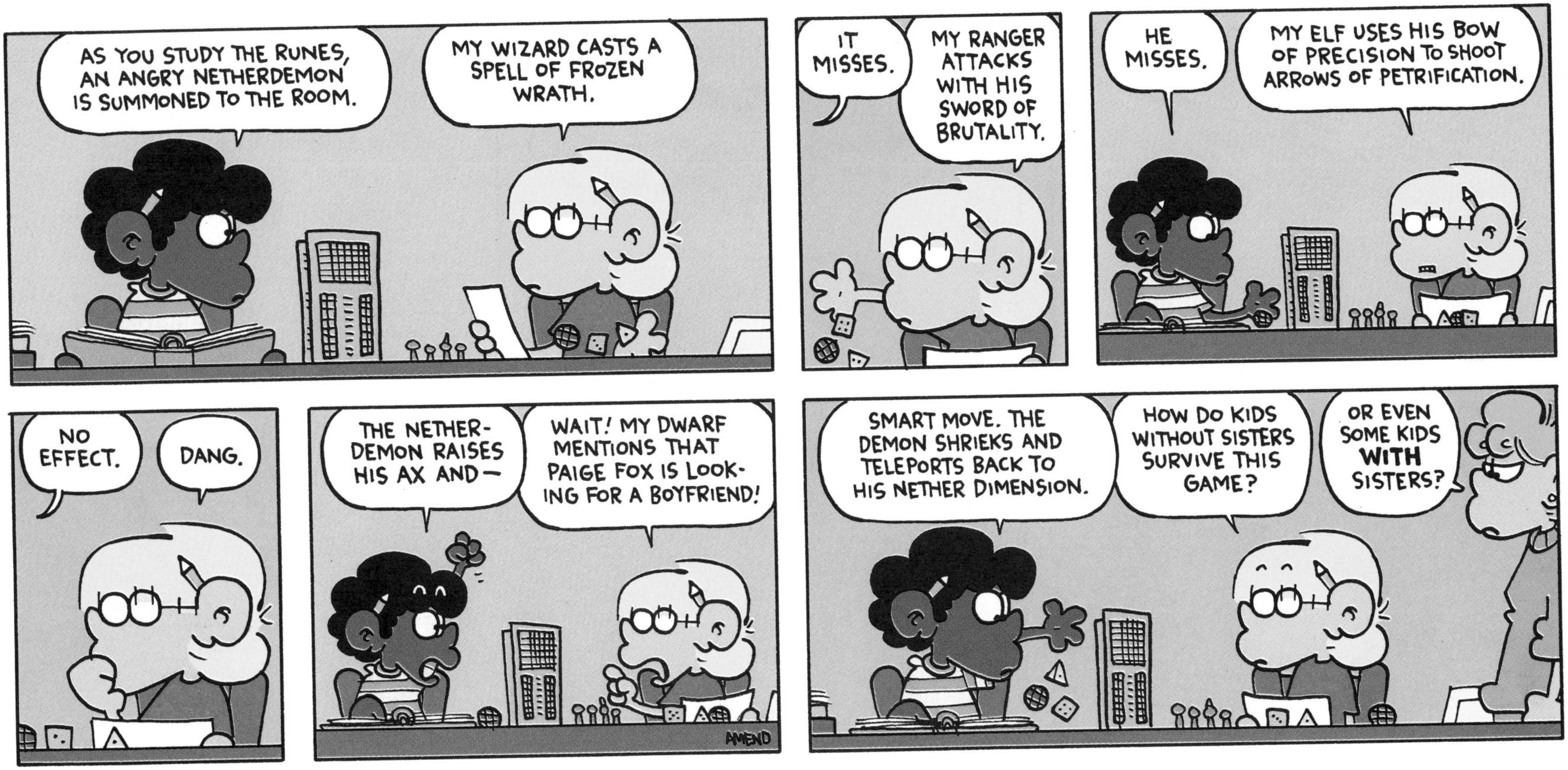
AS YOU STUDY THE RUNES, AN ANGRY NETHERDEMON IS SUMMONED TO THE ROOM.
MY WIZARD CASTS A SPELL OF FROZEN WRATH.
IT MISSES.
MY RANGER ATTACKS WITH HIS SWORD OF BRUTALITY.
HE MISSES.
MY ELF USES HIS BOW OF PRECISION TO SHOOT ARROWS OF PETRIFICATION.
NO EFFECT.
DANG.
THE NETHER-DEMON RAISES HIS AX AND—
WAIT! MY DWARF MENTIONS THAT PAIGE FOX IS LOOK-ING FOR A BOYFRIEND!
AMEND
SMART MOVE. THE DEMON SHRIEKS AND TELEPORTS BACK TO HIS NETHER DIMENSION.
HOW DO KIDS WITHOUT SISTERS SURVIVE THIS GAME?
OR EVEN SOME KIDS **WITH** SISTERS?

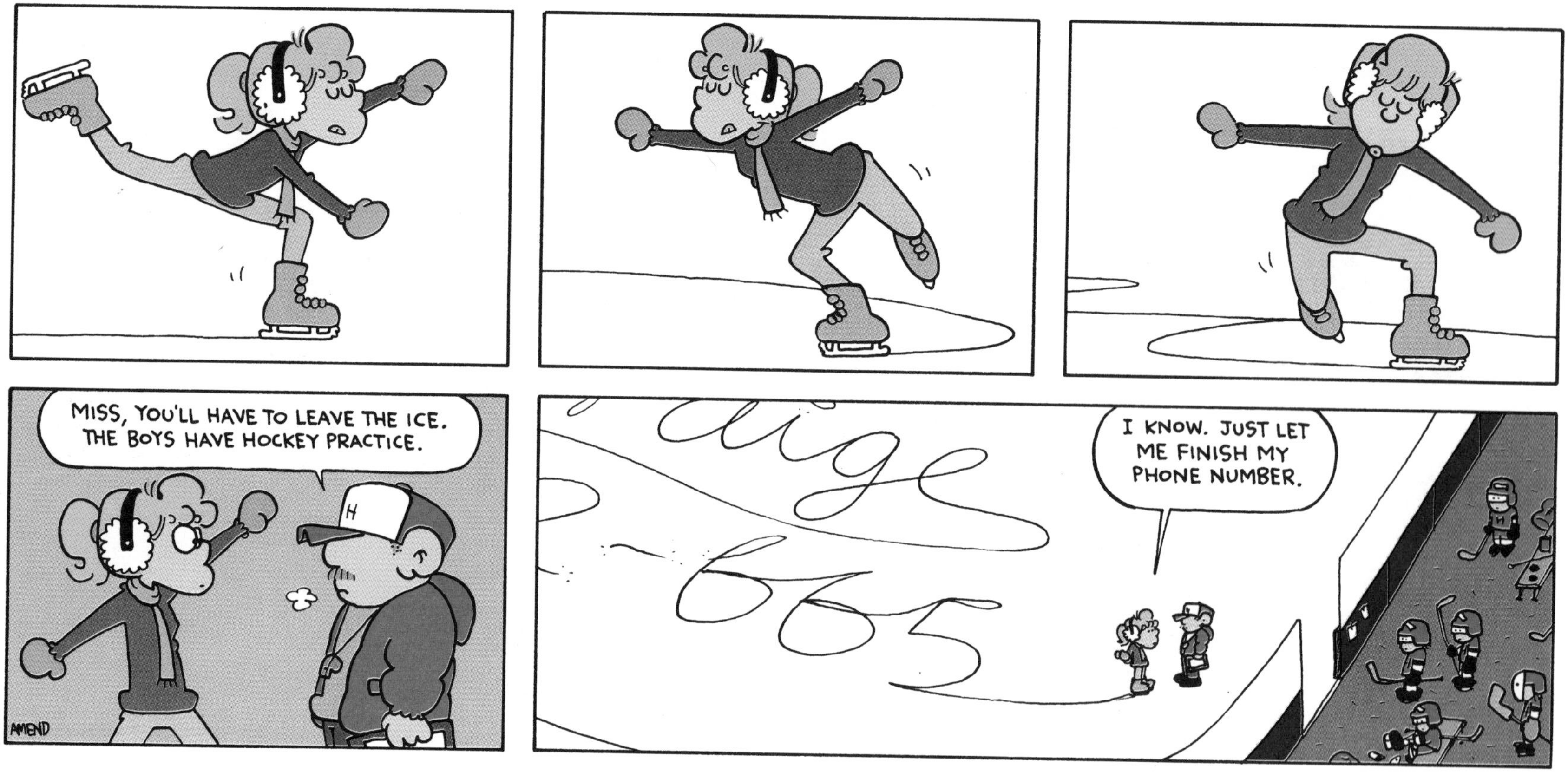
MISS, YOU'LL HAVE TO LEAVE THE ICE. THE BOYS HAVE HOCKEY PRACTICE.
AMEND
I KNOW. JUST LET ME FINISH MY PHONE NUMBER.

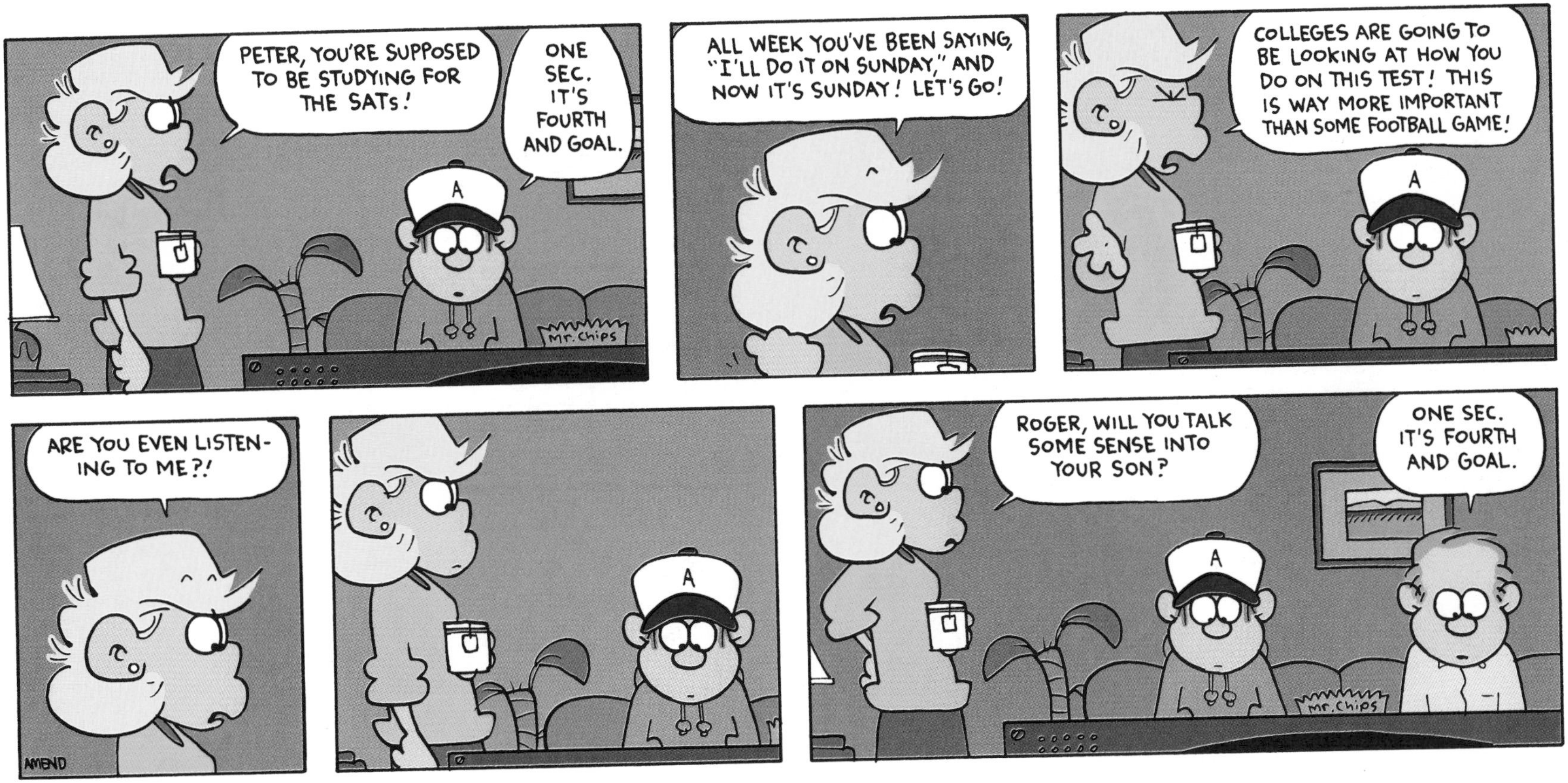
PETER, YOU'RE SUPPOSED TO BE STUDYING FOR THE SATs!
ONE SEC. IT'S FOURTH AND GOAL.
Mr. Chips
ALL WEEK YOU'VE BEEN SAYING, "I'LL DO IT ON SUNDAY," AND NOW IT'S SUNDAY! LET'S GO!
COLLEGES ARE GOING TO BE LOOKING AT HOW YOU DO ON THIS TEST! THIS IS WAY MORE IMPORTANT THAN SOME FOOTBALL GAME!
ARE YOU EVEN LISTEN-ING TO ME?!
AMEND
ROGER, WILL YOU TALK SOME SENSE INTO YOUR SON?
ONE SEC. IT'S FOURTH AND GOAL.
Mr. Chips

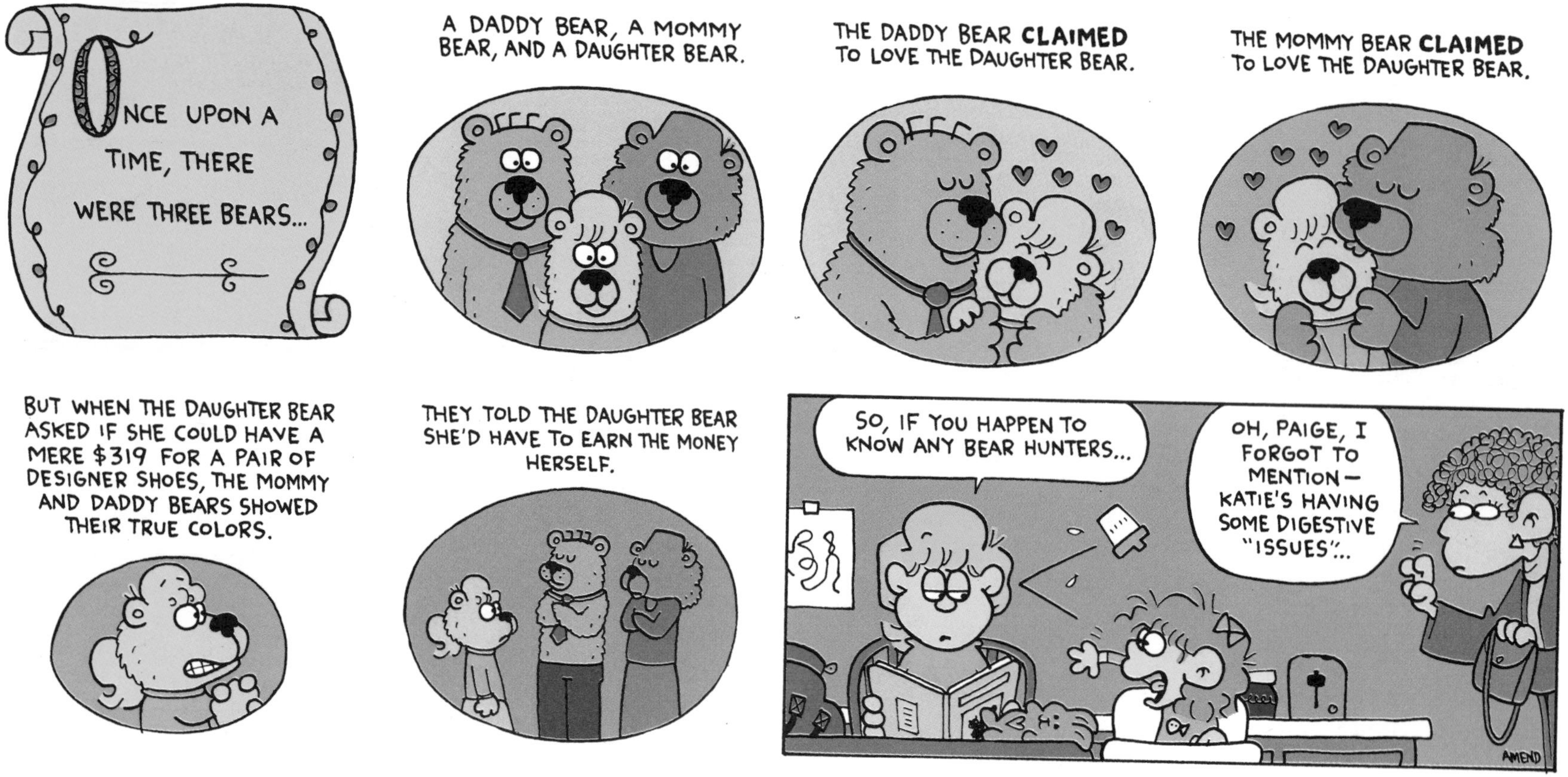
ONCE UPON A TIME, THERE WERE THREE BEARS...
A DADDY BEAR, A MOMMY BEAR, AND A DAUGHTER BEAR.
THE DADDY BEAR **CLAIMED** TO LOVE THE DAUGHTER BEAR.
THE MOMMY BEAR **CLAIMED** TO LOVE THE DAUGHTER BEAR.
BUT WHEN THE DAUGHTER BEAR ASKED IF SHE COULD HAVE A MERE $319 FOR A PAIR OF DESIGNER SHOES, THE MOMMY AND DADDY BEARS SHOWED THEIR TRUE COLORS.
THEY TOLD THE DAUGHTER BEAR SHE'D HAVE TO EARN THE MONEY HERSELF.
SO, IF YOU HAPPEN TO KNOW ANY BEAR HUNTERS...
OH, PAIGE, I FORGOT TO MENTION— KATIE'S HAVING SOME DIGESTIVE "ISSUES"...
AMEND

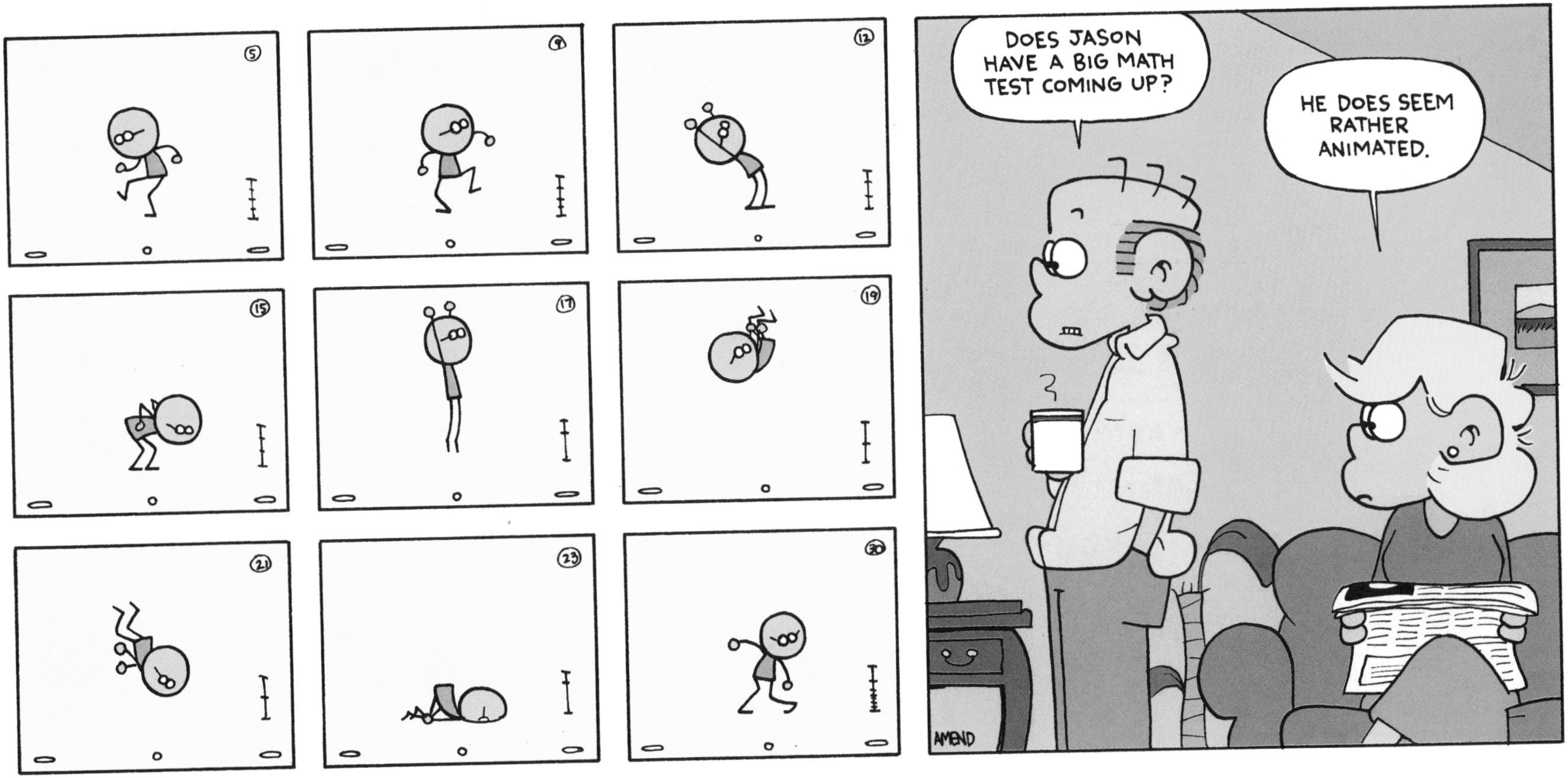
5
9
12
15
17
19
21
23
30
DOES JASON HAVE A BIG MATH TEST COMING UP?
HE DOES SEEM RATHER ANIMATED.
AMEND

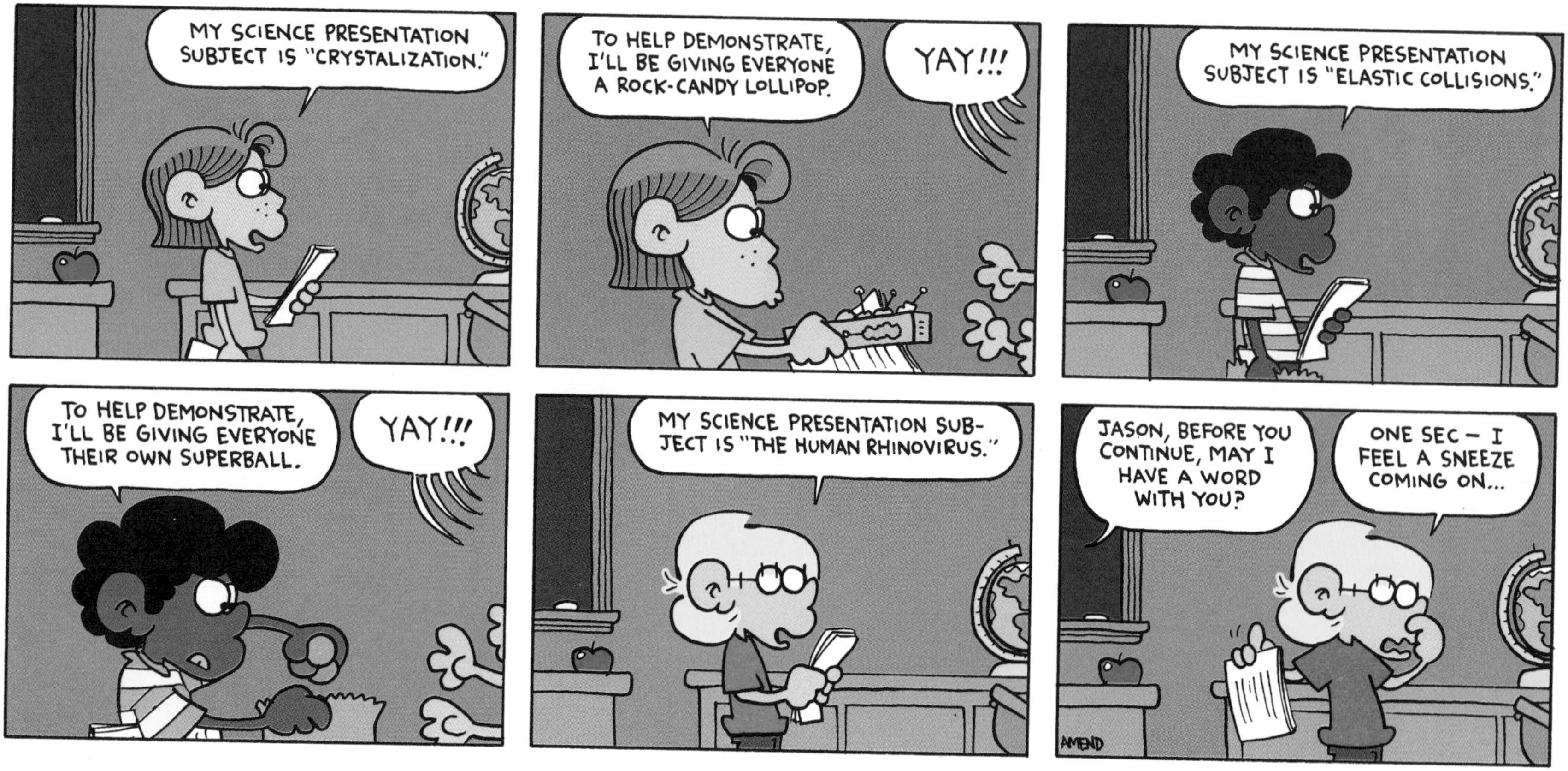

MY SCIENCE PRESENTATION SUBJECT IS "CRYSTALIZATION."
TO HELP DEMONSTRATE, I'LL BE GIVING EVERYONE A ROCK-CANDY LOLLIPOP.
YAY!!!
MY SCIENCE PRESENTATION SUBJECT IS "ELASTIC COLLISIONS."
TO HELP DEMONSTRATE, I'LL BE GIVING EVERYONE THEIR OWN SUPERBALL.
YAY!!!
MY SCIENCE PRESENTATION SUB-JECT IS "THE HUMAN RHINOVIRUS."
JASON, BEFORE YOU CONTINUE, MAY I HAVE A WORD WITH YOU?
ONE SEC – I FEEL A SNEEZE COMING ON...
AMEND

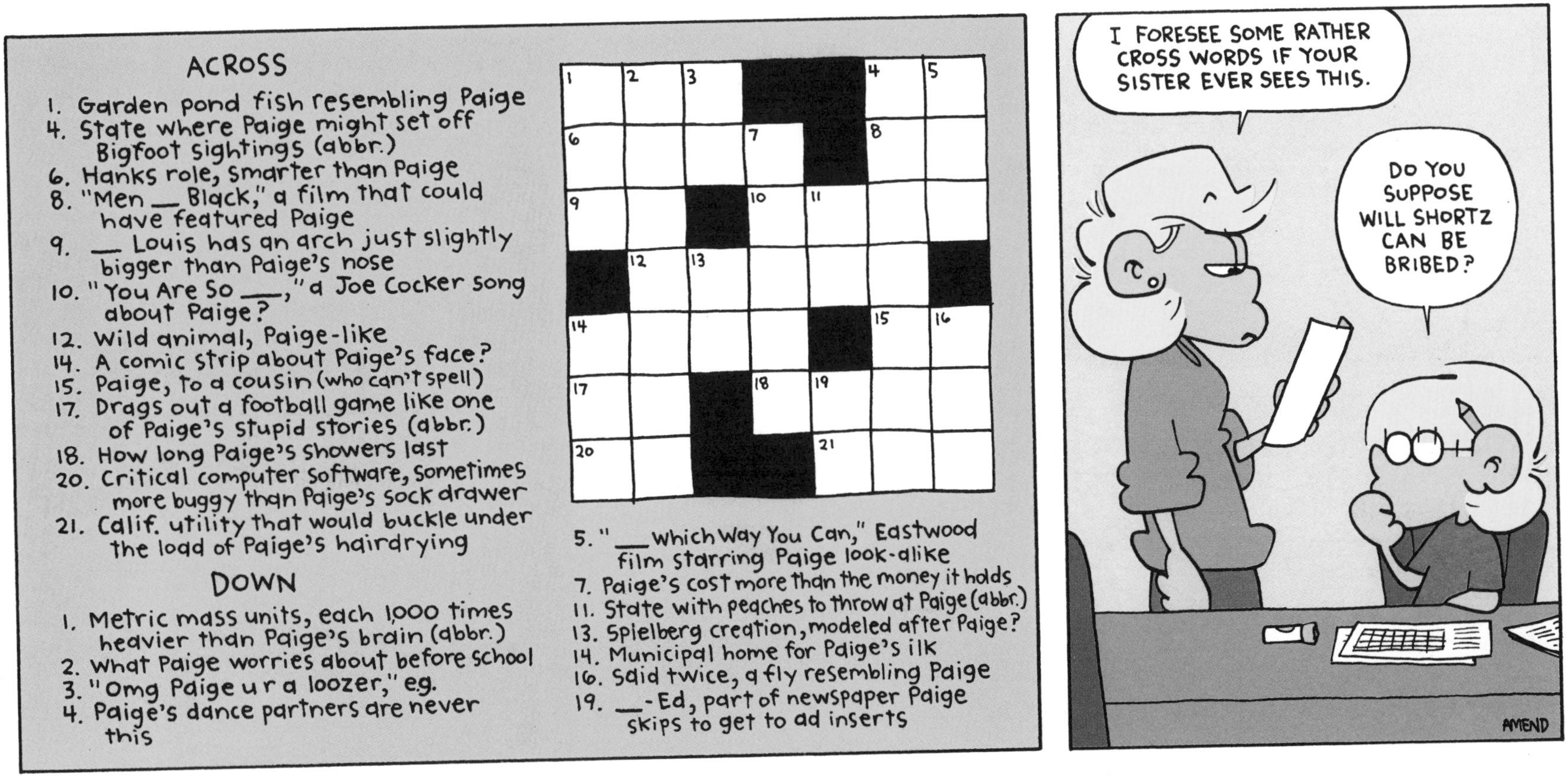
ACROSS
1. Garden pond fish resembling Paige
4. State where Paige might set off Bigfoot sightings (abbr.)
6. Hanks role, smarter than Paige
8. "Men __ Black," a film that could have featured Paige
9. __ Louis has an arch just slightly bigger than Paige's nose
10. "You Are So __," a Joe Cocker song about Paige?
12. Wild animal, Paige-like
14. A comic strip about Paige's face?
15. Paige, to a cousin (who can't spell)
17. Drags out a football game like one of Paige's stupid stories (abbr.)
18. How long Paige's showers last
20. Critical computer software, sometimes more buggy than Paige's sock drawer
21. Calif. utility that would buckle under the load of Paige's hairdrying
DOWN
1. Metric mass units, each 1,000 times heavier than Paige's brain (abbr.)
2. What Paige worries about before school
3. "Omg Paige u r a loozer," e.g.
4. Paige's dance partners are never this
5. "__ Which Way You Can," Eastwood film starring Paige look-alike
7. Paige's cost more than the money it holds
11. State with peaches to throw at Paige (abbr.)
13. Spielberg creation, modeled after Paige?
14. Municipal home for Paige's ilk
16. Said twice, a fly resembling Paige
19. __-Ed, part of newspaper Paige skips to get to ad inserts
1 2 3 4 5 6 7 8 9 10 11 12 13 14 15 16 17 18 19 20 21
I FORESEE SOME RATHER CROSS WORDS IF YOUR SISTER EVER SEES THIS.
DO YOU SUPPOSE WILL SHORTZ CAN BE BRIBED?
AMEND

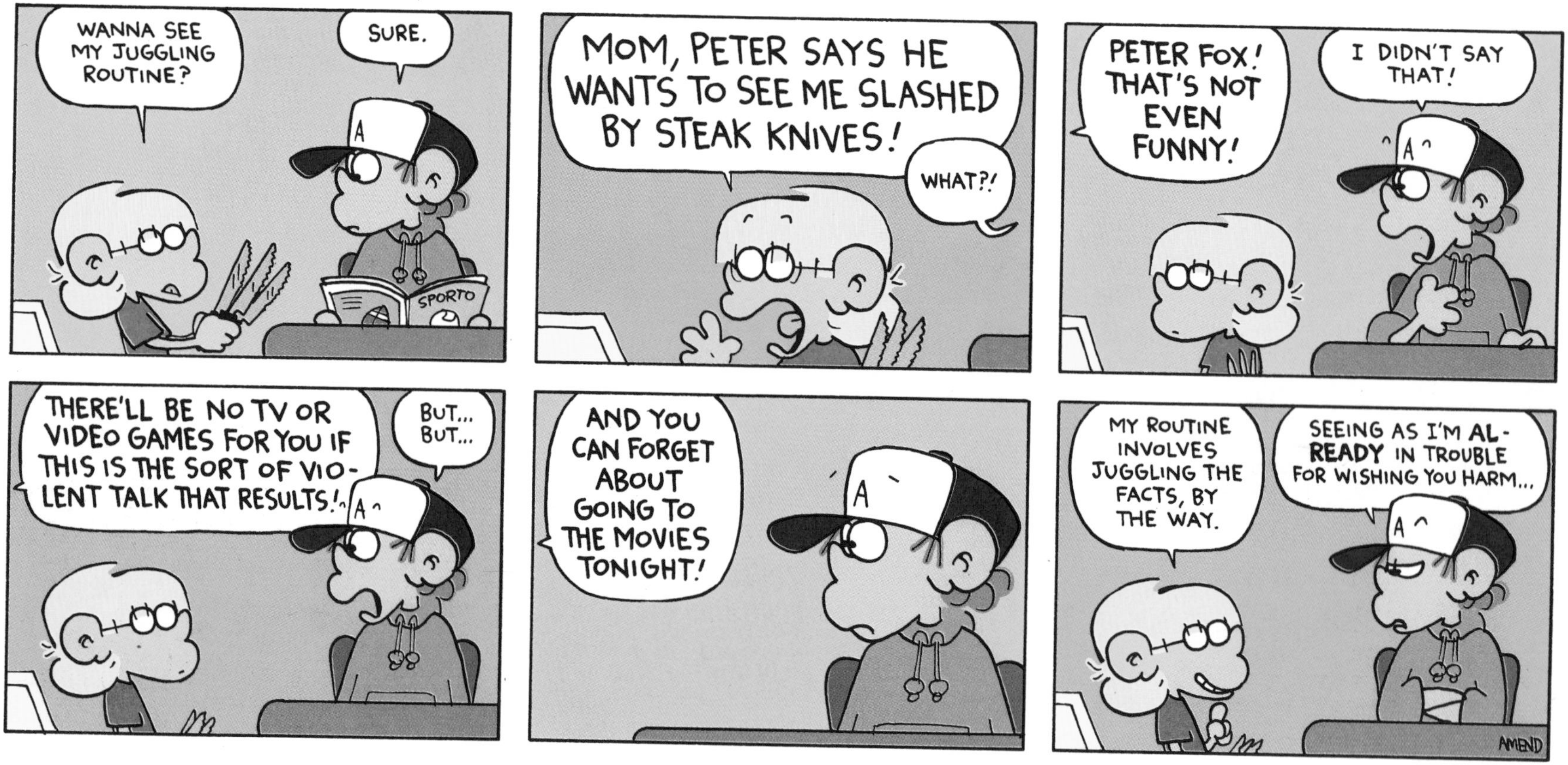
WANNA SEE MY JUGGLING ROUTINE?
SURE.
SPORTO
MOM, PETER SAYS HE WANTS TO SEE ME SLASHED BY STEAK KNIVES!
WHAT?!
PETER FOX! THAT'S NOT EVEN FUNNY!
I DIDN'T SAY THAT!
THERE'LL BE NO TV OR VIDEO GAMES FOR YOU IF THIS IS THE SORT OF VIO-LENT TALK THAT RESULTS!
BUT... BUT...
AND YOU CAN FORGET ABOUT GOING TO THE MOVIES TONIGHT!
MY ROUTINE INVOLVES JUGGLING THE FACTS, BY THE WAY.
SEEING AS I'M **AL-READY** IN TROUBLE FOR WISHING YOU HARM...
AMEND

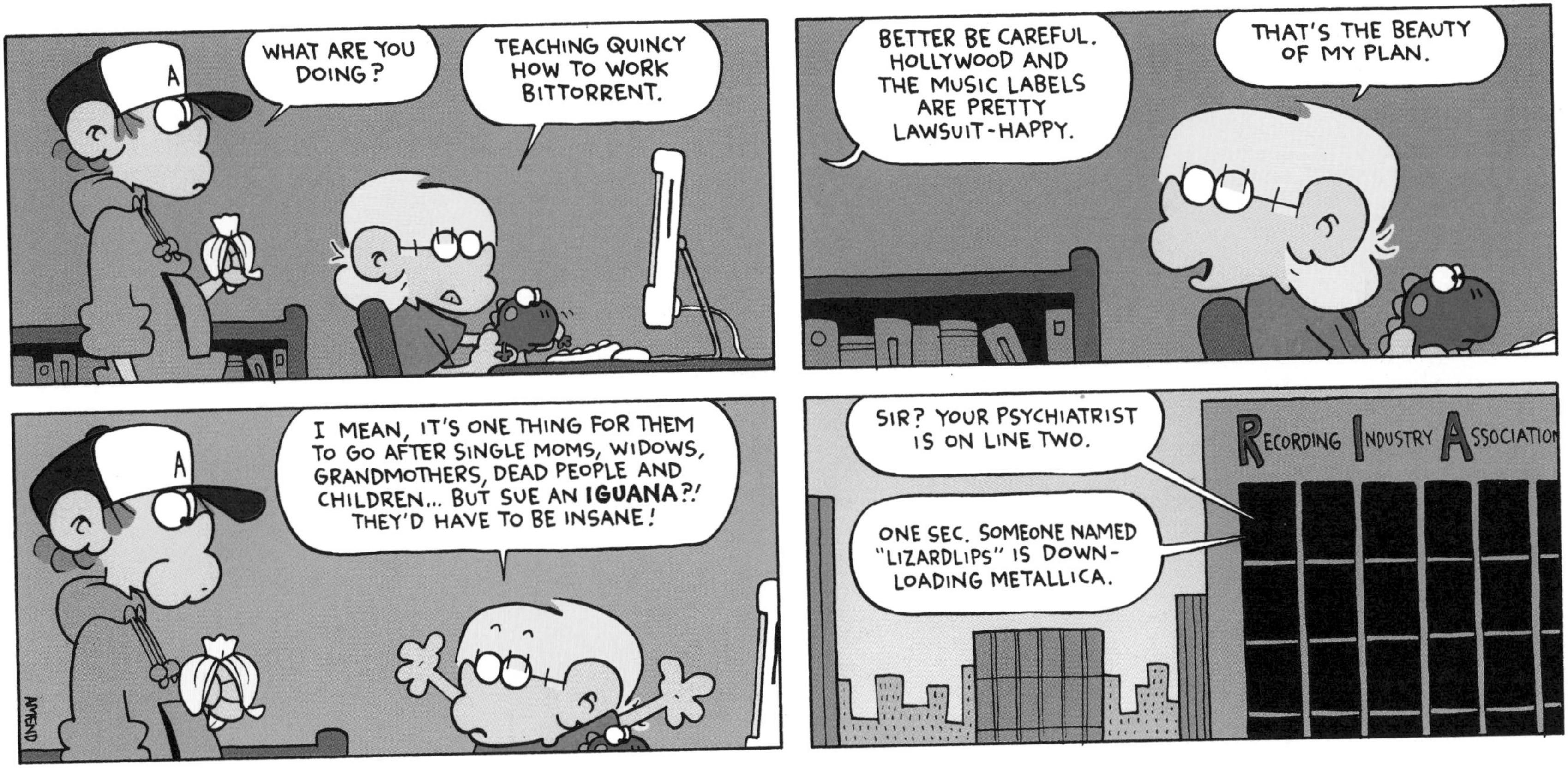
WHAT ARE YOU DOING?
TEACHING QUINCY HOW TO WORK BITTORRENT.
BETTER BE CAREFUL. HOLLYWOOD AND THE MUSIC LABELS ARE PRETTY LAWSUIT-HAPPY.
THAT'S THE BEAUTY OF MY PLAN.
I MEAN, IT'S ONE THING FOR THEM TO GO AFTER SINGLE MOMS, WIDOWS, GRANDMOTHERS, DEAD PEOPLE AND CHILDREN... BUT SUE AN **IGUANA**?! THEY'D HAVE TO BE INSANE!
AMEND
RECORDING INDUSTRY ASSOCIATION
SIR? YOUR PSYCHIATRIST IS ON LINE TWO.
ONE SEC. SOMEONE NAMED "LIZARDLIPS" IS DOWNLOADING METALLICA.

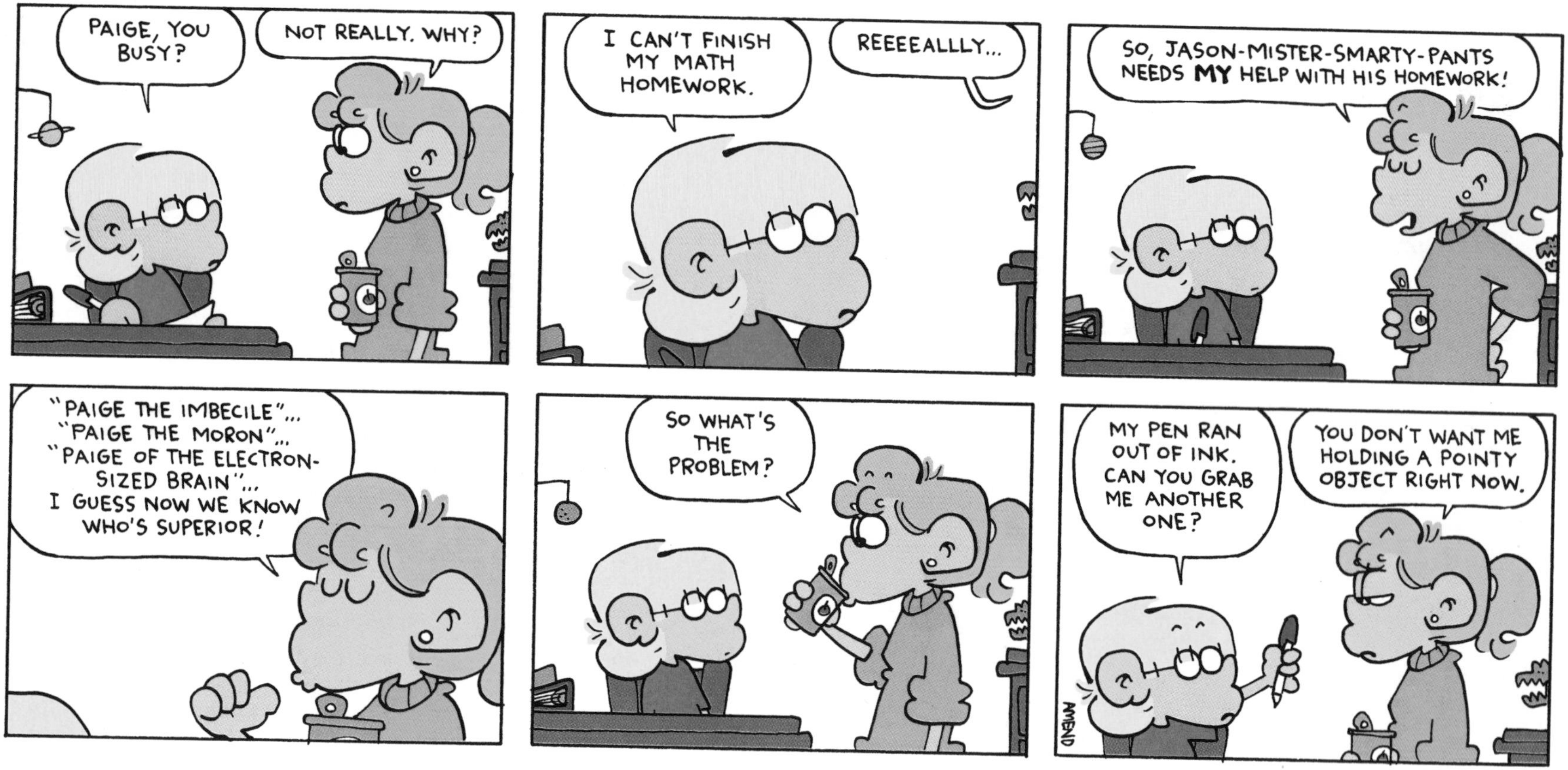
PAIGE, YOU BUSY?
NOT REALLY. WHY?
I CAN'T FINISH MY MATH HOMEWORK.
REEEEALLLY...
SO, JASON-MISTER-SMARTY-PANTS NEEDS **MY** HELP WITH HIS HOMEWORK!
"PAIGE THE IMBECILE"... "PAIGE THE MORON"... "PAIGE OF THE ELECTRON-SIZED BRAIN"... I GUESS NOW WE KNOW WHO'S SUPERIOR!
SO WHAT'S THE PROBLEM?
MY PEN RAN OUT OF INK. CAN YOU GRAB ME ANOTHER ONE?
YOU DON'T WANT ME HOLDING A POINTY OBJECT RIGHT NOW.
AMEND

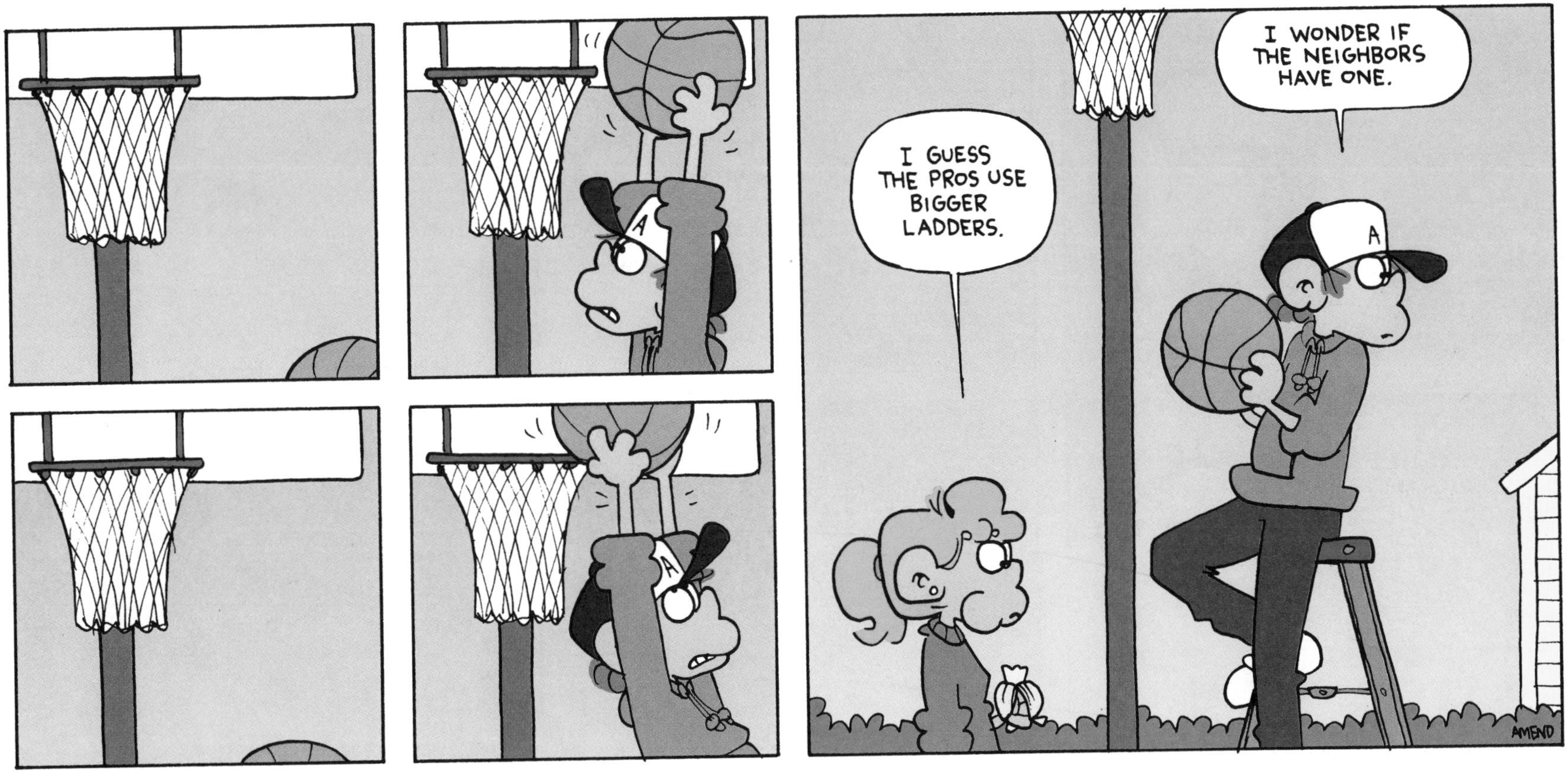
I GUESS THE PROS USE BIGGER LADDERS.
I WONDER IF THE NEIGHBORS HAVE ONE.
AMEND

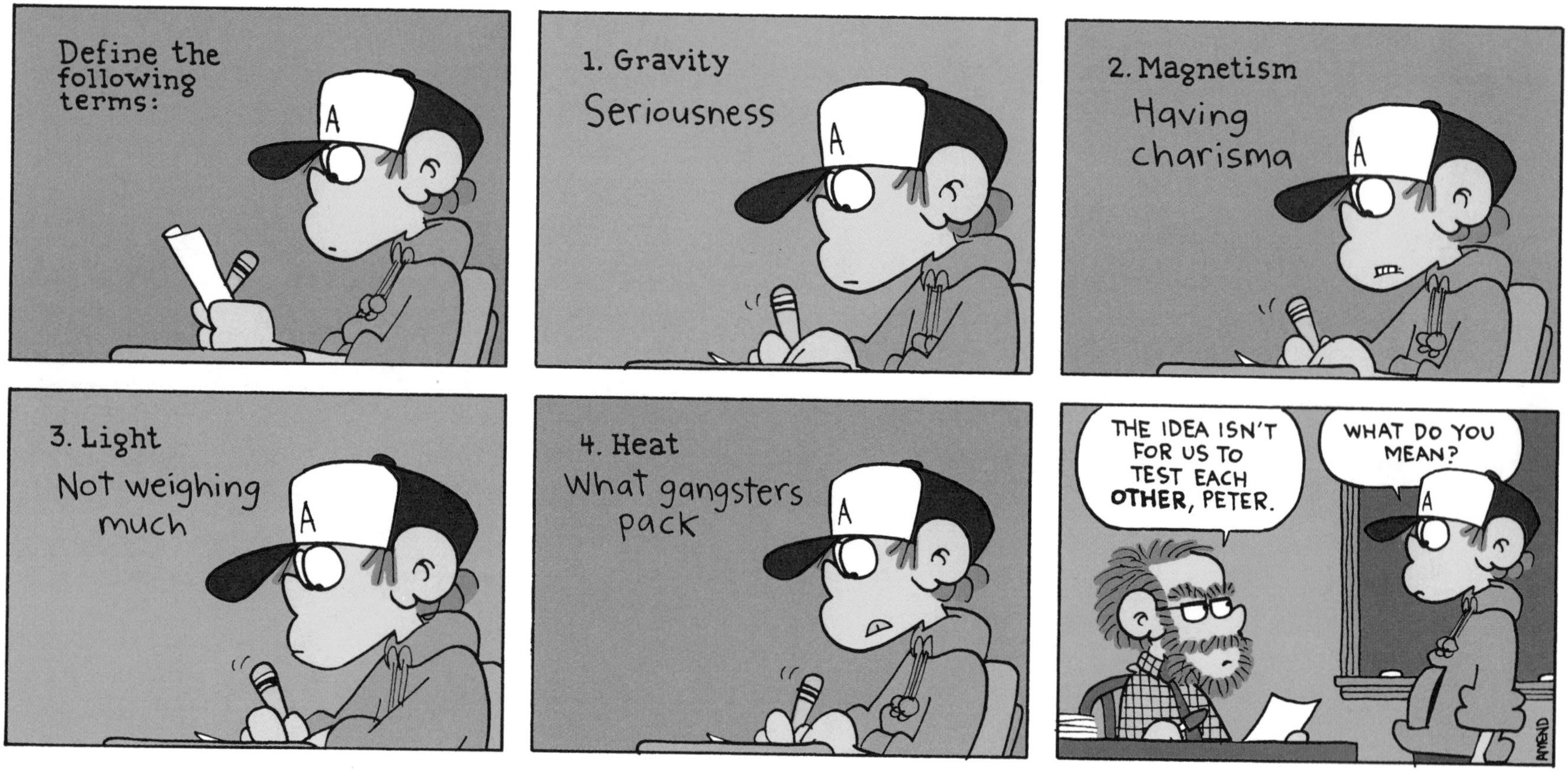
Define the following terms:
1. Gravity
Seriousness
2. Magnetism
Having charisma
3. Light
Not weighing much
4. Heat
What gangsters pack
THE IDEA ISN'T FOR US TO TEST EACH OTHER, PETER.
WHAT DO YOU MEAN?
AMEND

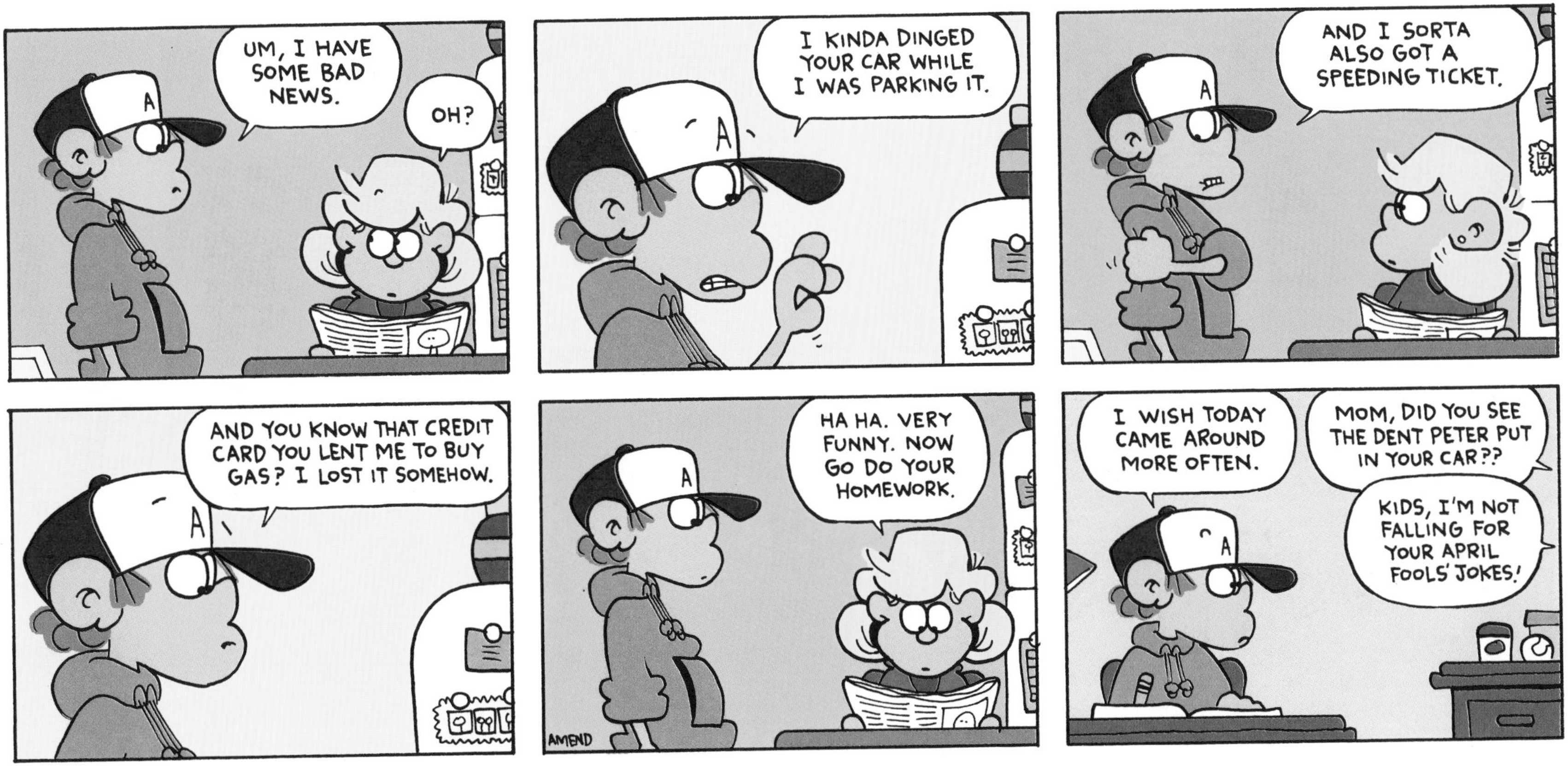
UM, I HAVE SOME BAD NEWS.
OH?
I KINDA DINGED YOUR CAR WHILE I WAS PARKING IT.
AND I SORTA ALSO GOT A SPEEDING TICKET.
AND YOU KNOW THAT CREDIT CARD YOU LENT ME TO BUY GAS? I LOST IT SOMEHOW.
HA HA. VERY FUNNY. NOW GO DO YOUR HOMEWORK.
AMEND
I WISH TODAY CAME AROUND MORE OFTEN.
MOM, DID YOU SEE THE DENT PETER PUT IN YOUR CAR??
KIDS, I'M NOT FALLING FOR YOUR APRIL FOOLS' JOKES!

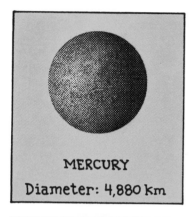

MERCURY
Diameter: 4,880 km
VENUS
Diameter: 12,100 km
EARTH
Diameter: 12,756 km
MARS
Diameter: 6,794 km
JUPITER
Diameter: 142,800 km
The Death Star owns them all!!!!!!
I UNDERSTAND IT WAS YOUR TURN TO RUN THE SLIDE PROJECTOR AT SCHOOL TODAY.
HOW'D YOU KNOW?
THYME
AMEND

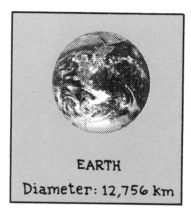

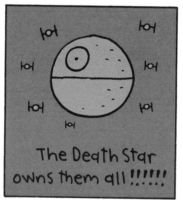

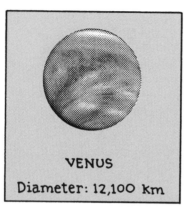

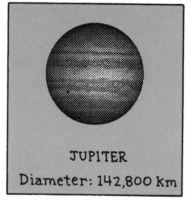

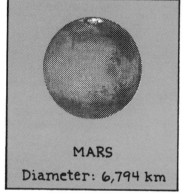

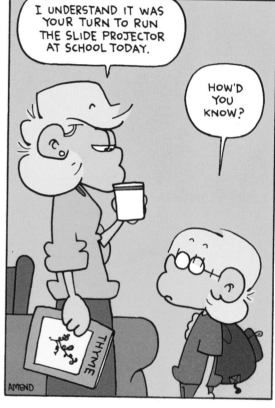

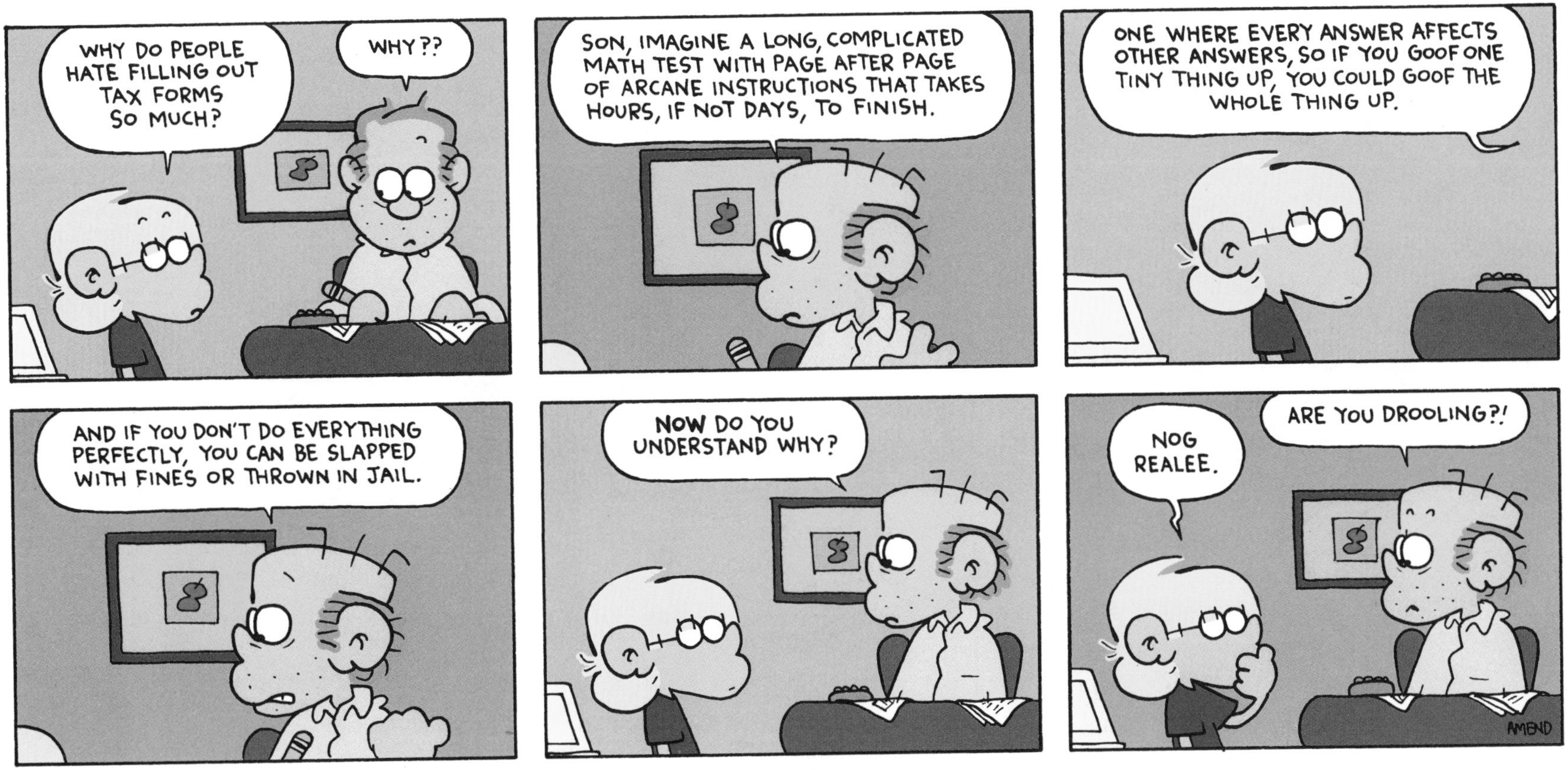
WHY DO PEOPLE HATE FILLING OUT TAX FORMS SO MUCH?
WHY??
SON, IMAGINE A LONG, COMPLICATED MATH TEST WITH PAGE AFTER PAGE OF ARCANE INSTRUCTIONS THAT TAKES HOURS, IF NOT DAYS, TO FINISH.
ONE WHERE EVERY ANSWER AFFECTS OTHER ANSWERS, SO IF YOU GOOF ONE TINY THING UP, YOU COULD GOOF THE WHOLE THING UP.
AND IF YOU DON'T DO EVERYTHING PERFECTLY, YOU CAN BE SLAPPED WITH FINES OR THROWN IN JAIL.
NOW DO YOU UNDERSTAND WHY?
NOG REALEE.
ARE YOU DROOLING?!
AMEND

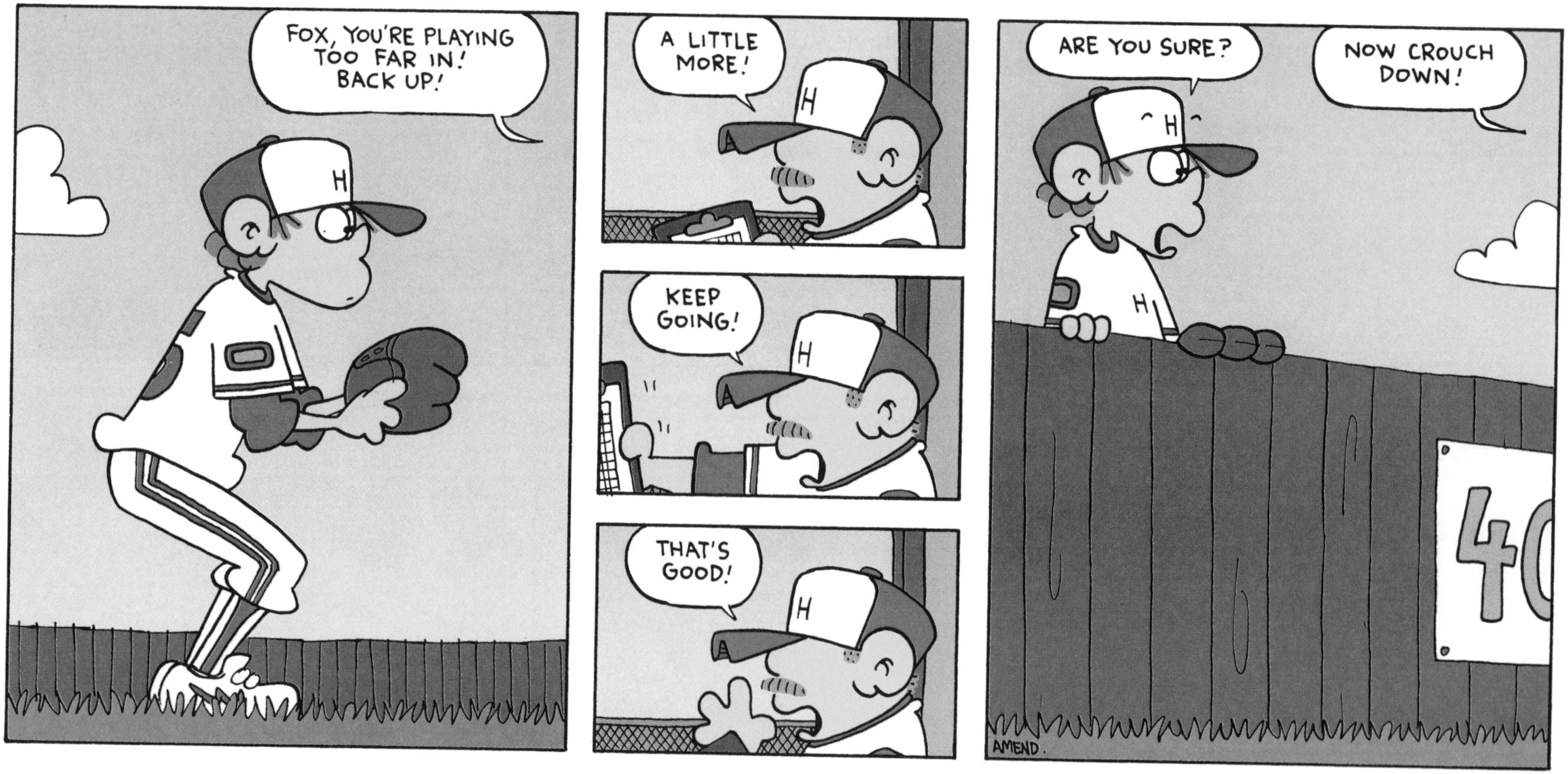
FOX, YOU'RE PLAYING TOO FAR IN! BACK UP!
A LITTLE MORE!
KEEP GOING!
THAT'S GOOD!
ARE YOU SURE?
NOW CROUCH DOWN!
40
AMEND.

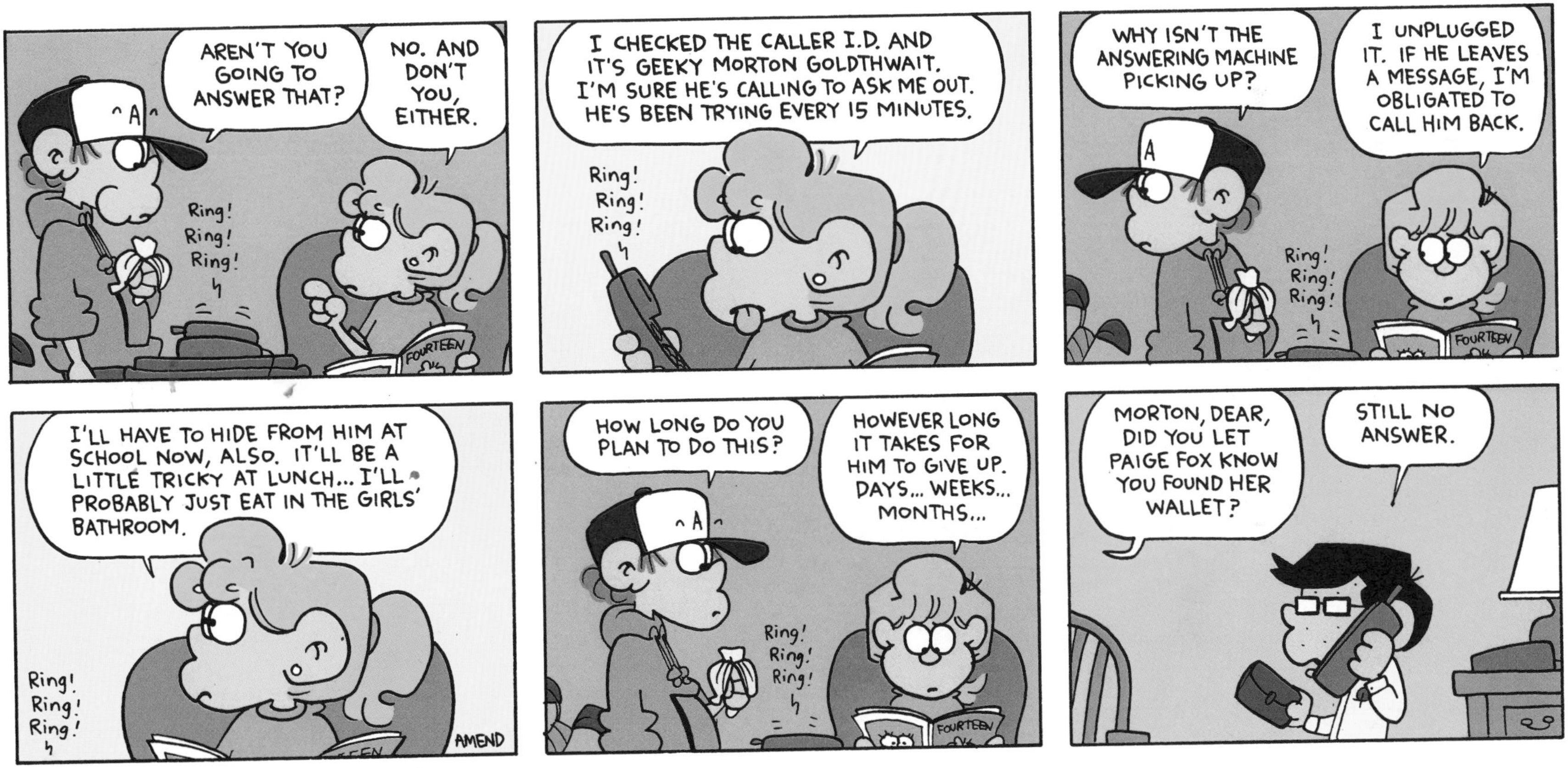
AREN'T YOU GOING TO ANSWER THAT?
NO. AND DON'T YOU, EITHER.
Ring! Ring! Ring!
FOURTEEN
I CHECKED THE CALLER I.D. AND IT'S GEEKY MORTON GOLDTHWAIT. I'M SURE HE'S CALLING TO ASK ME OUT. HE'S BEEN TRYING EVERY 15 MINUTES.
Ring! Ring! Ring!
WHY ISN'T THE ANSWERING MACHINE PICKING UP?
I UNPLUGGED IT. IF HE LEAVES A MESSAGE, I'M OBLIGATED TO CALL HIM BACK.
Ring! Ring! Ring!
FOURTEEN
I'LL HAVE TO HIDE FROM HIM AT SCHOOL NOW, ALSO. IT'LL BE A LITTLE TRICKY AT LUNCH... I'LL PROBABLY JUST EAT IN THE GIRLS' BATHROOM.
Ring! Ring! Ring!
AMEND
HOW LONG DO YOU PLAN TO DO THIS?
HOWEVER LONG IT TAKES FOR HIM TO GIVE UP. DAYS... WEEKS... MONTHS...
Ring! Ring! Ring!
FOURTEEN
MORTON, DEAR, DID YOU LET PAIGE FOX KNOW YOU FOUND HER WALLET?
STILL NO ANSWER.

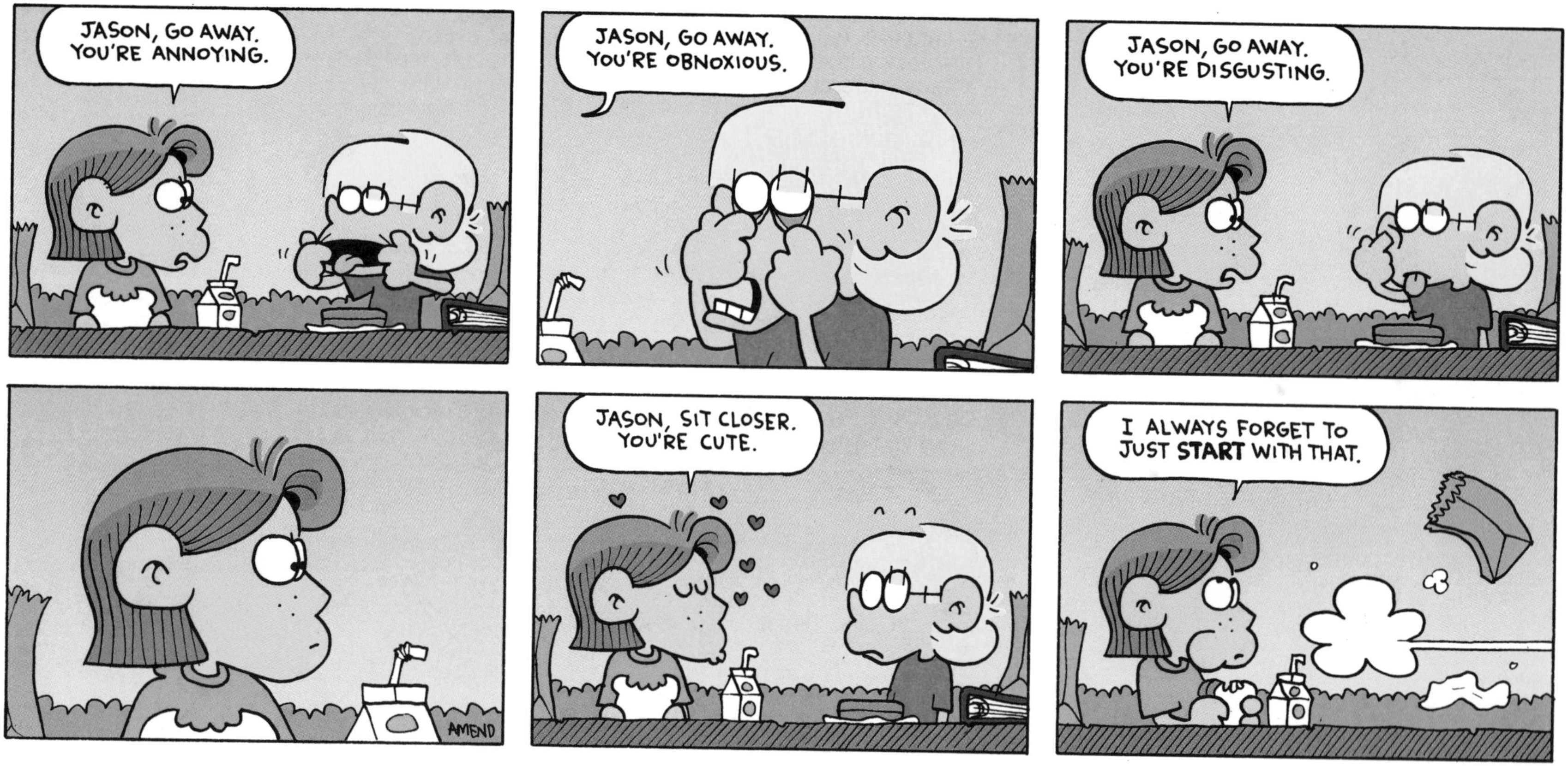
JASON, GO AWAY. YOU'RE ANNOYING.
JASON, GO AWAY. YOU'RE OBNOXIOUS.
JASON, GO AWAY. YOU'RE DISGUSTING.
AMEND
JASON, SIT CLOSER. YOU'RE CUTE.
I ALWAYS FORGET TO JUST START WITH THAT.

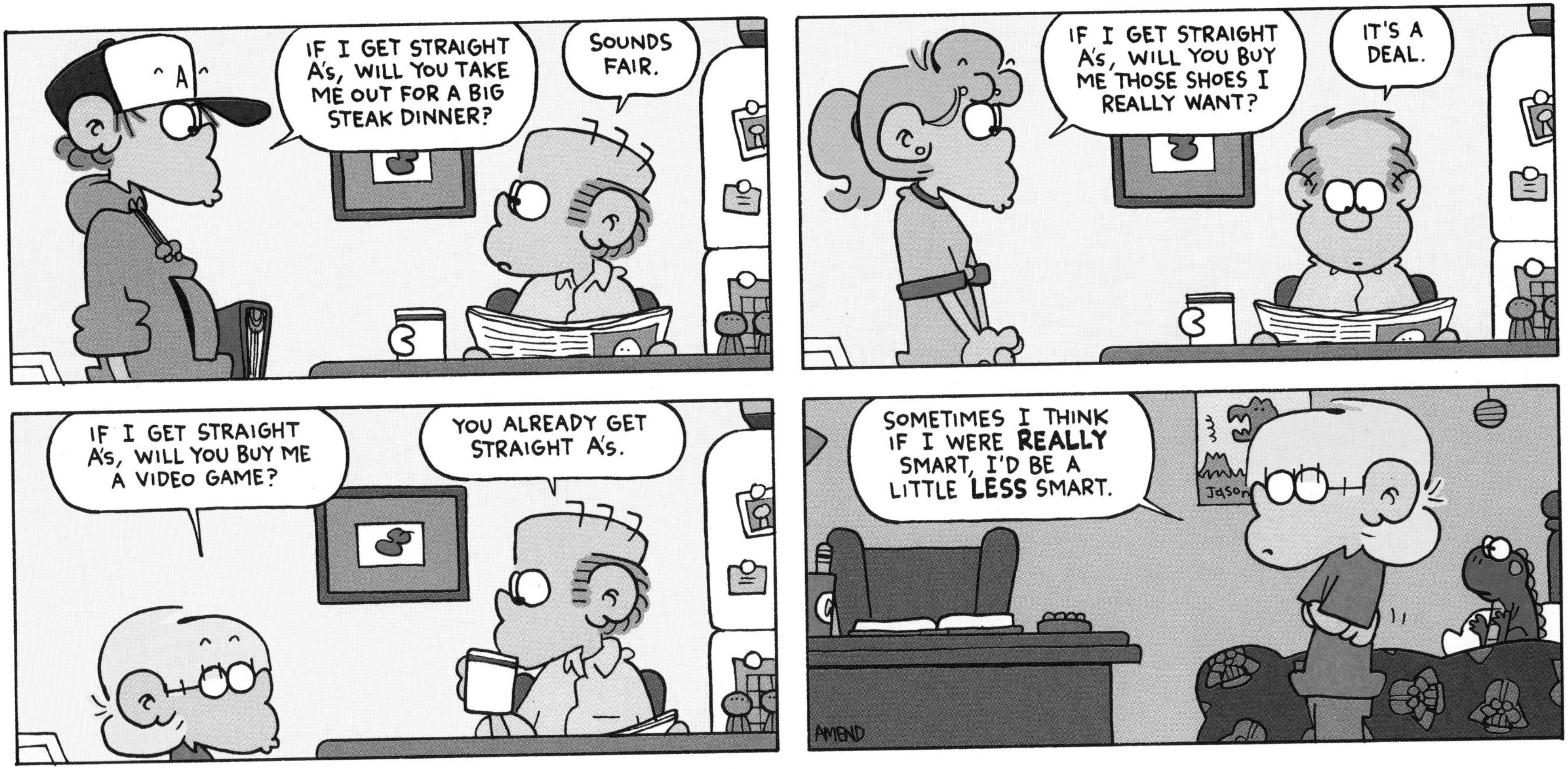
IF I GET STRAIGHT A's, WILL YOU TAKE ME OUT FOR A BIG STEAK DINNER?
SOUNDS FAIR.
IF I GET STRAIGHT A's, WILL YOU BUY ME THOSE SHOES I REALLY WANT?
IT'S A DEAL.
IF I GET STRAIGHT A's, WILL YOU BUY ME A VIDEO GAME?
YOU ALREADY GET STRAIGHT A's.
SOMETIMES I THINK IF I WERE **REALLY** SMART, I'D BE A LITTLE **LESS** SMART.
Jason
AMEND

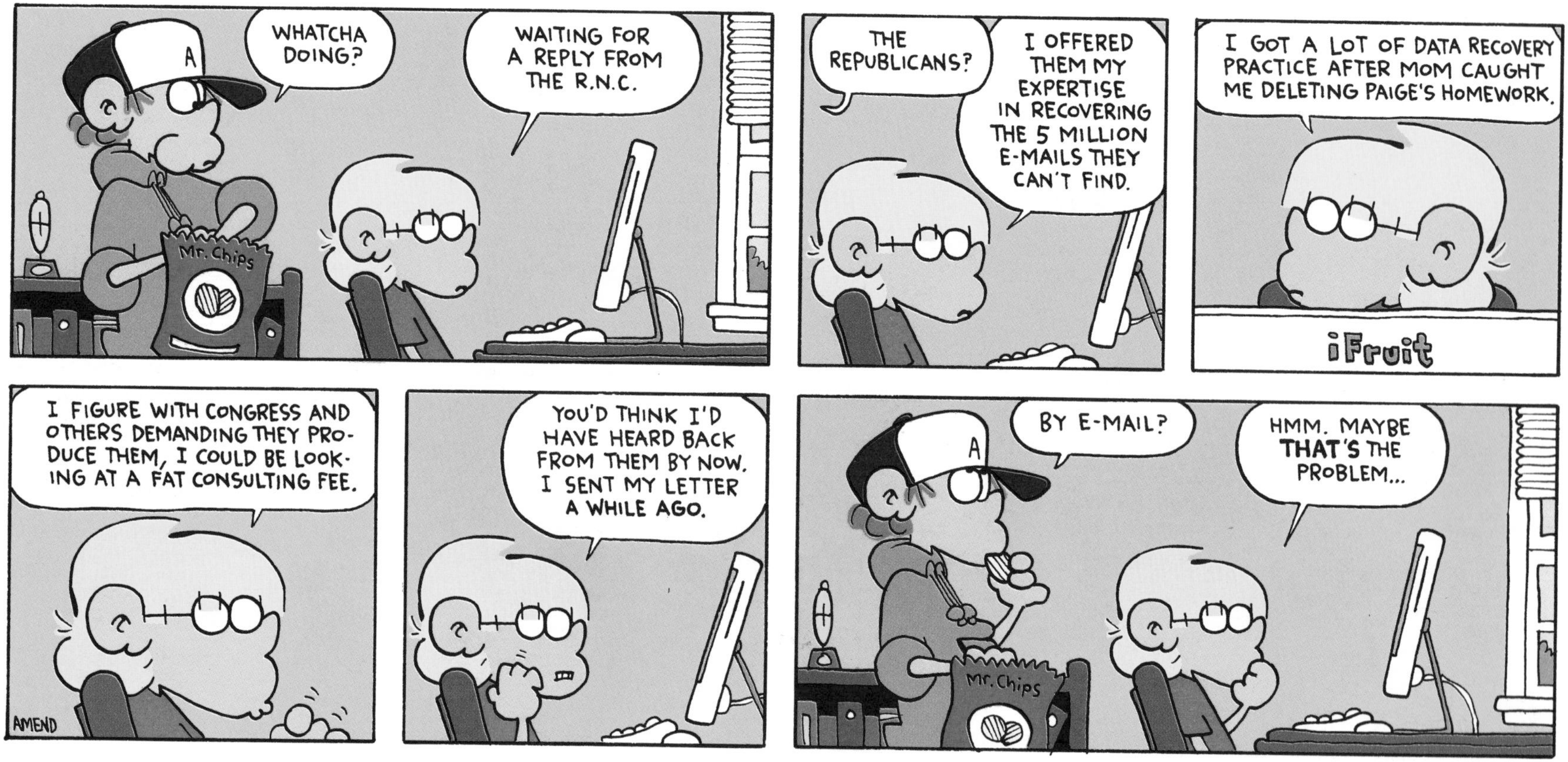
WHATCHA DOING?
WAITING FOR A REPLY FROM THE R.N.C.
THE REPUBLICANS?
I OFFERED THEM MY EXPERTISE IN RECOVERING THE 5 MILLION E-MAILS THEY CAN'T FIND.
I GOT A LOT OF DATA RECOVERY PRACTICE AFTER MOM CAUGHT ME DELETING PAIGE'S HOMEWORK.
iFruit
I FIGURE WITH CONGRESS AND OTHERS DEMANDING THEY PRODUCE THEM, I COULD BE LOOKING AT A FAT CONSULTING FEE.
AMEND
YOU'D THINK I'D HAVE HEARD BACK FROM THEM BY NOW. I SENT MY LETTER A WHILE AGO.
BY E-MAIL?
HMM. MAYBE **THAT'S** THE PROBLEM...
Mr. Chips

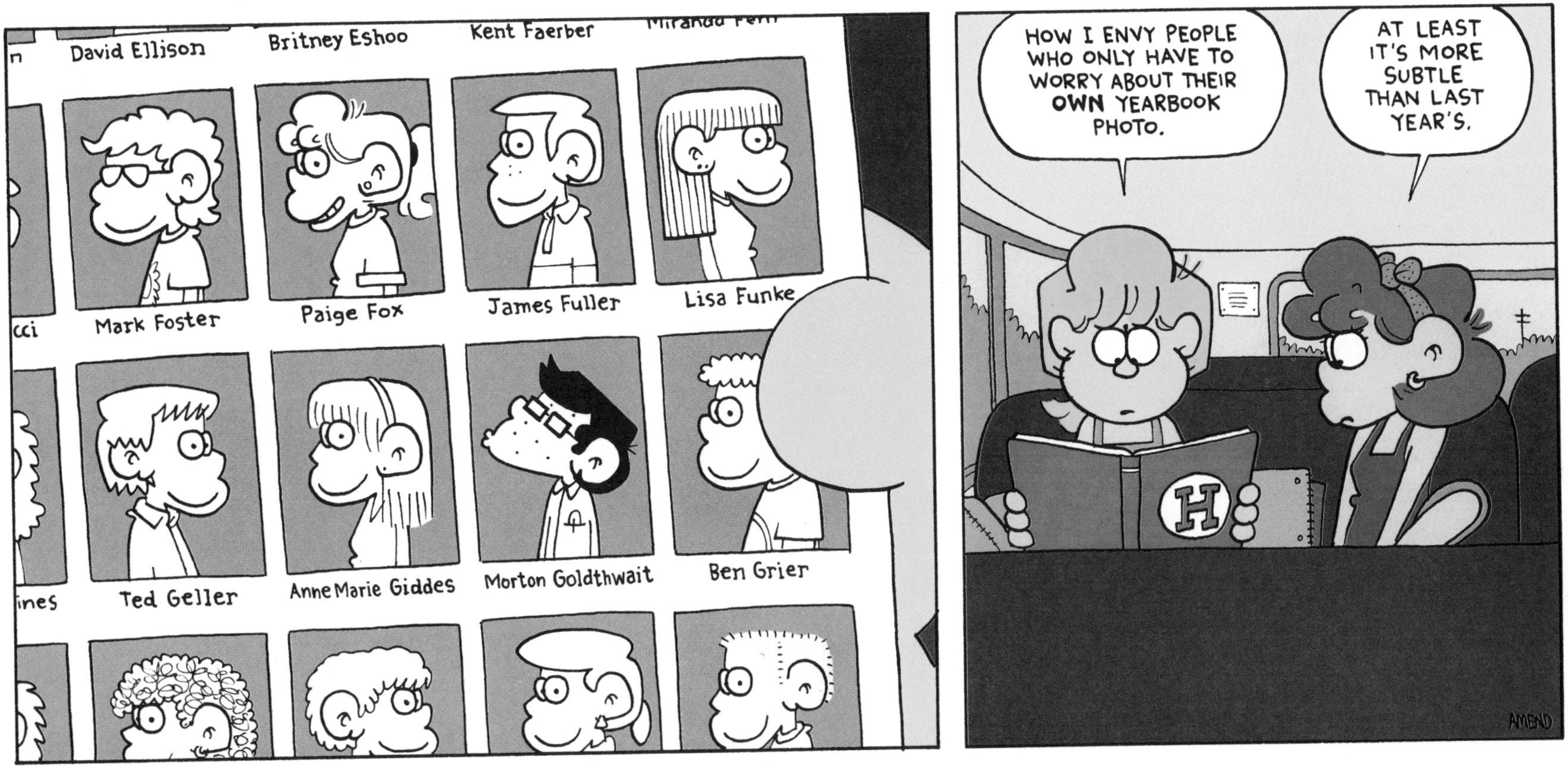
David Ellison
Britney Eshoo
Kent Faerber
Mark Foster
Paige Fox
James Fuller
Lisa Funke
Ted Geller
AnneMarie Giddes
Morton Goldthwait
Ben Grier
HOW I ENVY PEOPLE WHO ONLY HAVE TO WORRY ABOUT THEIR **OWN** YEARBOOK PHOTO.
AT LEAST IT'S MORE SUBTLE THAN LAST YEAR'S.
AMEND

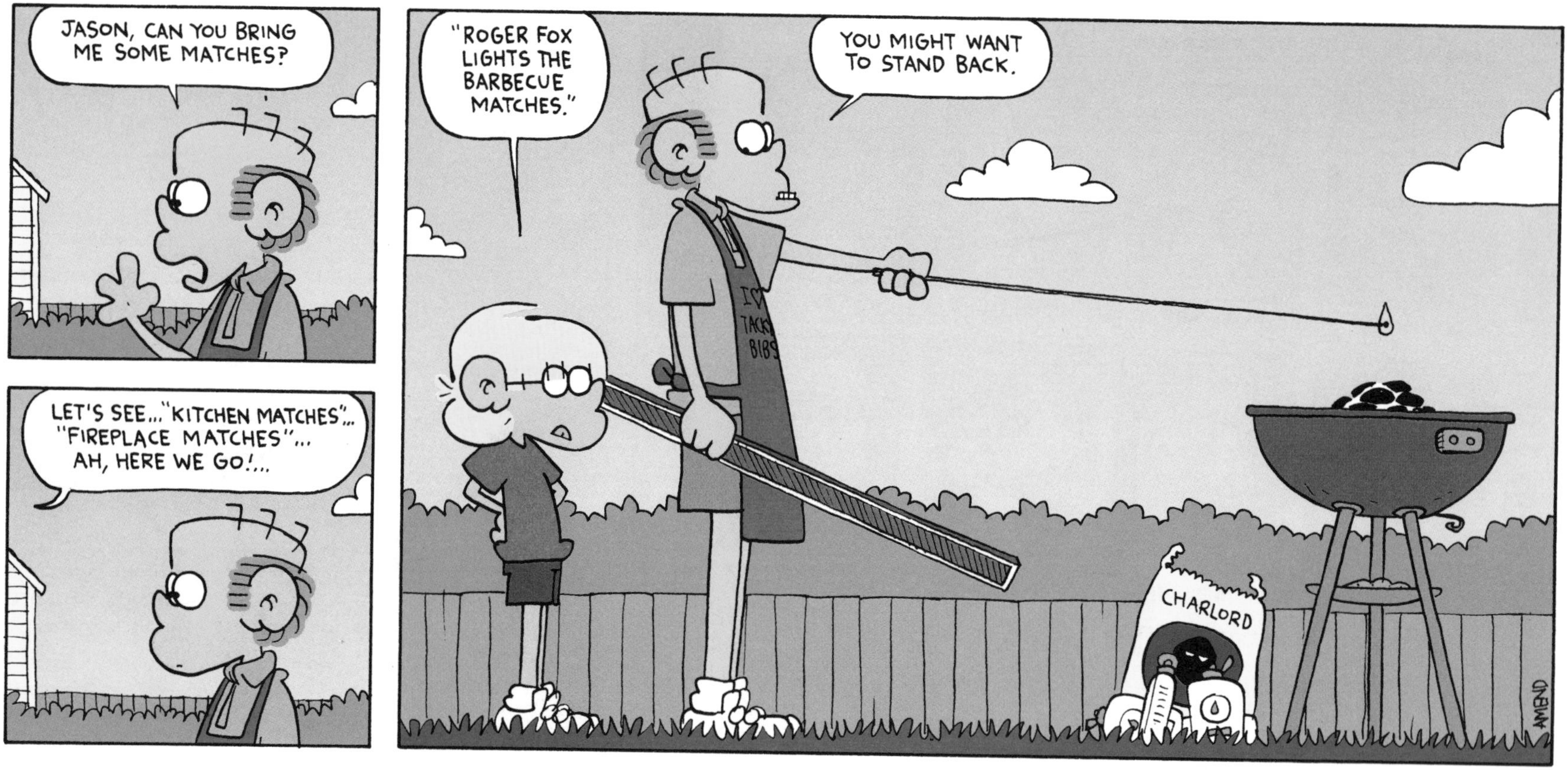
JASON, CAN YOU BRING ME SOME MATCHES?
LET'S SEE... "KITCHEN MATCHES"... "FIREPLACE MATCHES"... AH, HERE WE GO!...
"ROGER FOX LIGHTS THE BARBECUE MATCHES."
YOU MIGHT WANT TO STAND BACK.
I ♡ TACKY BIBS
CHARLORD
AMEND

THE MOMENT OF INERTIA FOR A SOLID SPHERE IS $\frac{2}{5}MR^2$...

THE MOMENT OF INERTIA FOR A HOLLOW SPHERE IS $\frac{2}{3}MR^2$...

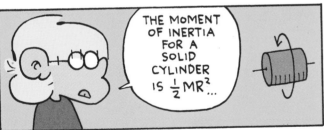

THE MOMENT OF INERTIA FOR A SOLID CYLINDER IS $\frac{1}{2}MR^2$...

MEANWHILE, THE MOMENT OF INERTIA FOR **US** IS...

THE FIRST NANOSECOND OF SUMMER VACATION, OF COURSE.

I WISH YOU BOYS WOULD GET OFF THAT SOFA!

CHIP-OS

AMEND

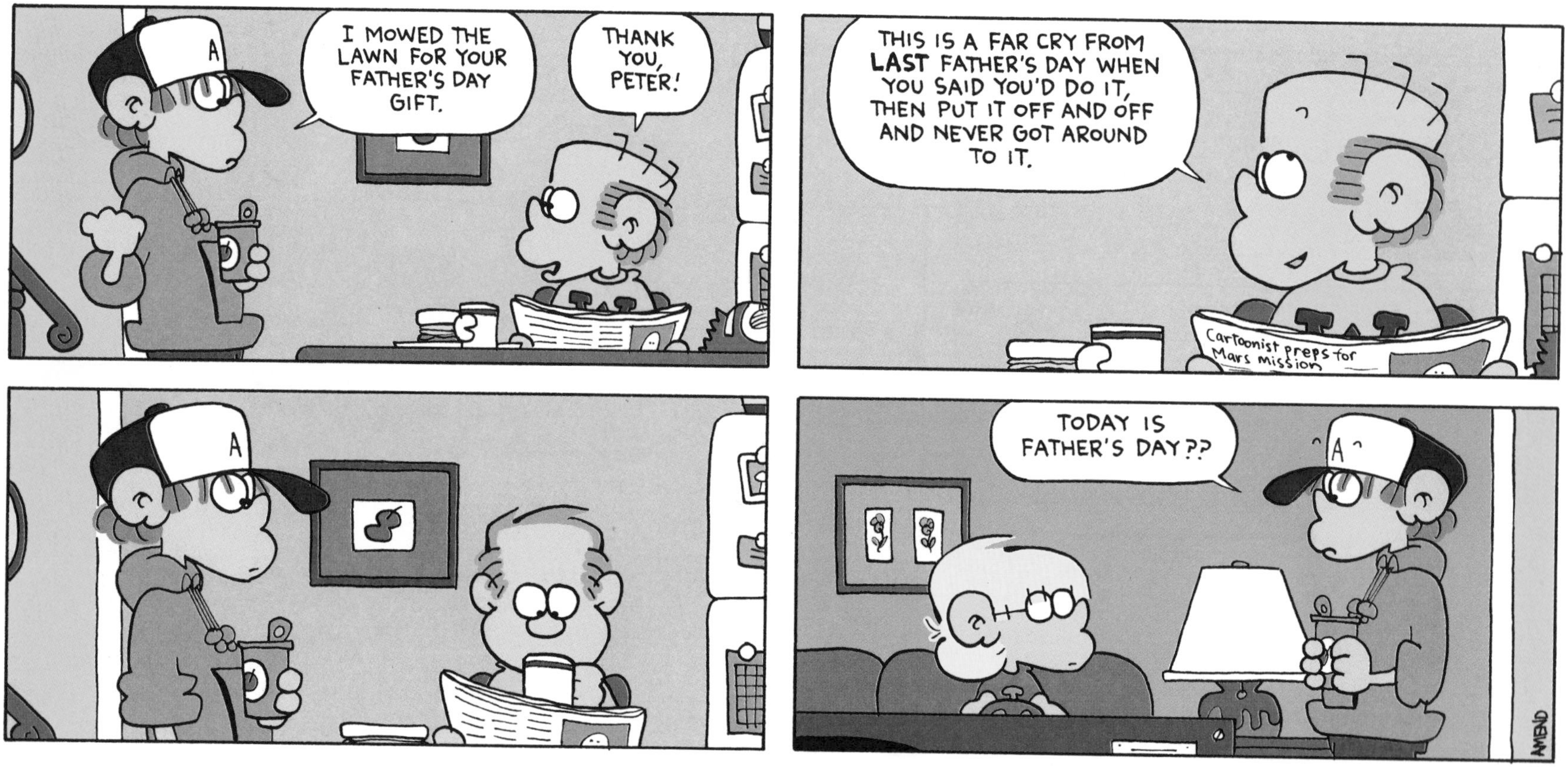
I MOWED THE LAWN FOR YOUR FATHER'S DAY GIFT.
THANK YOU, PETER!
THIS IS A FAR CRY FROM **LAST** FATHER'S DAY WHEN YOU SAID YOU'D DO IT, THEN PUT IT OFF AND OFF AND NEVER GOT AROUND TO IT.
Cartoonist preps for Mars mission
TODAY IS FATHER'S DAY??
AMEND

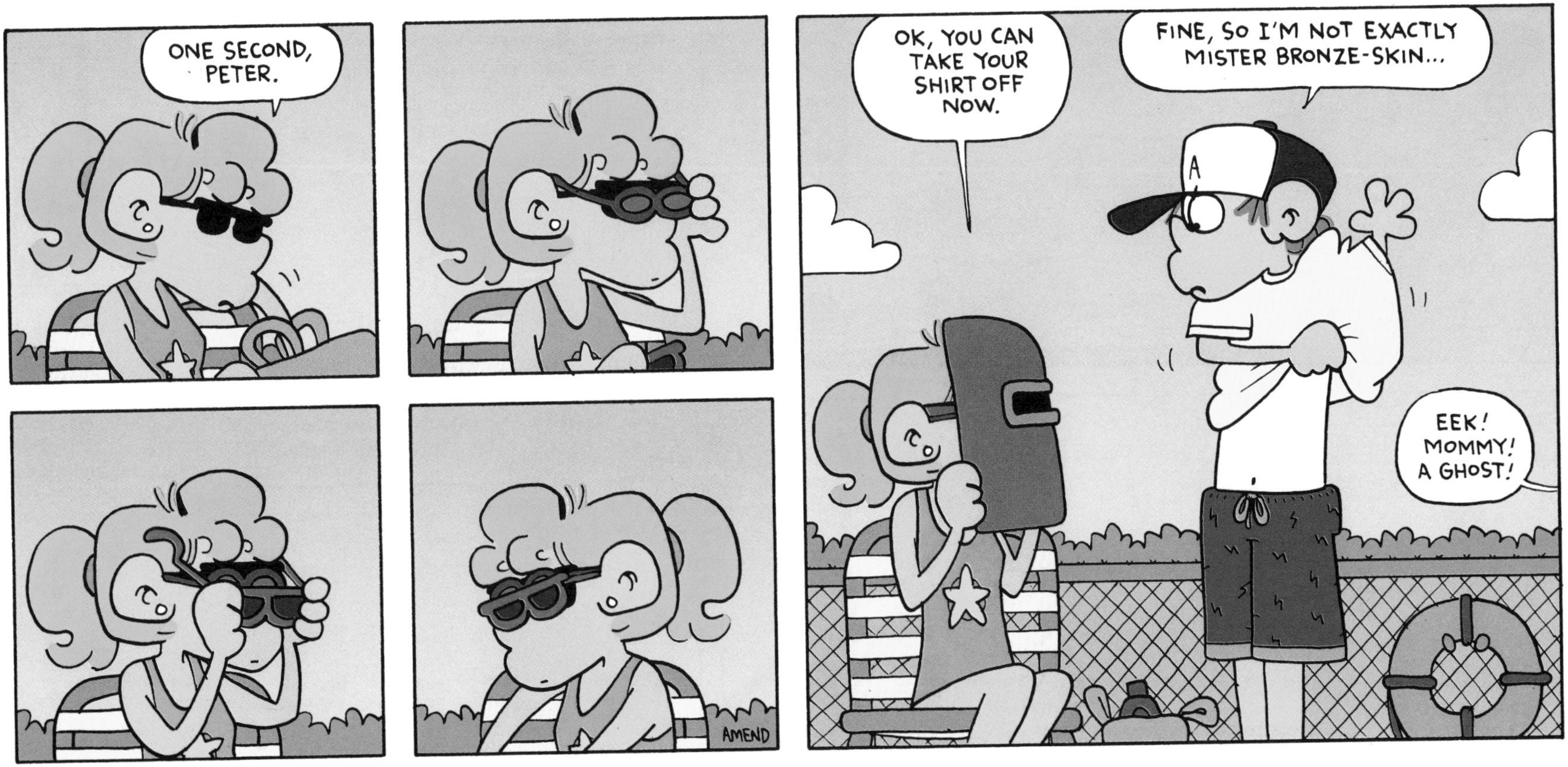
ONE SECOND, PETER.
AMEND
OK, YOU CAN TAKE YOUR SHIRT OFF NOW.
FINE, SO I'M NOT EXACTLY MISTER BRONZE-SKIN...
EEK! MOMMY! A GHOST!

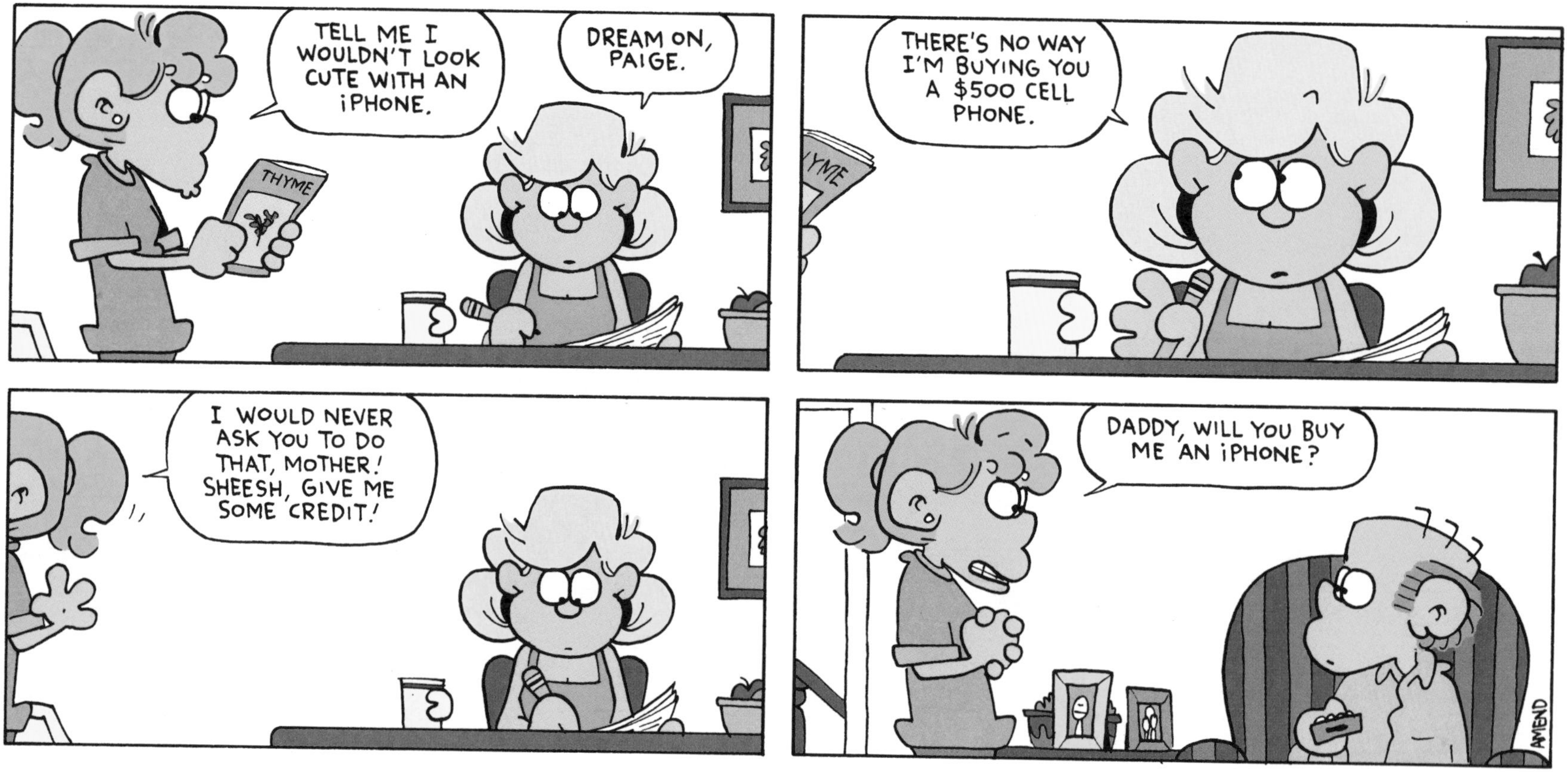
TELL ME I WOULDN'T LOOK CUTE WITH AN iPHONE.
DREAM ON, PAIGE.
THYME
THERE'S NO WAY I'M BUYING YOU A $500 CELL PHONE.
I WOULD NEVER ASK YOU TO DO THAT, MOTHER! SHEESH, GIVE ME SOME CREDIT!
DADDY, WILL YOU BUY ME AN iPHONE?
AMEND

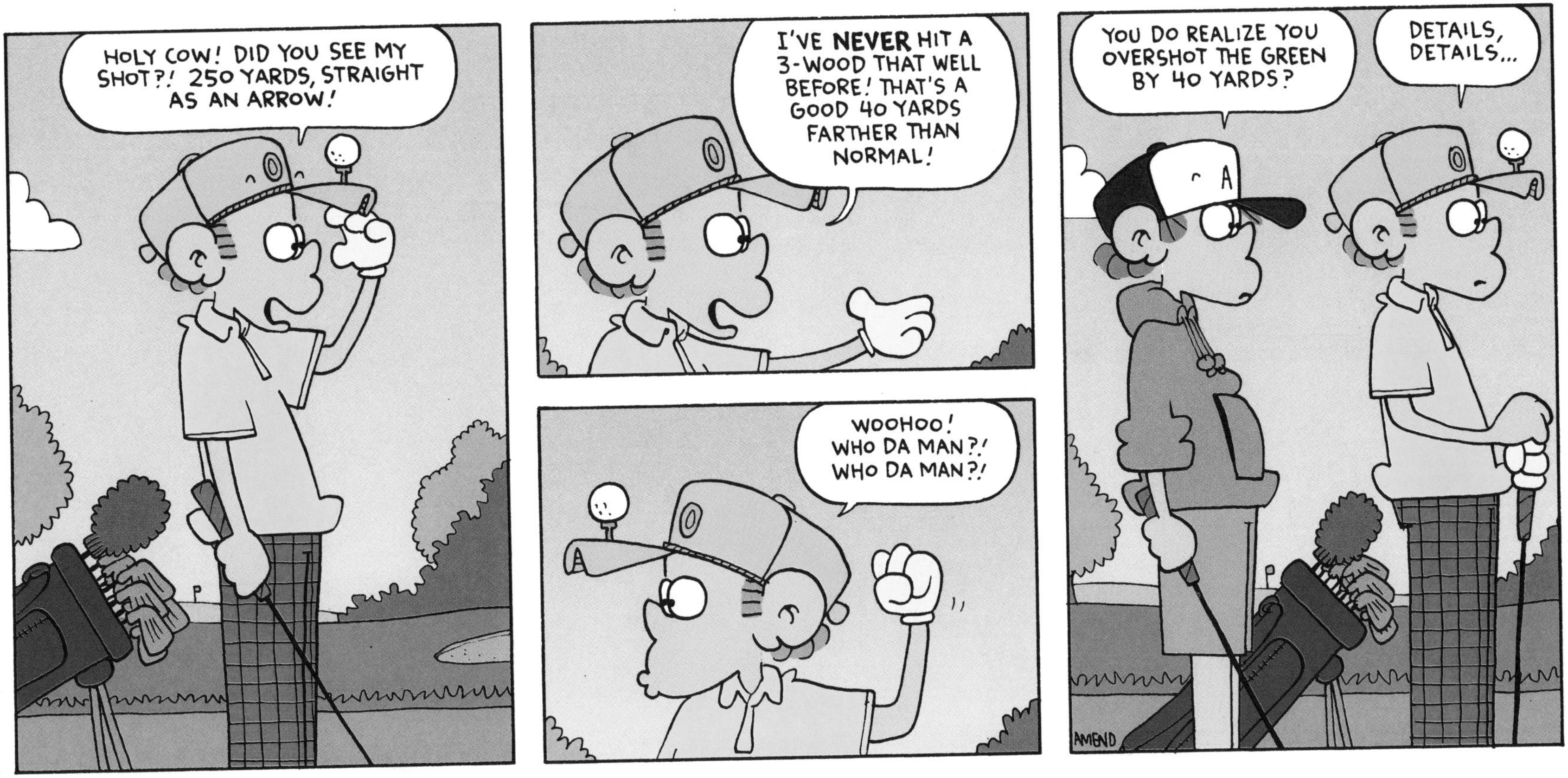
HOLY COW! DID YOU SEE MY SHOT?! 250 YARDS, STRAIGHT AS AN ARROW!
I'VE **NEVER** HIT A 3-WOOD THAT WELL BEFORE! THAT'S A GOOD 40 YARDS FARTHER THAN NORMAL!
WOOHOO! WHO DA MAN?! WHO DA MAN?!
YOU DO REALIZE YOU OVERSHOT THE GREEN BY 40 YARDS?
DETAILS, DETAILS...
AMEND

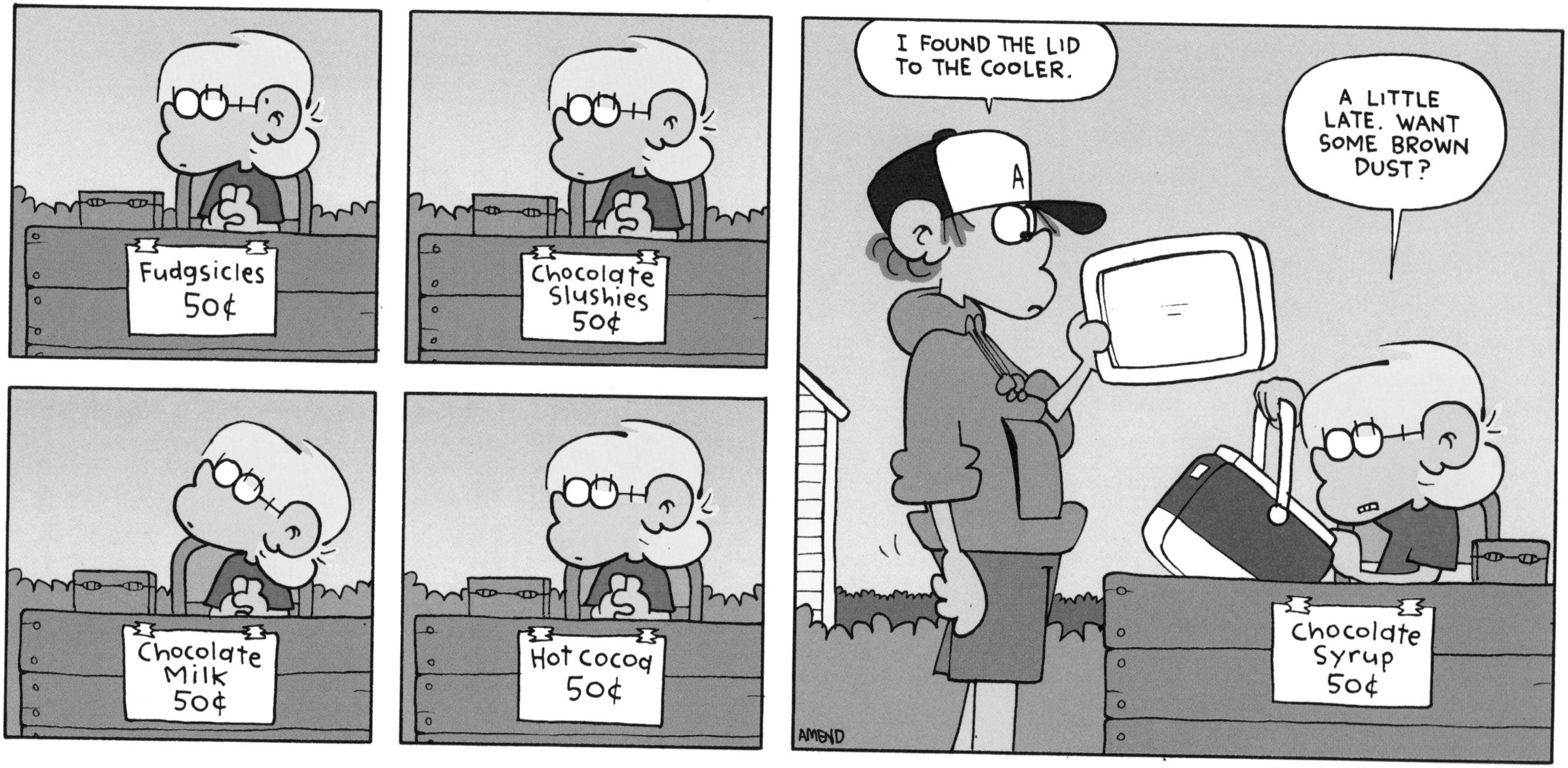
Fudgsicles 50¢
Chocolate Slushies 50¢
Chocolate Milk 50¢
Hot cocoa 50¢
I FOUND THE LID TO THE COOLER.
A LITTLE LATE. WANT SOME BROWN DUST?
Chocolate Syrup 50¢
AMEND

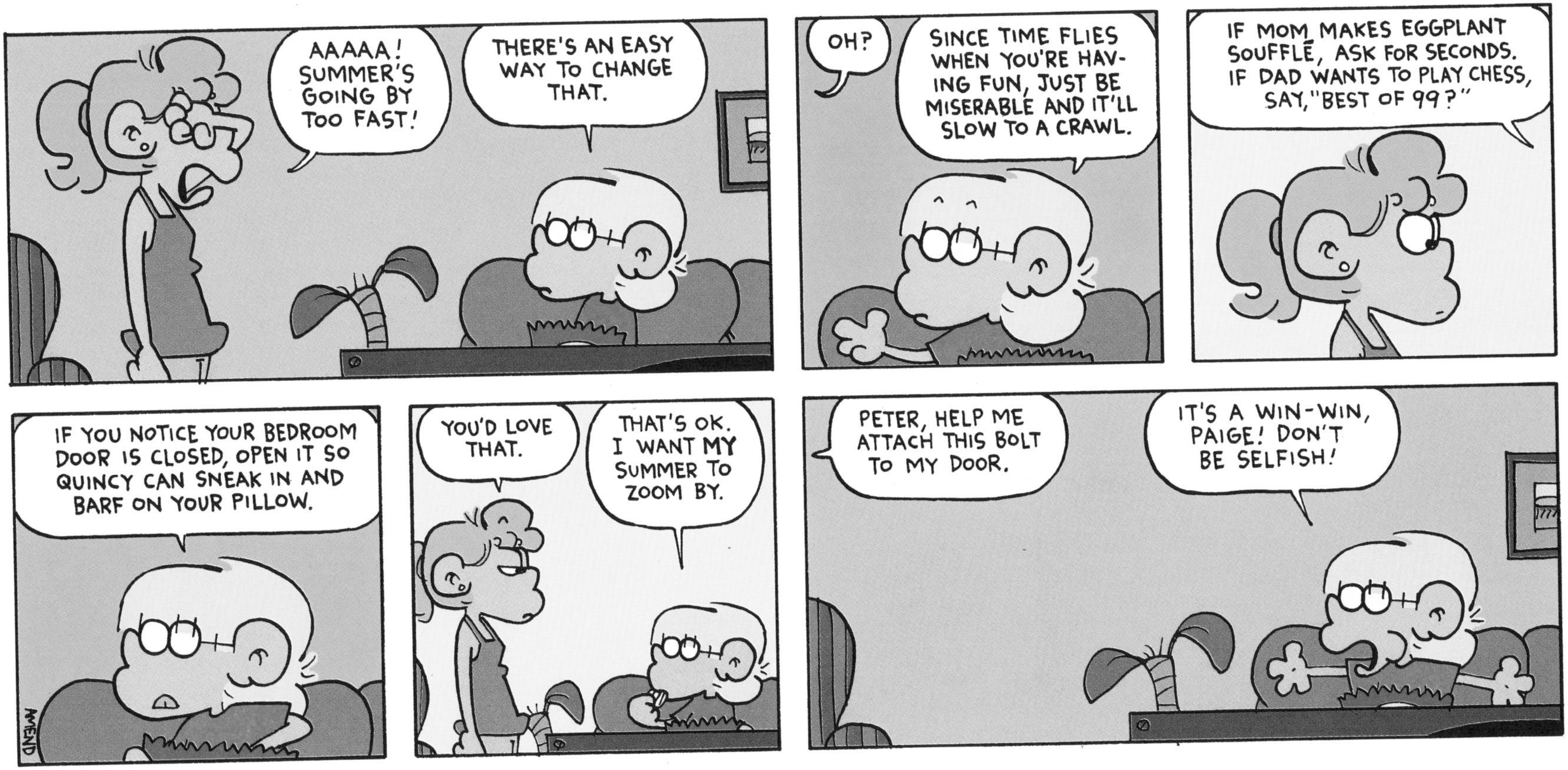
AAAAA! SUMMER'S GOING BY TOO FAST!
THERE'S AN EASY WAY TO CHANGE THAT.
OH?
SINCE TIME FLIES WHEN YOU'RE HAV-ING FUN, JUST BE MISERABLE AND IT'LL SLOW TO A CRAWL.
IF MOM MAKES EGGPLANT SOUFFLÉ, ASK FOR SECONDS. IF DAD WANTS TO PLAY CHESS, SAY, "BEST OF 99?"
IF YOU NOTICE YOUR BEDROOM DOOR IS CLOSED, OPEN IT SO QUINCY CAN SNEAK IN AND BARF ON YOUR PILLOW.
AMEND
YOU'D LOVE THAT.
THAT'S OK. I WANT MY SUMMER TO ZOOM BY.
PETER, HELP ME ATTACH THIS BOLT TO MY DOOR.
IT'S A WIN-WIN, PAIGE! DON'T BE SELFISH!

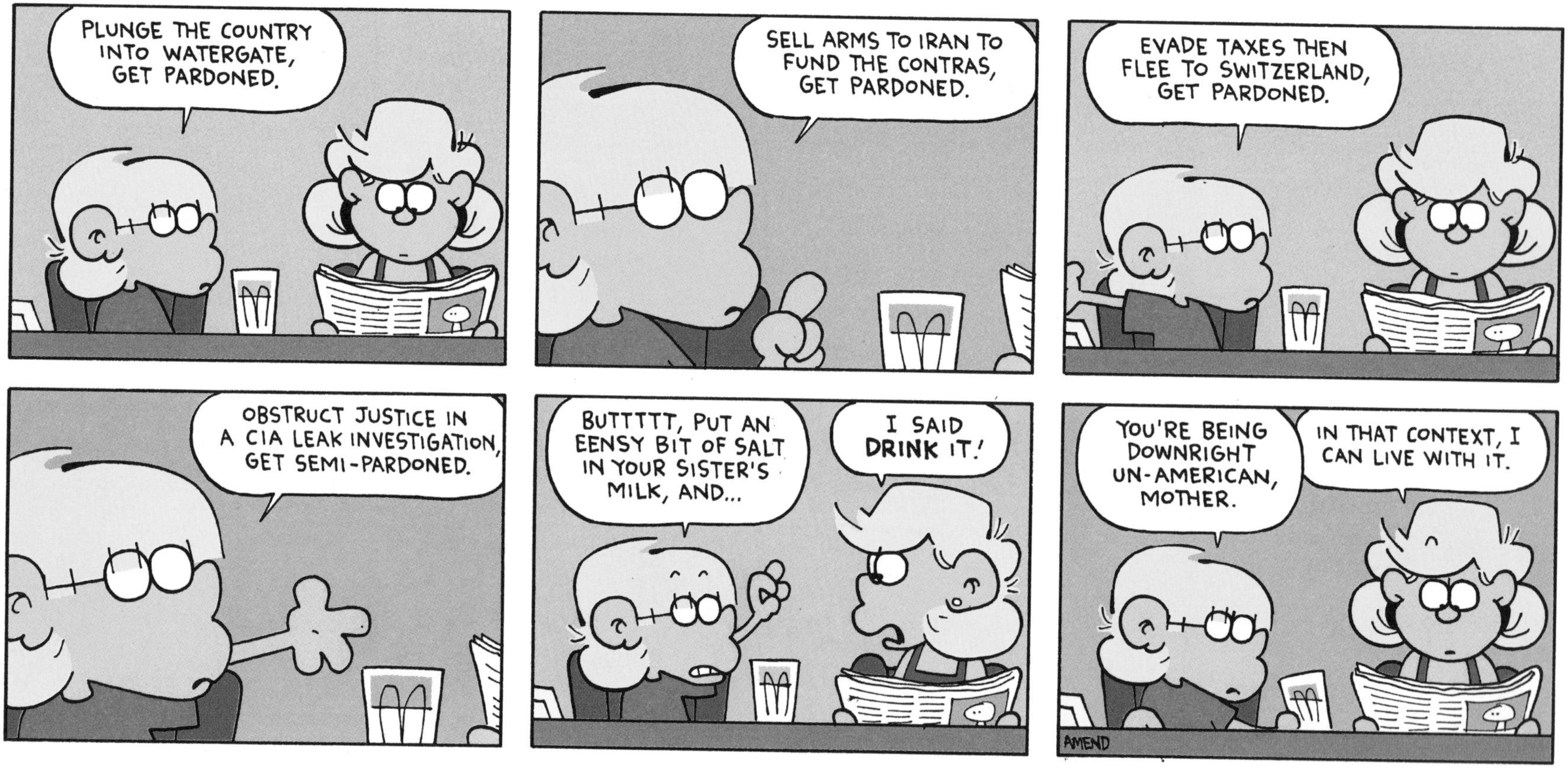
PLUNGE THE COUNTRY INTO WATERGATE, GET PARDONED.
SELL ARMS TO IRAN TO FUND THE CONTRAS, GET PARDONED.
EVADE TAXES THEN FLEE TO SWITZERLAND, GET PARDONED.
OBSTRUCT JUSTICE IN A CIA LEAK INVESTIGATION, GET SEMI-PARDONED.
BUTTTTT, PUT AN EENSY BIT OF SALT IN YOUR SISTER'S MILK, AND...
I SAID DRINK IT!
YOU'RE BEING DOWNRIGHT UN-AMERICAN, MOTHER.
IN THAT CONTEXT, I CAN LIVE WITH IT.
AMEND

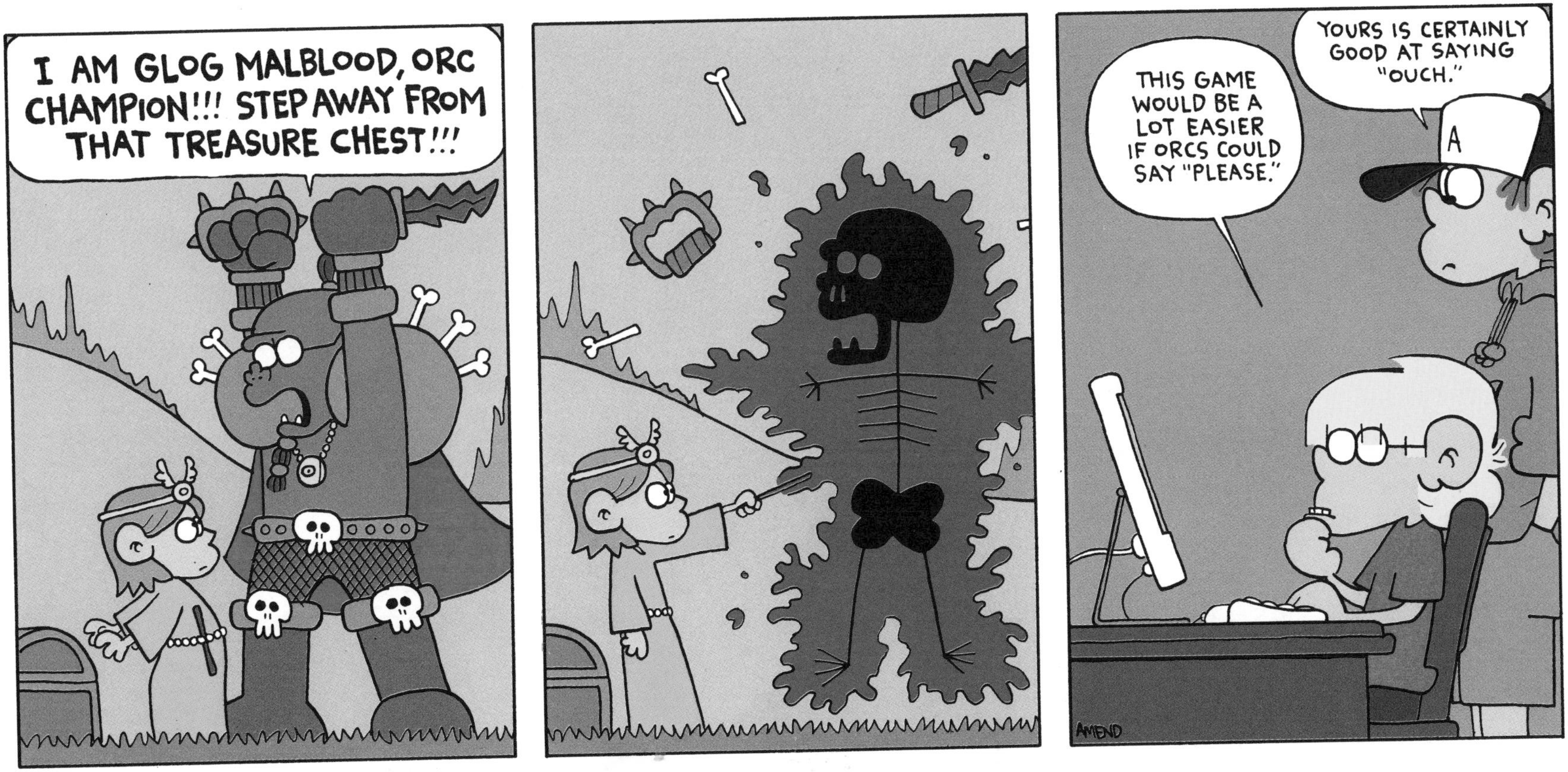
I AM GLOG MALBLOOD, ORC CHAMPION!!! STEP AWAY FROM THAT TREASURE CHEST!!!
THIS GAME WOULD BE A LOT EASIER IF ORCS COULD SAY "PLEASE."
YOURS IS CERTAINLY GOOD AT SAYING "OUCH."
A
AMEND

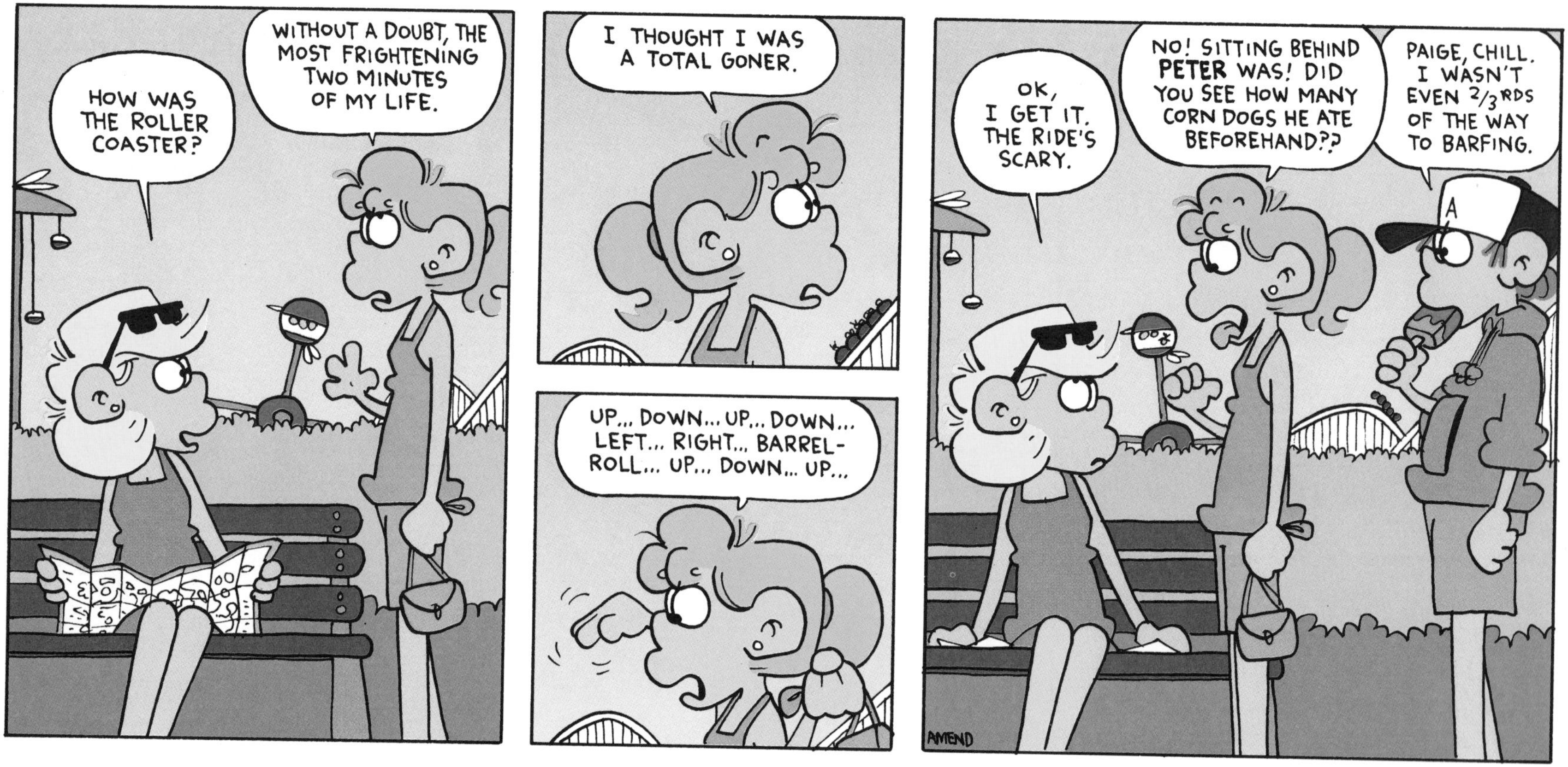
HOW WAS THE ROLLER COASTER?
WITHOUT A DOUBT, THE MOST FRIGHTENING TWO MINUTES OF MY LIFE.
I THOUGHT I WAS A TOTAL GONER.
UP... DOWN... UP... DOWN... LEFT... RIGHT... BARREL-ROLL... UP... DOWN... UP...
OK, I GET IT. THE RIDE'S SCARY.
NO! SITTING BEHIND PETER WAS! DID YOU SEE HOW MANY CORN DOGS HE ATE BEFOREHAND??
PAIGE, CHILL. I WASN'T EVEN 2/3RDS OF THE WAY TO BARFING.
AMEND

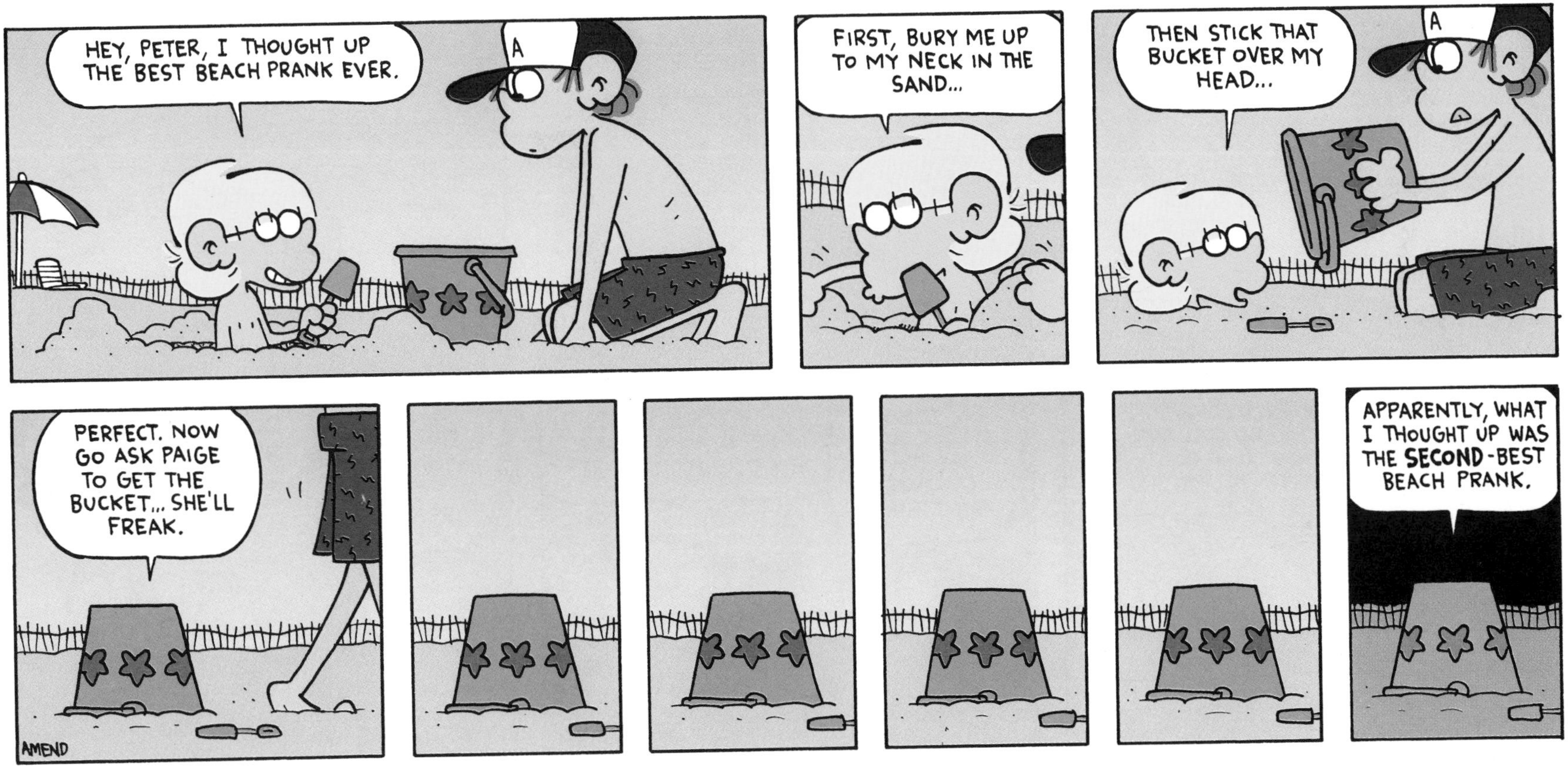
HEY, PETER, I THOUGHT UP THE BEST BEACH PRANK EVER.
FIRST, BURY ME UP TO MY NECK IN THE SAND...
THEN STICK THAT BUCKET OVER MY HEAD...
PERFECT. NOW GO ASK PAIGE TO GET THE BUCKET... SHE'LL FREAK.
AMEND
APPARENTLY, WHAT I THOUGHT UP WAS THE **SECOND**-BEST BEACH PRANK.

CHECK OUT THE UBER-COOL CALCULATOR I GOT FOR SCHOOL!
I THOUGHT YOU SAID CALCULATORS ARE FOR WIMPS.
THIS ONE'S DIFFERENT— NOTICE ANYTHING?
IT ONLY HAS THREE BUTTONS.
YUP. "ZERO," "ONE" AND "ENTER."
YOU HAVE TO INPUT EVERYTHING IN BINARY FORMAT, AND TO DO CALCULATIONS, YOU HAVE TO WRITE YOUR OWN ROUTINES IN MACHINE LANGUAGE, BIT BY BIT.
I'LL DEMON-STRATE. ASK ME TO COMPUTE SOMETHING.
ON A SCALE OF ONE TO TEN, HOW DORKY DO I THINK YOU ARE?
IT'S A CALCULATOR, NOT A MIND-READER.
I'LL HELP YOU OUT— PUSH THESE TWO KEYS...
AMEND

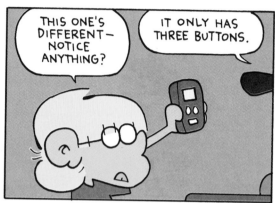

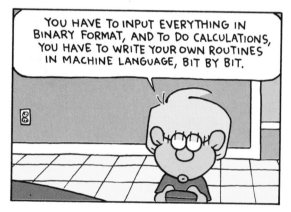

RUMBLE RUMBLE

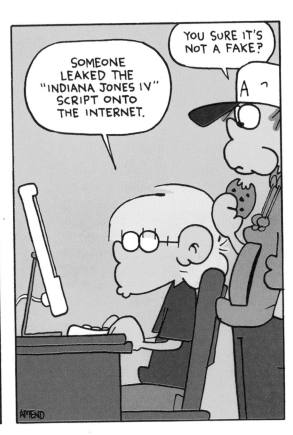

SOMEONE LEAKED THE "INDIANA JONES IV" SCRIPT ONTO THE INTERNET.

YOU SURE IT'S NOT A FAKE?

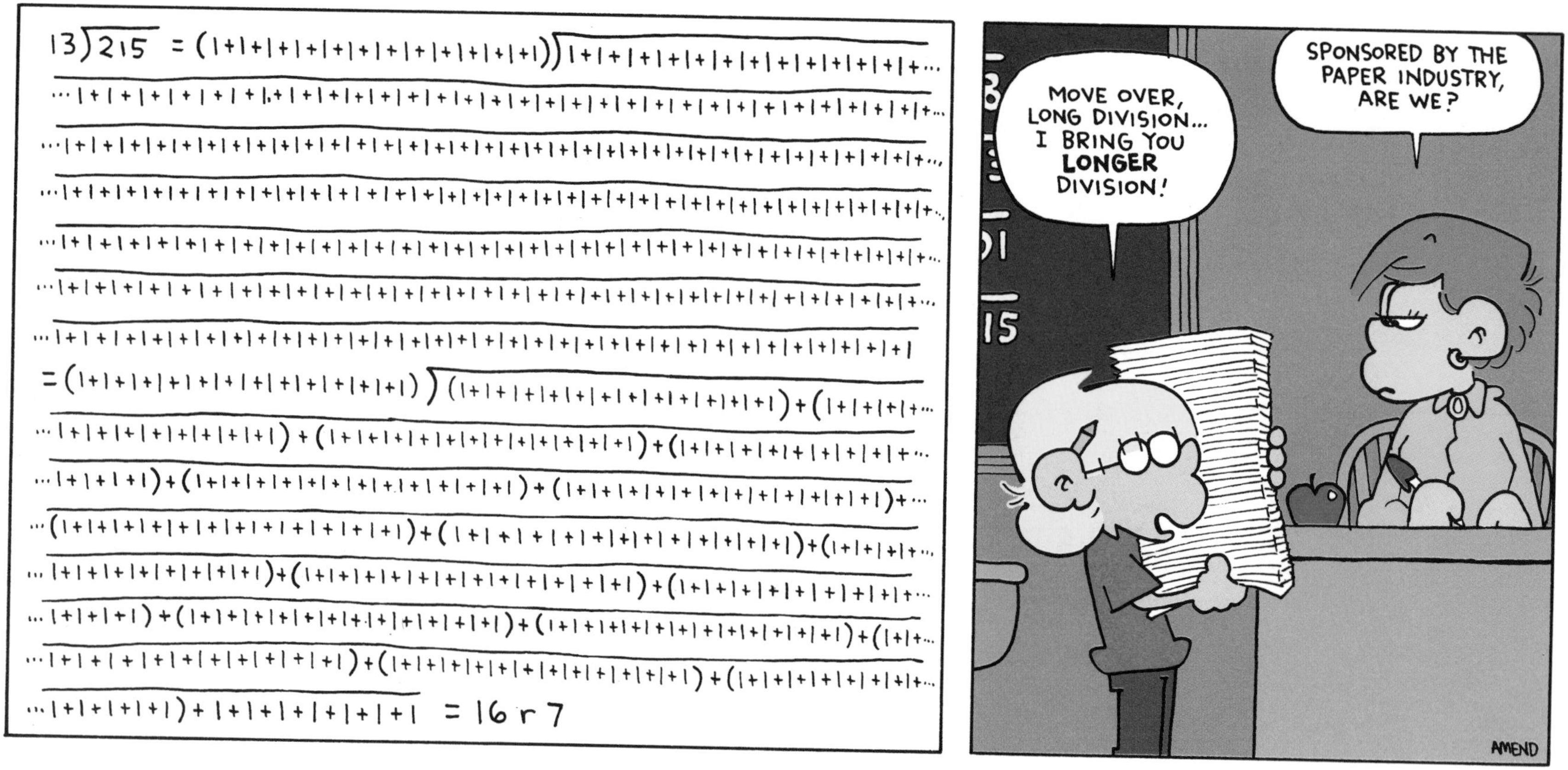
13)215
= 16 r 7
MOVE OVER, LONG DIVISION... I BRING YOU **LONGER** DIVISION!
SPONSORED BY THE PAPER INDUSTRY, ARE WE?
AMEND

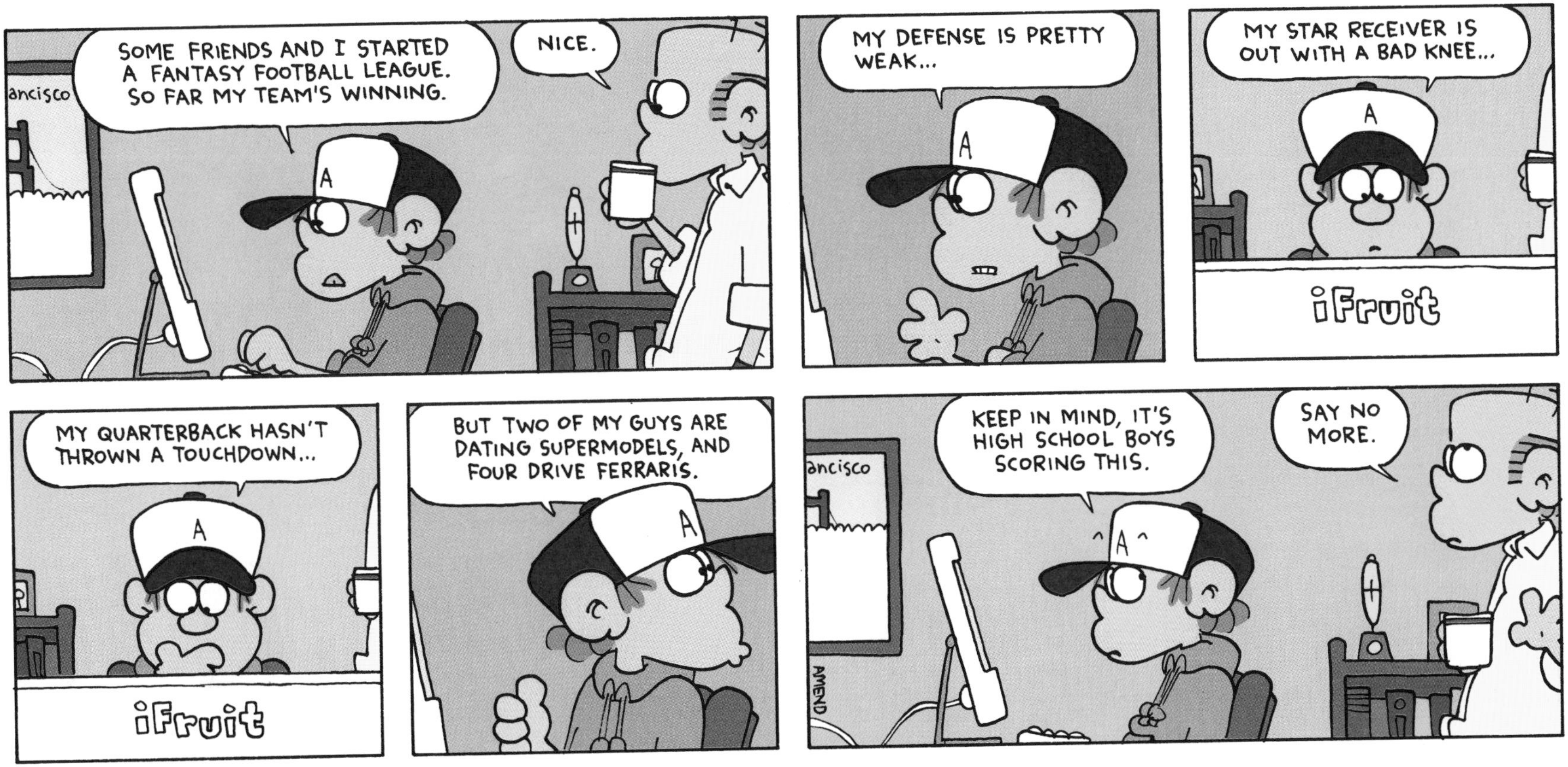
ancisco
SOME FRIENDS AND I STARTED A FANTASY FOOTBALL LEAGUE. SO FAR MY TEAM'S WINNING.
NICE.
MY DEFENSE IS PRETTY WEAK...
MY STAR RECEIVER IS OUT WITH A BAD KNEE...
iFruit
MY QUARTERBACK HASN'T THROWN A TOUCHDOWN...
iFruit
BUT TWO OF MY GUYS ARE DATING SUPERMODELS, AND FOUR DRIVE FERRARIS.
ancisco
KEEP IN MIND, IT'S HIGH SCHOOL BOYS SCORING THIS.
SAY NO MORE.
AMEND

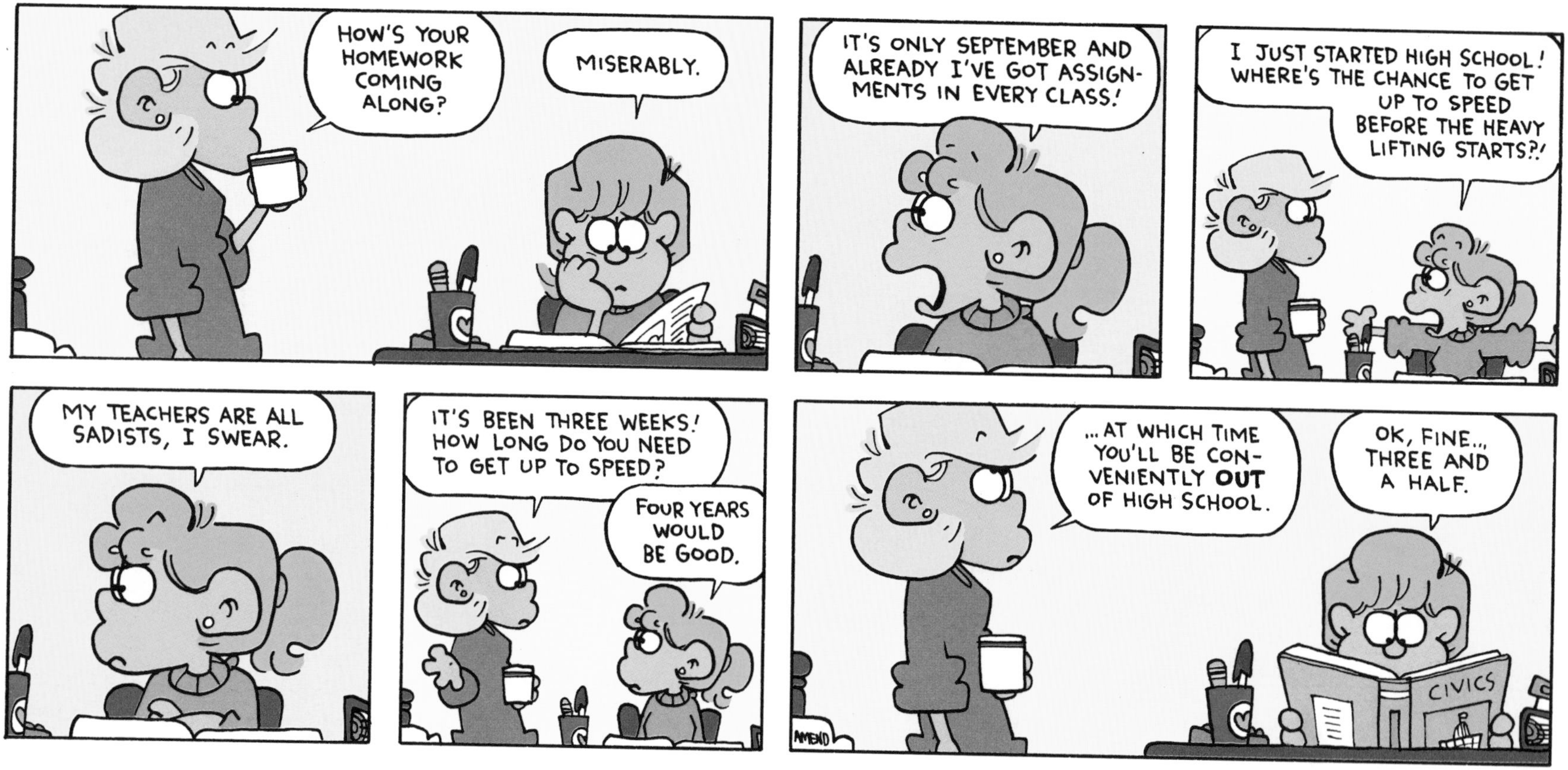

HOW'S YOUR HOMEWORK COMING ALONG?
MISERABLY.
IT'S ONLY SEPTEMBER AND ALREADY I'VE GOT ASSIGNMENTS IN EVERY CLASS!
I JUST STARTED HIGH SCHOOL! WHERE'S THE CHANCE TO GET UP TO SPEED BEFORE THE HEAVY LIFTING STARTS?!
MY TEACHERS ARE ALL SADISTS, I SWEAR.
IT'S BEEN THREE WEEKS! HOW LONG DO YOU NEED TO GET UP TO SPEED?
FOUR YEARS WOULD BE GOOD.
...AT WHICH TIME YOU'LL BE CONVENIENTLY **OUT** OF HIGH SCHOOL.
OK, FINE... THREE AND A HALF.
CIVICS
AMEND

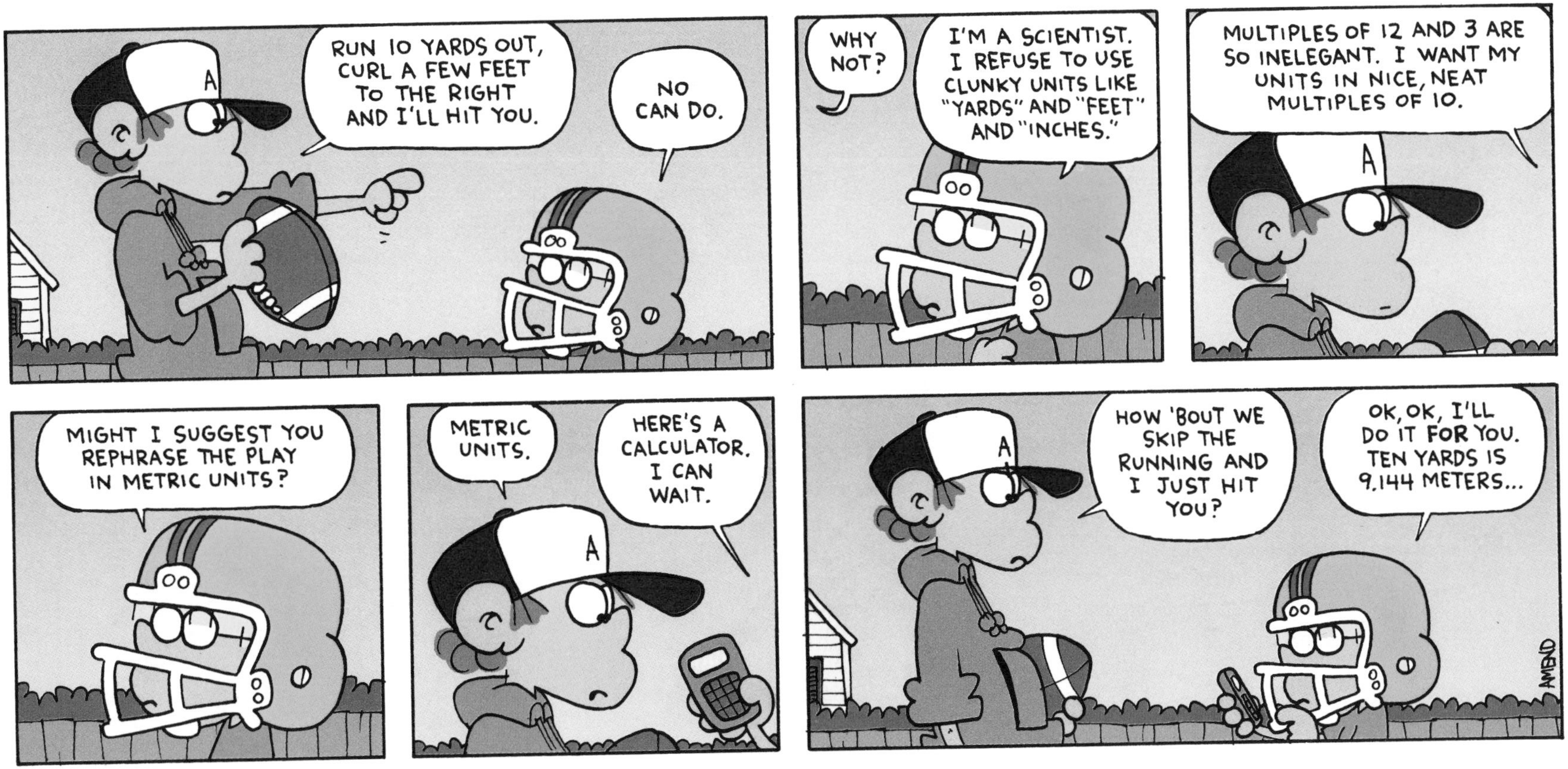
RUN 10 YARDS OUT, CURL A FEW FEET TO THE RIGHT AND I'LL HIT YOU.
NO CAN DO.
WHY NOT?
I'M A SCIENTIST. I REFUSE TO USE CLUNKY UNITS LIKE "YARDS" AND "FEET" AND "INCHES."
MULTIPLES OF 12 AND 3 ARE SO INELEGANT. I WANT MY UNITS IN NICE, NEAT MULTIPLES OF 10.
MIGHT I SUGGEST YOU REPHRASE THE PLAY IN METRIC UNITS?
METRIC UNITS.
HERE'S A CALCULATOR. I CAN WAIT.
HOW 'BOUT WE SKIP THE RUNNING AND I JUST HIT YOU?
OK, OK, I'LL DO IT **FOR** YOU. TEN YARDS IS 9.144 METERS...
AMEND

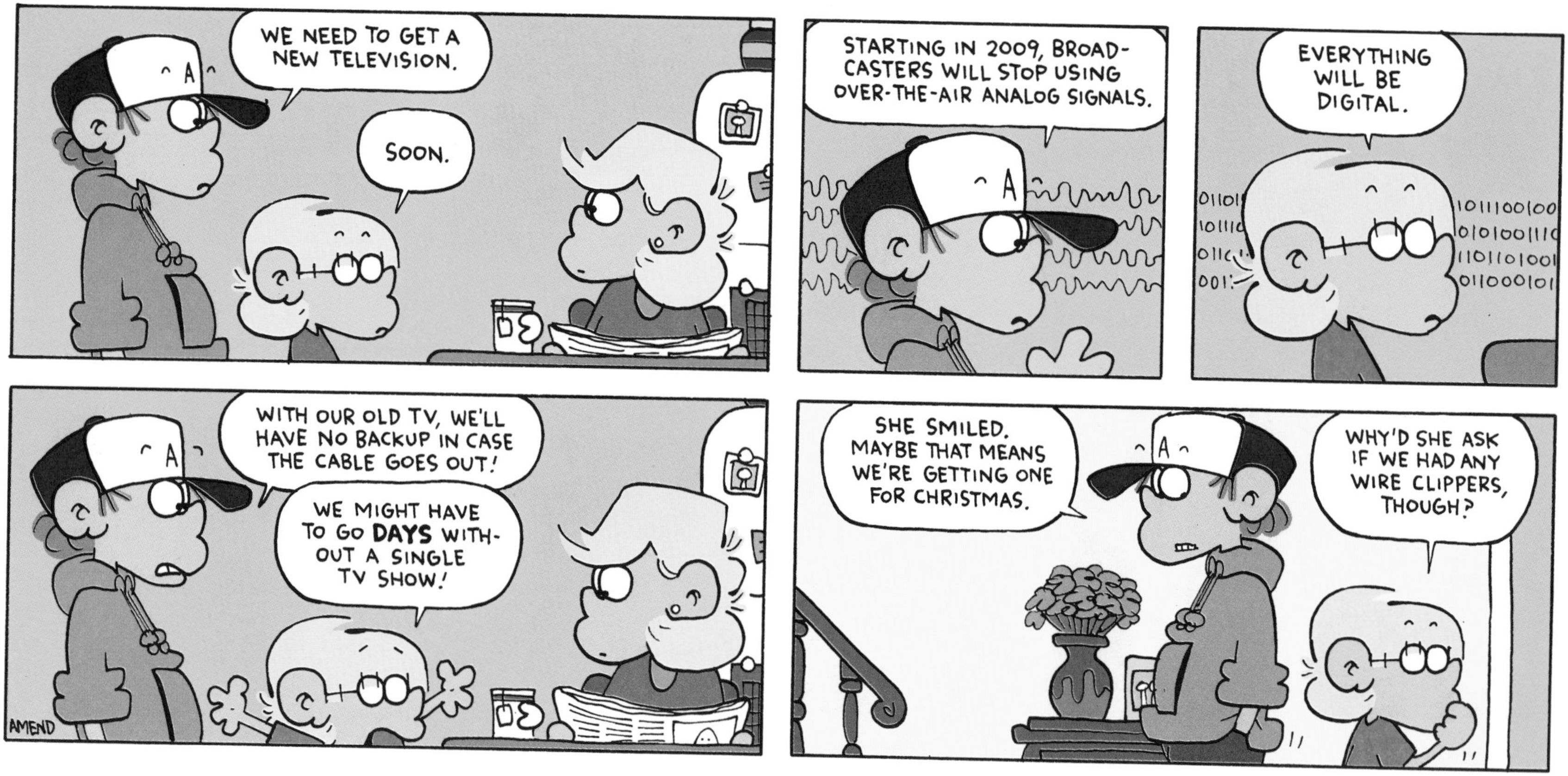
WE NEED TO GET A NEW TELEVISION.
SOON.
STARTING IN 2009, BROADCASTERS WILL STOP USING OVER-THE-AIR ANALOG SIGNALS.
EVERYTHING WILL BE DIGITAL.
01101 10110 0110 001
1011100100 0101001110 1101101001 011000101
WITH OUR OLD TV, WE'LL HAVE NO BACKUP IN CASE THE CABLE GOES OUT!
WE MIGHT HAVE TO GO **DAYS** WITHOUT A SINGLE TV SHOW!
AMEND
SHE SMILED. MAYBE THAT MEANS WE'RE GETTING ONE FOR CHRISTMAS.
WHY'D SHE ASK IF WE HAD ANY WIRE CLIPPERS, THOUGH?

MOM WANTS YOU TO CLEAN YOUR ROOM.

I'M WORKING ON IT.

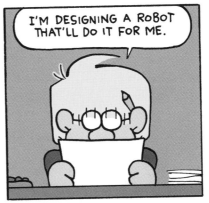

I'M DESIGNING A ROBOT THAT'LL DO IT FOR ME.

IT'LL MAKE MY BED, PICK UP MY CLOTHES, ORGANIZE MY CLOSET...

ITS SELF-CLEANING VACUUM SYSTEM IS PRETTY INNOVATIVE. I MIGHT GO FOR A PATENT.

AMEND

JASON, DO YOU HAVE ANY IDEA HOW LONG IT'LL TAKE TO BUILD A ROBOT?! MONTHS! YEARS!

WOULDN'T IT BE A TAD EASIER TO JUST CLEAN IT YOURSELF??

YOU OBVIOUSLY HAVEN'T SEEN MY CLOSET LATELY.

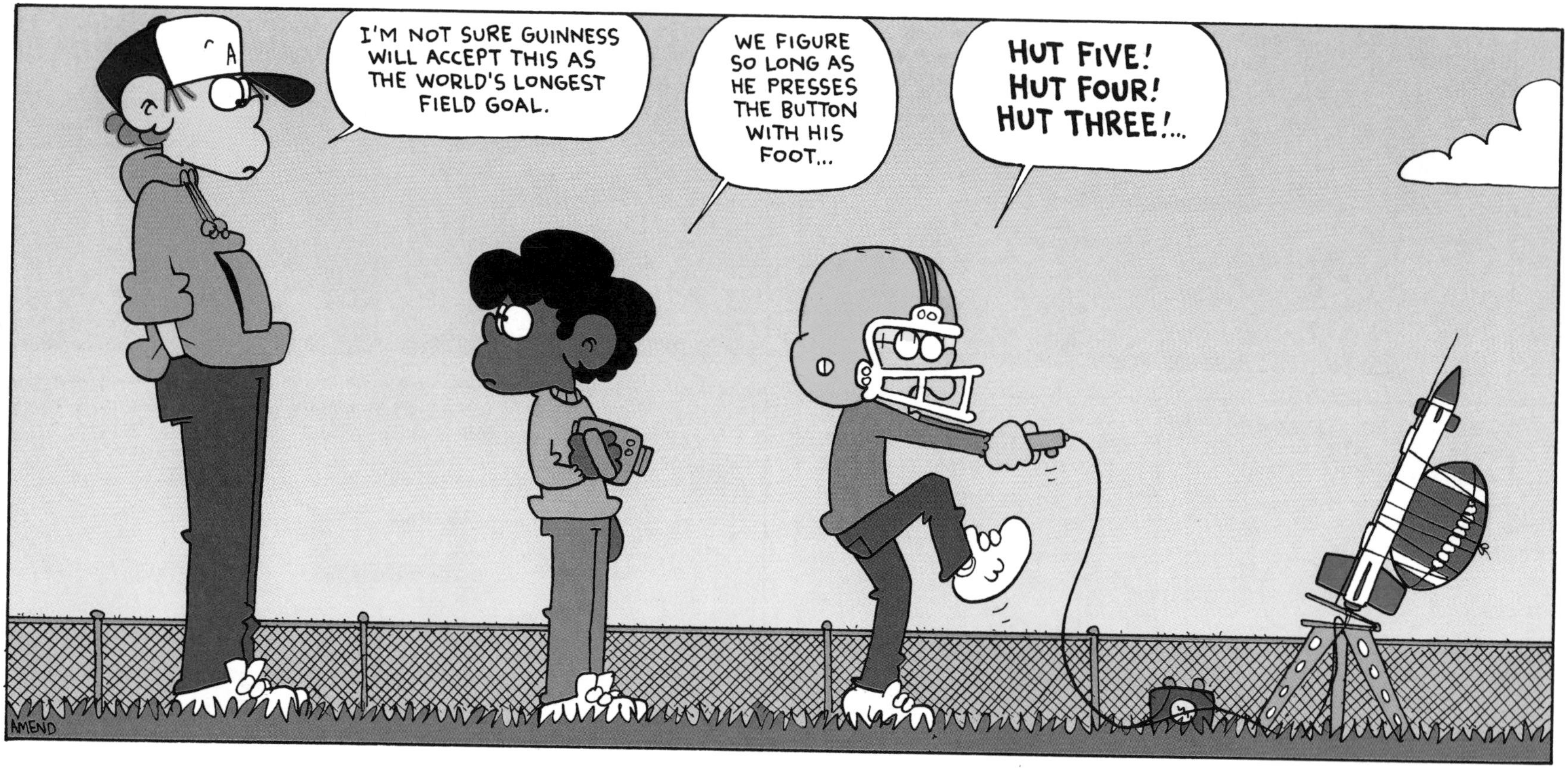
I'M NOT SURE GUINNESS WILL ACCEPT THIS AS THE WORLD'S LONGEST FIELD GOAL.
WE FIGURE SO LONG AS HE PRESSES THE BUTTON WITH HIS FOOT...
HUT FIVE! HUT FOUR! HUT THREE!...
AMEND

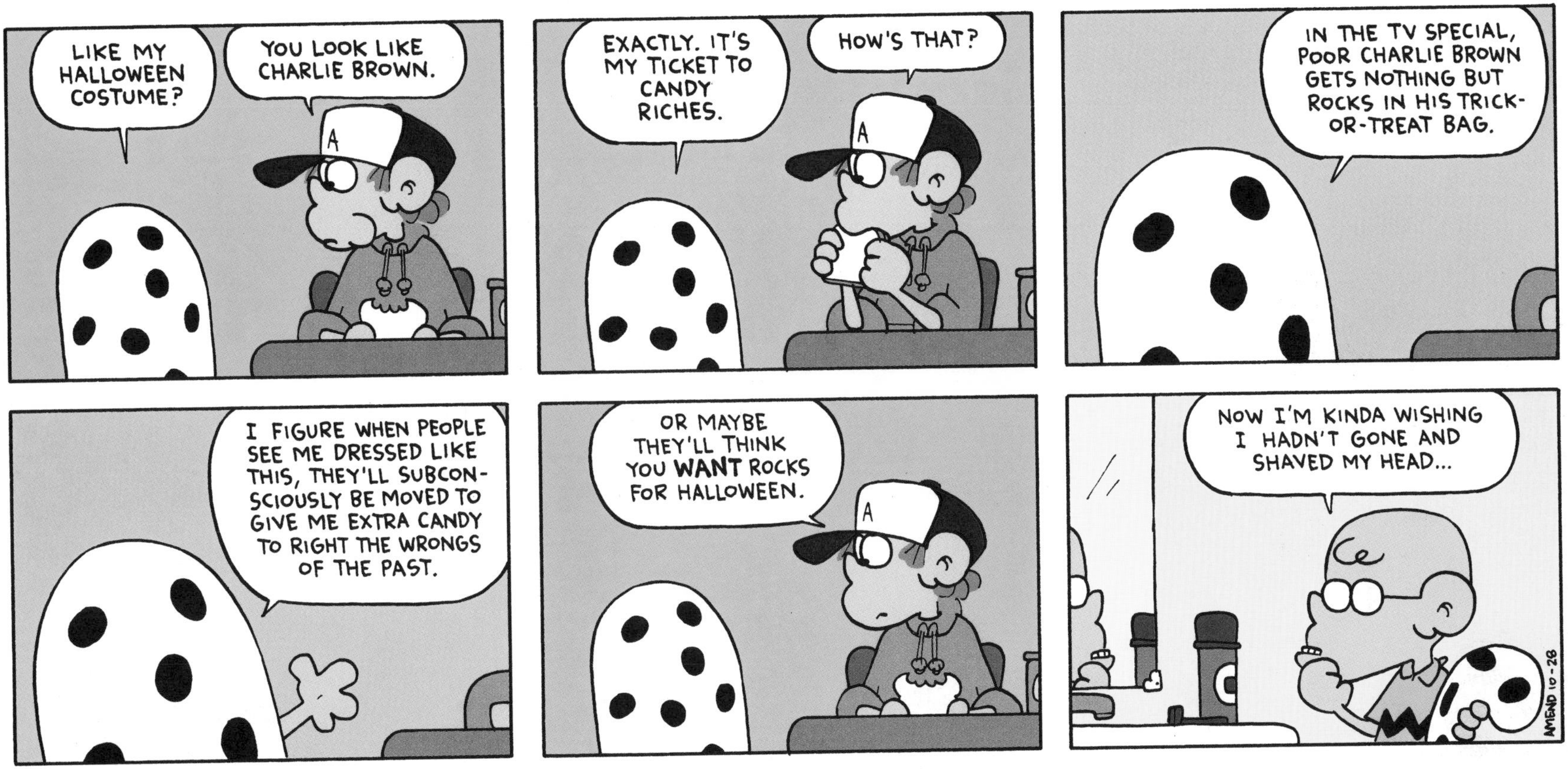
LIKE MY HALLOWEEN COSTUME?
YOU LOOK LIKE CHARLIE BROWN.
EXACTLY. IT'S MY TICKET TO CANDY RICHES.
HOW'S THAT?
IN THE TV SPECIAL, POOR CHARLIE BROWN GETS NOTHING BUT ROCKS IN HIS TRICK-OR-TREAT BAG.
I FIGURE WHEN PEOPLE SEE ME DRESSED LIKE THIS, THEY'LL SUBCONSCIOUSLY BE MOVED TO GIVE ME EXTRA CANDY TO RIGHT THE WRONGS OF THE PAST.
OR MAYBE THEY'LL THINK YOU WANT ROCKS FOR HALLOWEEN.
NOW I'M KINDA WISHING I HADN'T GONE AND SHAVED MY HEAD...
AMEND 10-28

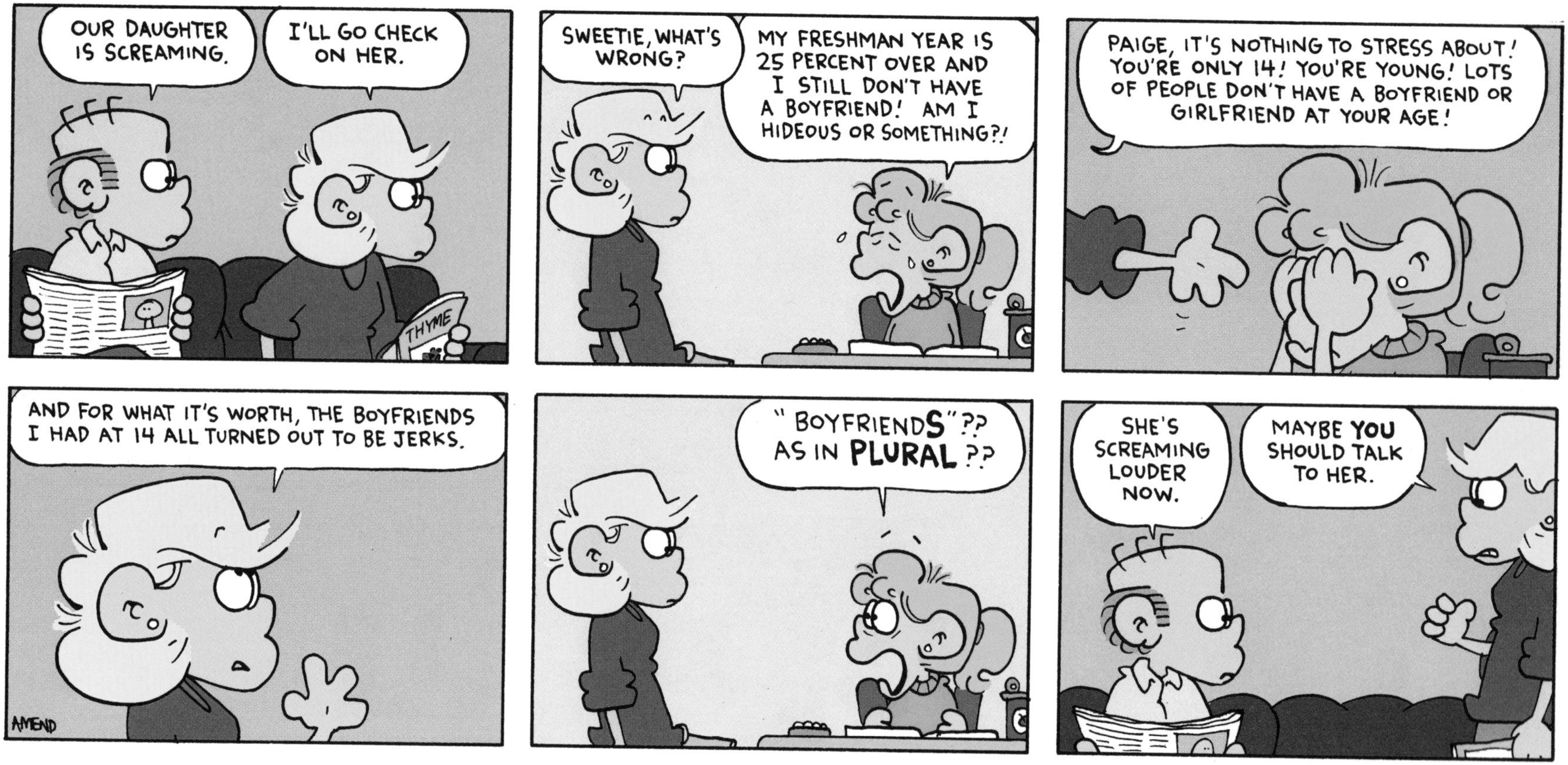
OUR DAUGHTER IS SCREAMING.
I'LL GO CHECK ON HER.
THYME
SWEETIE, WHAT'S WRONG?
MY FRESHMAN YEAR IS 25 PERCENT OVER AND I STILL DON'T HAVE A BOYFRIEND! AM I HIDEOUS OR SOMETHING?!
PAIGE, IT'S NOTHING TO STRESS ABOUT! YOU'RE ONLY 14! YOU'RE YOUNG! LOTS OF PEOPLE DON'T HAVE A BOYFRIEND OR GIRLFRIEND AT YOUR AGE!
AND FOR WHAT IT'S WORTH, THE BOYFRIENDS I HAD AT 14 ALL TURNED OUT TO BE JERKS.
AMEND
"BOYFRIENDS"?? AS IN PLURAL??
SHE'S SCREAMING LOUDER NOW.
MAYBE YOU SHOULD TALK TO HER.

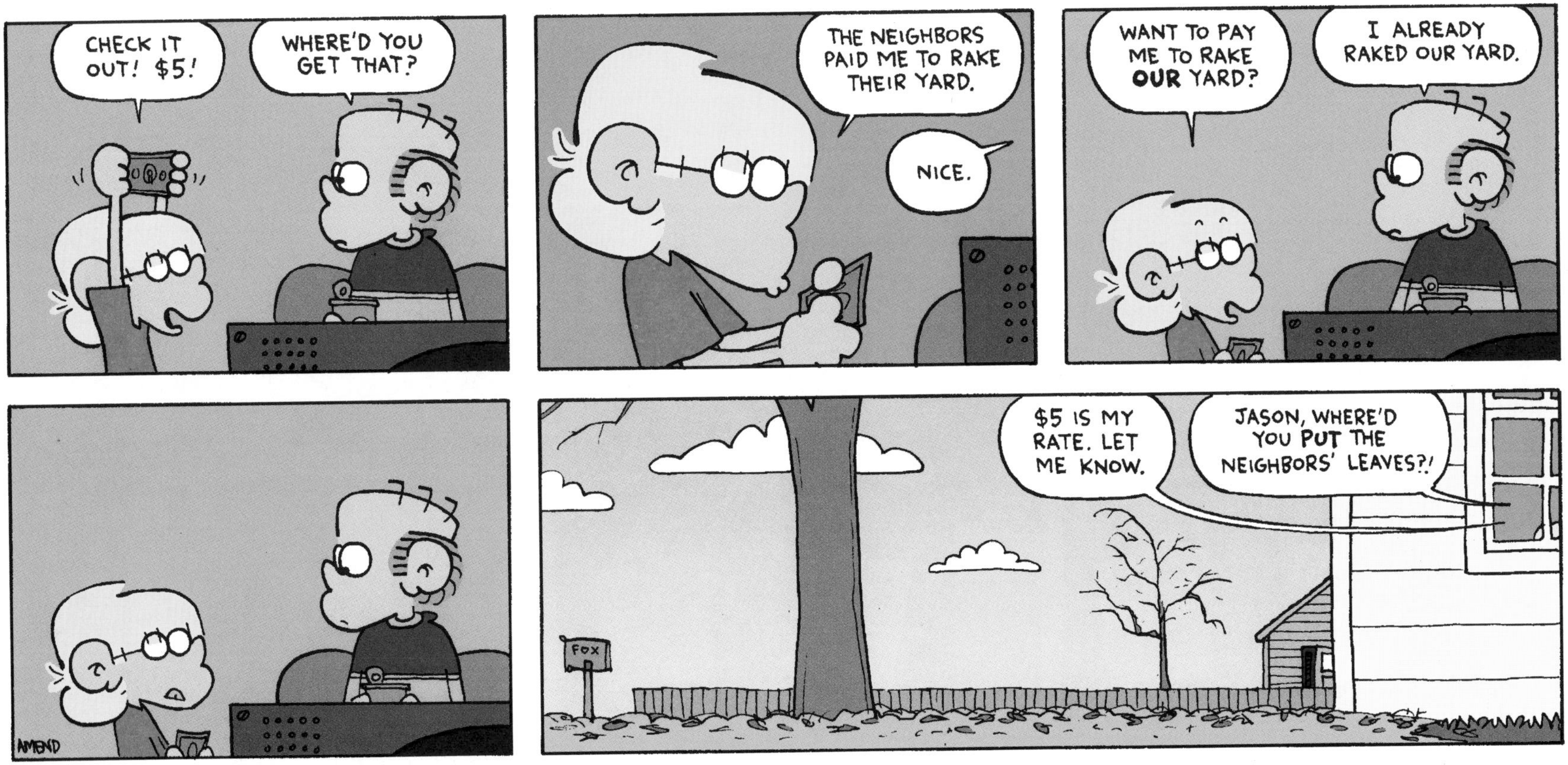
CHECK IT OUT! $5!
WHERE'D YOU GET THAT?
THE NEIGHBORS PAID ME TO RAKE THEIR YARD.
NICE.
WANT TO PAY ME TO RAKE **OUR** YARD?
I ALREADY RAKED OUR YARD.
AMEND
$5 IS MY RATE. LET ME KNOW.
JASON, WHERE'D YOU **PUT** THE NEIGHBORS' LEAVES?!
FOX

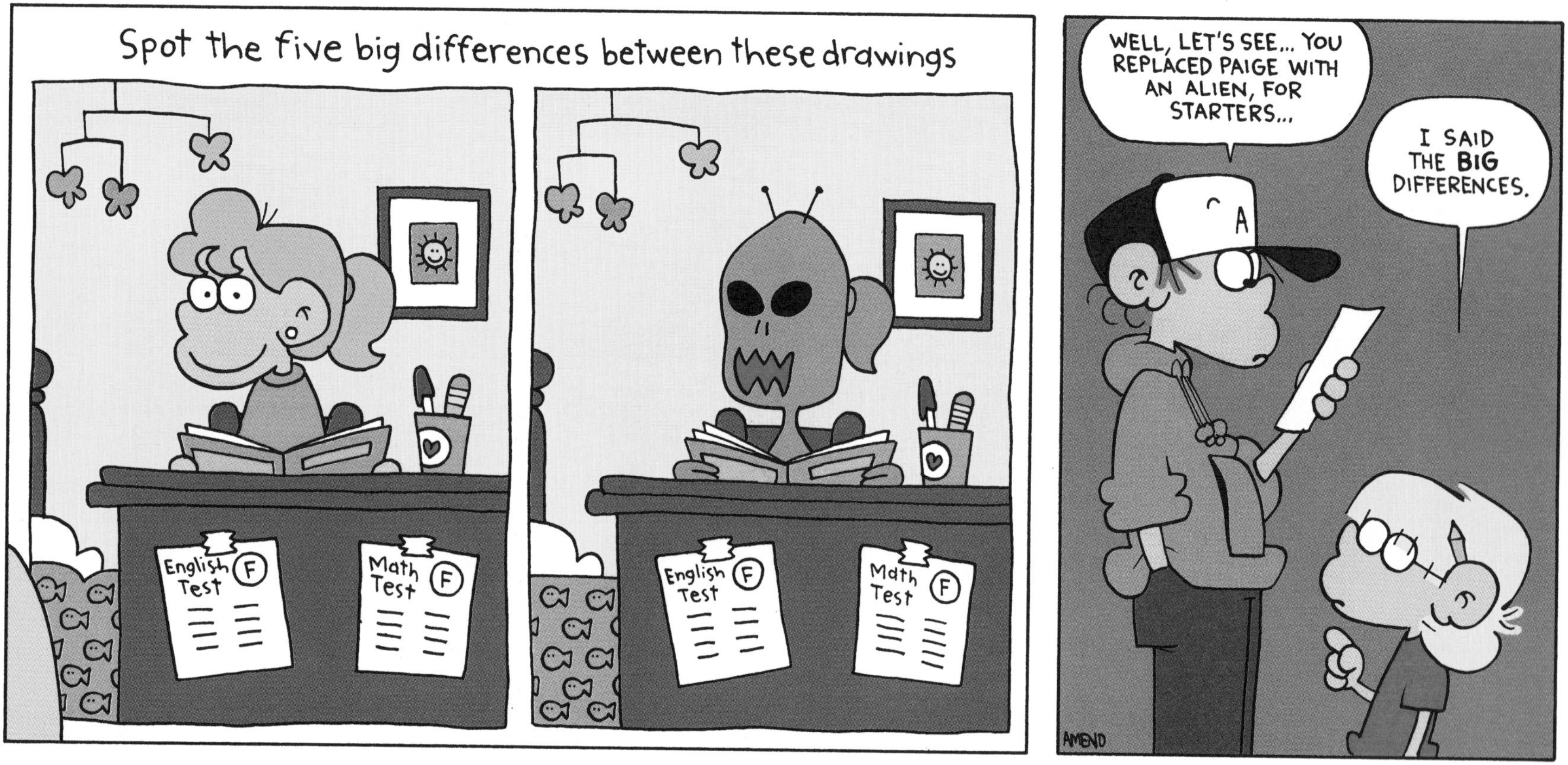
Spot the five big differences between these drawings
English Test F
Math Test F
English Test F
Math Test F
WELL, LET'S SEE... YOU REPLACED PAIGE WITH AN ALIEN, FOR STARTERS...
I SAID THE BIG DIFFERENCES.
A
AMEND

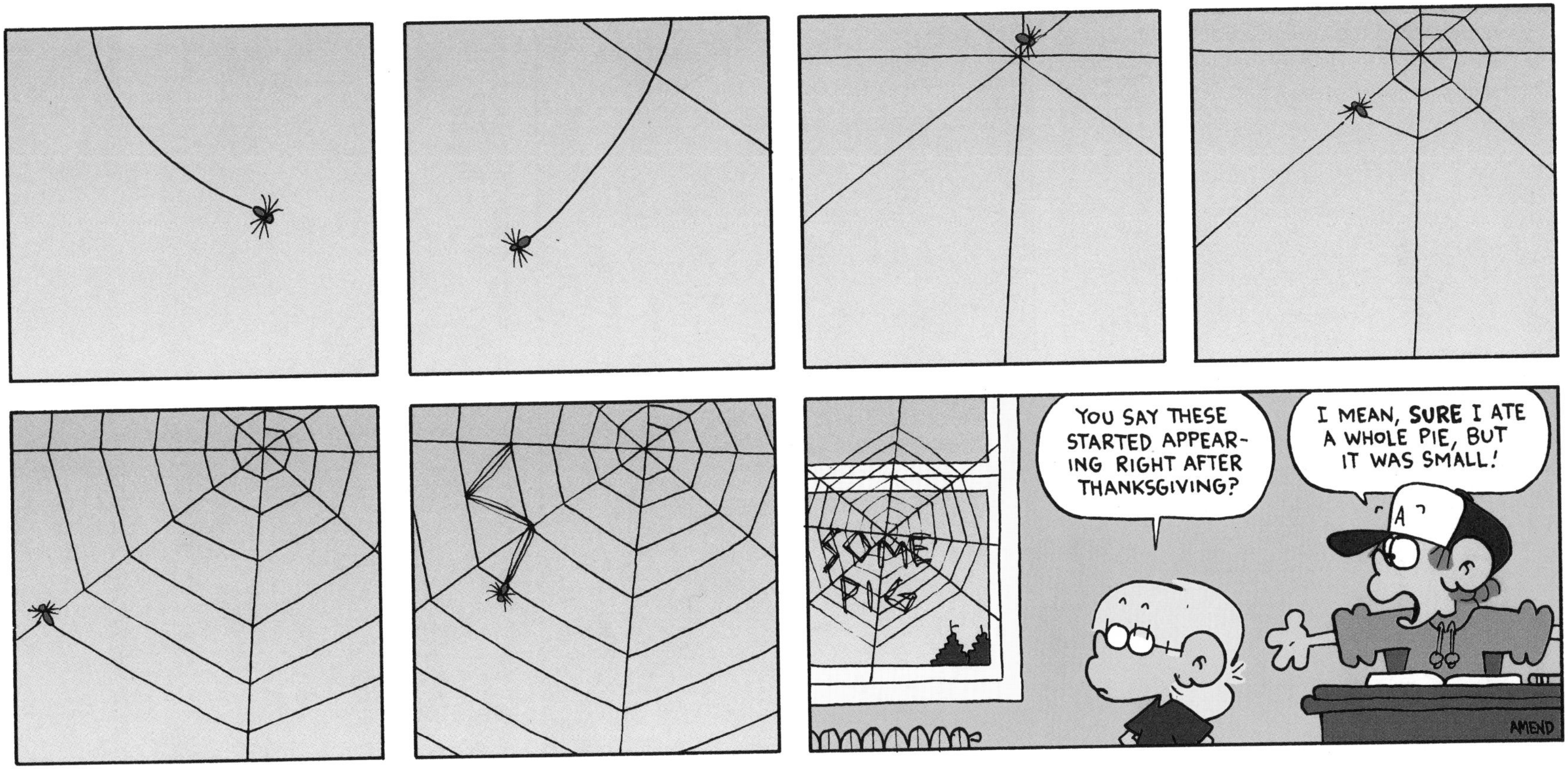
SOME PIG
YOU SAY THESE STARTED APPEAR-ING RIGHT AFTER THANKSGIVING?
I MEAN, SURE I ATE A WHOLE PIE, BUT IT WAS SMALL!
A
AMEND

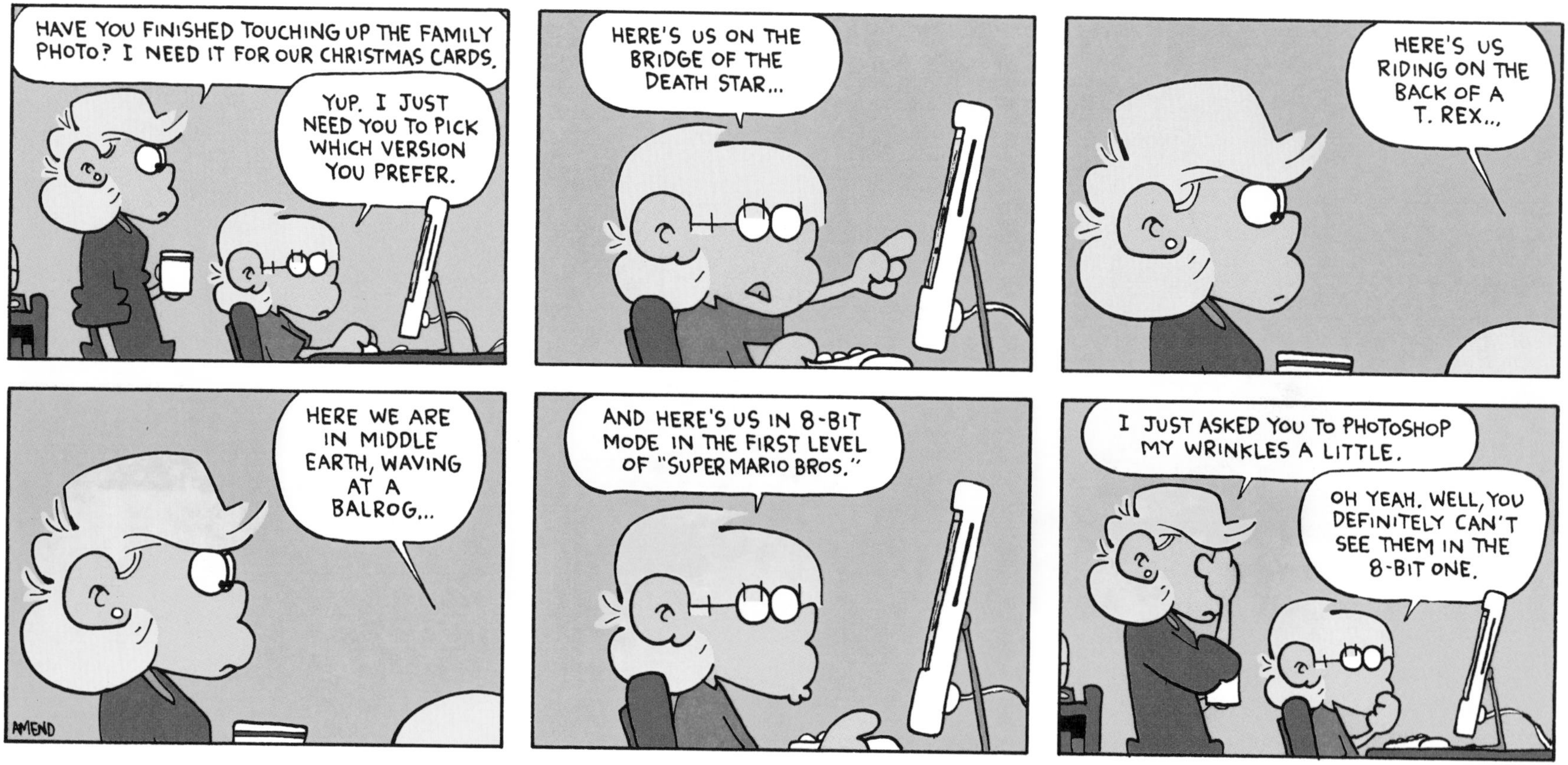
HAVE YOU FINISHED TOUCHING UP THE FAMILY PHOTO? I NEED IT FOR OUR CHRISTMAS CARDS.
YUP. I JUST NEED YOU TO PICK WHICH VERSION YOU PREFER.
HERE'S US ON THE BRIDGE OF THE DEATH STAR...
HERE'S US RIDING ON THE BACK OF A T. REX...
HERE WE ARE IN MIDDLE EARTH, WAVING AT A BALROG...
AND HERE'S US IN 8-BIT MODE IN THE FIRST LEVEL OF "SUPER MARIO BROS."
I JUST ASKED YOU TO PHOTOSHOP MY WRINKLES A LITTLE.
OH YEAH. WELL, YOU DEFINITELY CAN'T SEE THEM IN THE 8-BIT ONE.
AMEND

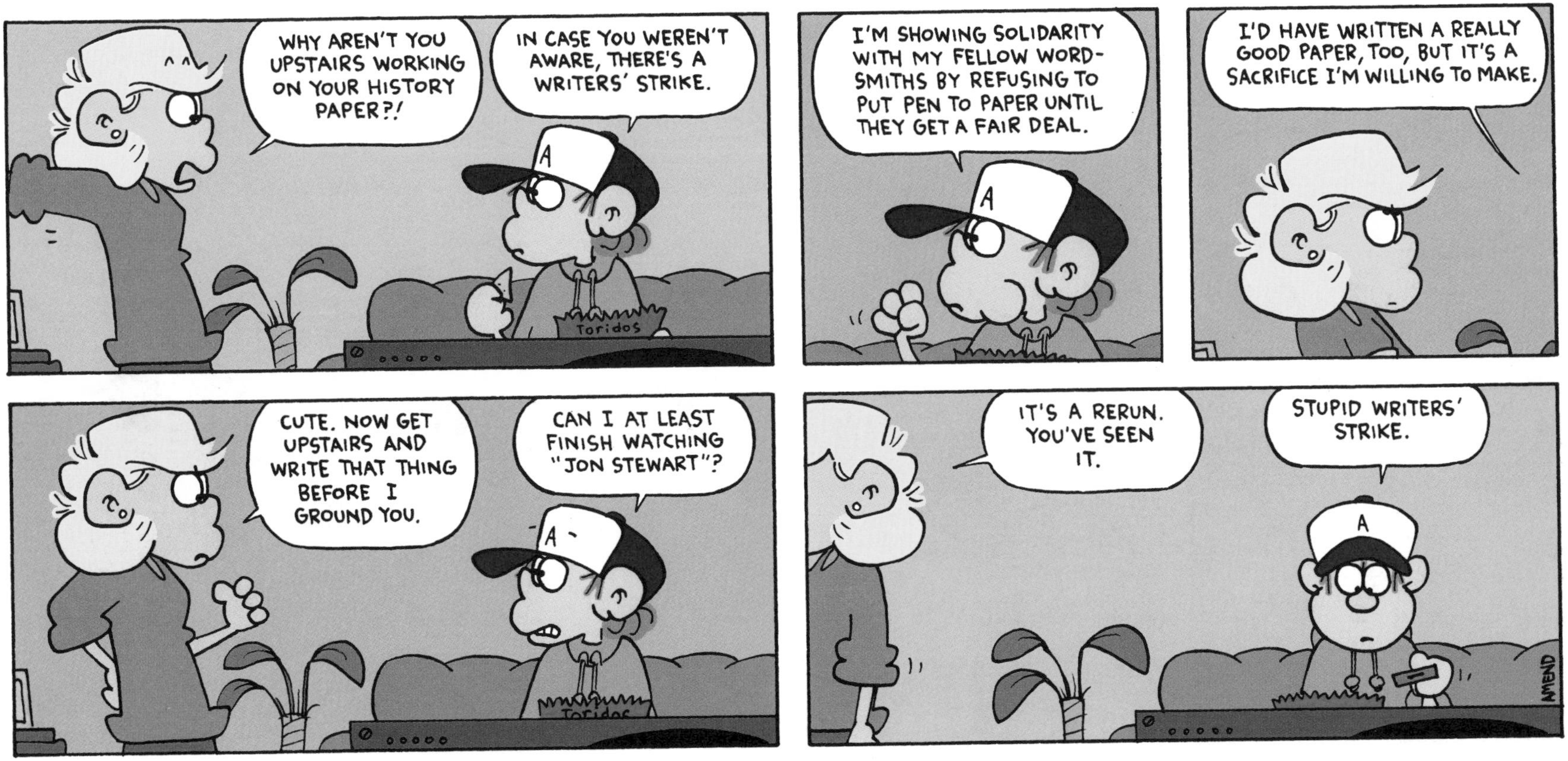
WHY AREN'T YOU UPSTAIRS WORKING ON YOUR HISTORY PAPER?!
IN CASE YOU WEREN'T AWARE, THERE'S A WRITERS' STRIKE.
Toridos
I'M SHOWING SOLIDARITY WITH MY FELLOW WORD-SMITHS BY REFUSING TO PUT PEN TO PAPER UNTIL THEY GET A FAIR DEAL.
I'D HAVE WRITTEN A REALLY GOOD PAPER, TOO, BUT IT'S A SACRIFICE I'M WILLING TO MAKE.
CUTE. NOW GET UPSTAIRS AND WRITE THAT THING BEFORE I GROUND YOU.
CAN I AT LEAST FINISH WATCHING "JON STEWART"?
IT'S A RERUN. YOU'VE SEEN IT.
STUPID WRITERS' STRIKE.
AMEND

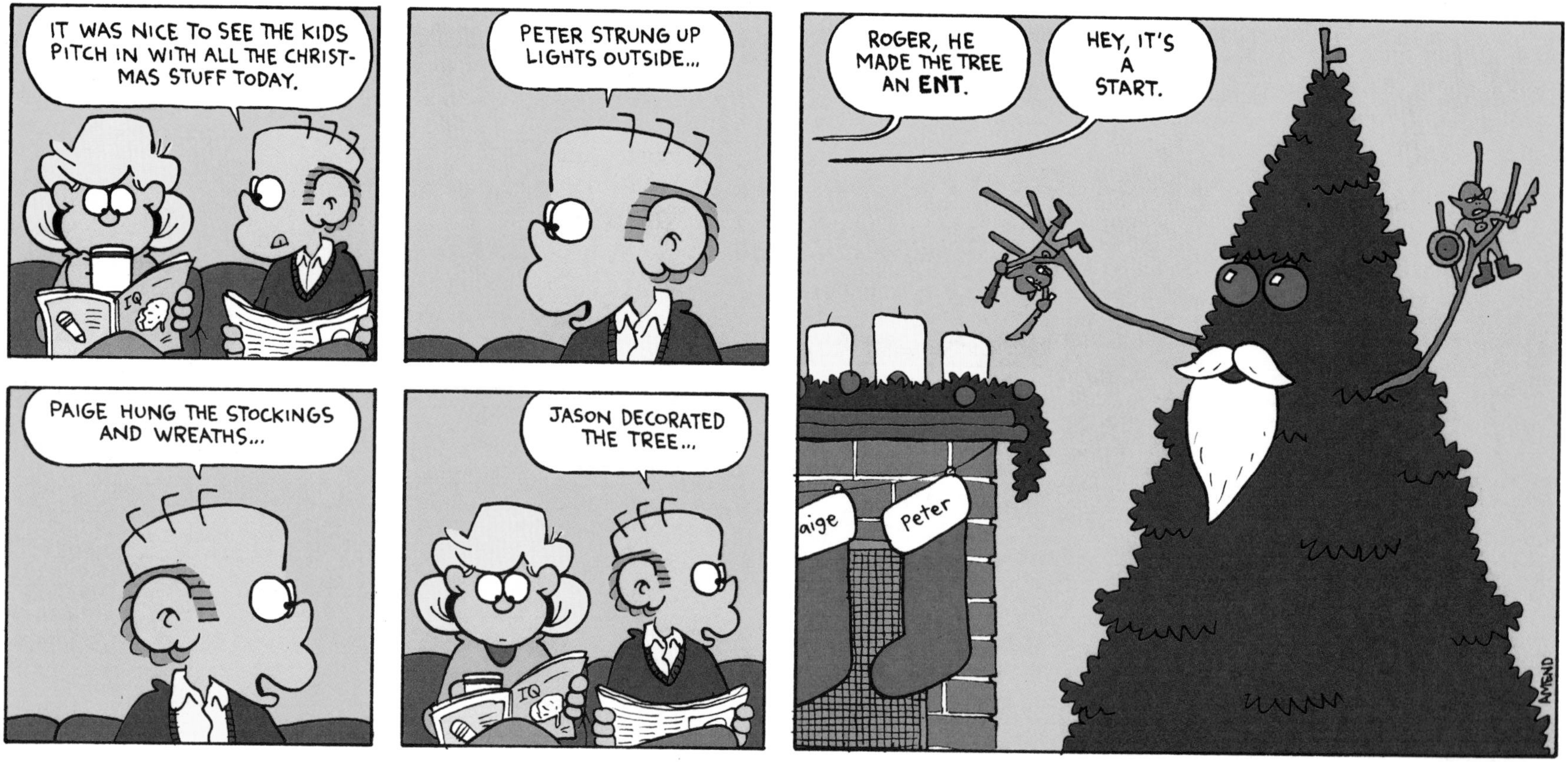
IT WAS NICE TO SEE THE KIDS PITCH IN WITH ALL THE CHRIST-MAS STUFF TODAY.
IQ
PETER STRUNG UP LIGHTS OUTSIDE...
PAIGE HUNG THE STOCKINGS AND WREATHS...
JASON DECORATED THE TREE...
IQ
ROGER, HE MADE THE TREE AN **ENT**.
HEY, IT'S A START.
aige
Peter
AMEND

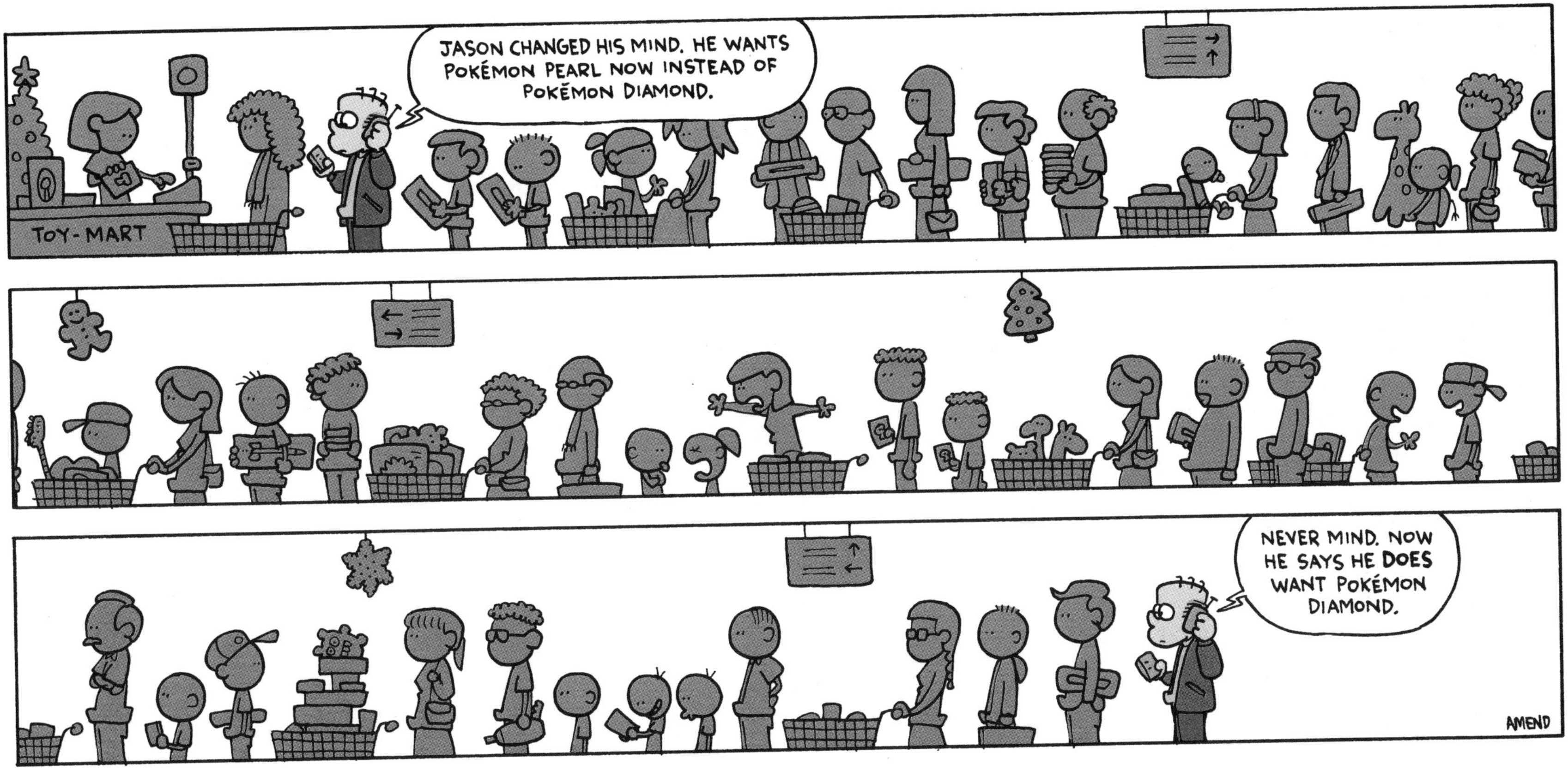

JASON CHANGED HIS MIND. HE WANTS POKÉMON PEARL NOW INSTEAD OF POKÉMON DIAMOND.
TOY-MART
NEVER MIND. NOW HE SAYS HE **DOES** WANT POKÉMON DIAMOND.
AMEND

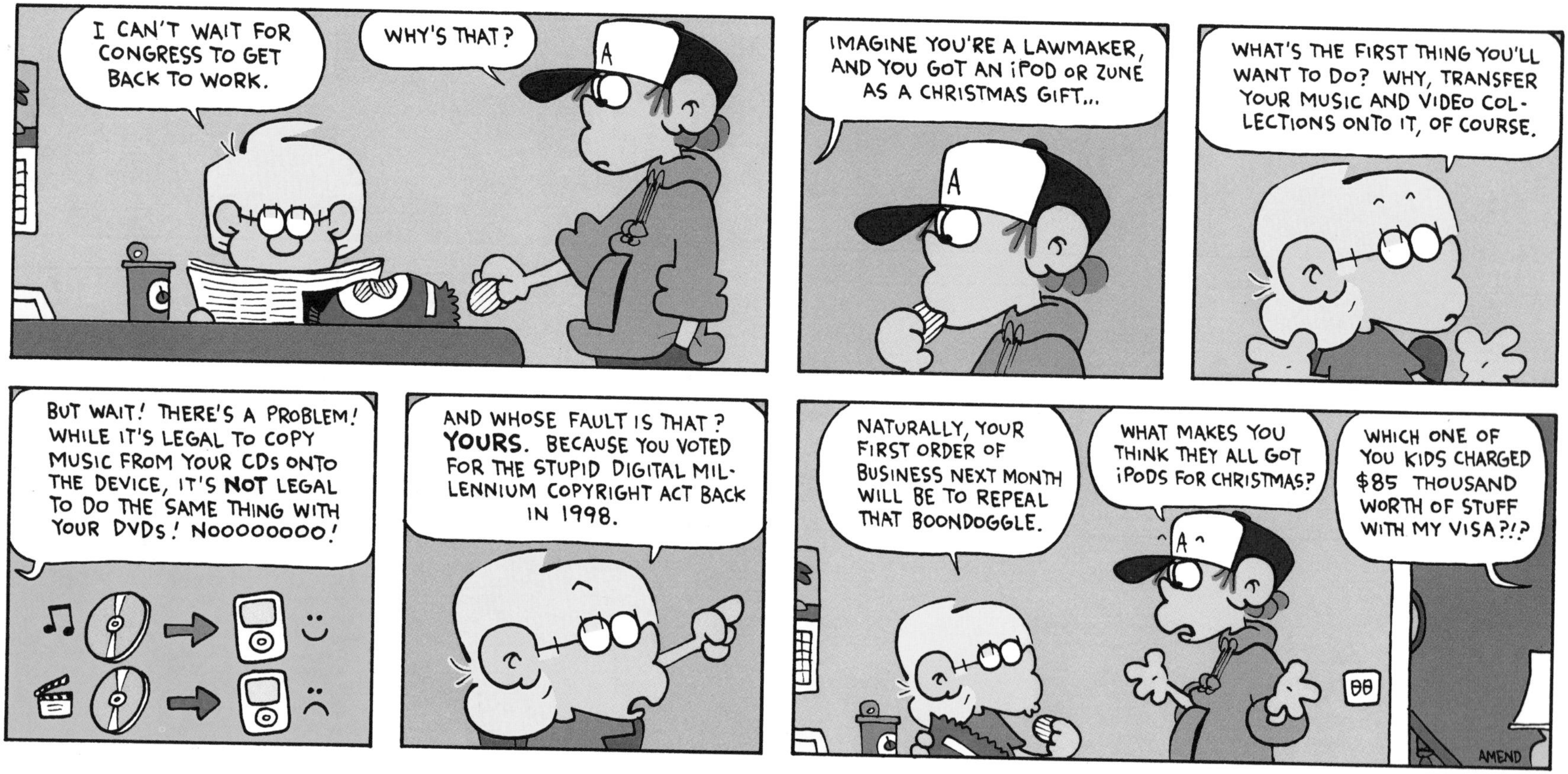
I CAN'T WAIT FOR CONGRESS TO GET BACK TO WORK.
WHY'S THAT?
IMAGINE YOU'RE A LAWMAKER, AND YOU GOT AN iPOD OR ZUNE AS A CHRISTMAS GIFT...
WHAT'S THE FIRST THING YOU'LL WANT TO DO? WHY, TRANSFER YOUR MUSIC AND VIDEO COLLECTIONS ONTO IT, OF COURSE.
BUT WAIT! THERE'S A PROBLEM! WHILE IT'S LEGAL TO COPY MUSIC FROM YOUR CDs ONTO THE DEVICE, IT'S NOT LEGAL TO DO THE SAME THING WITH YOUR DVDs! NOOOOOOOO!
AND WHOSE FAULT IS THAT? YOURS. BECAUSE YOU VOTED FOR THE STUPID DIGITAL MILLENNIUM COPYRIGHT ACT BACK IN 1998.
NATURALLY, YOUR FIRST ORDER OF BUSINESS NEXT MONTH WILL BE TO REPEAL THAT BOONDOGGLE.
WHAT MAKES YOU THINK THEY ALL GOT iPODS FOR CHRISTMAS?
WHICH ONE OF YOU KIDS CHARGED $85 THOUSAND WORTH OF STUFF WITH MY VISA?!?
AMEND

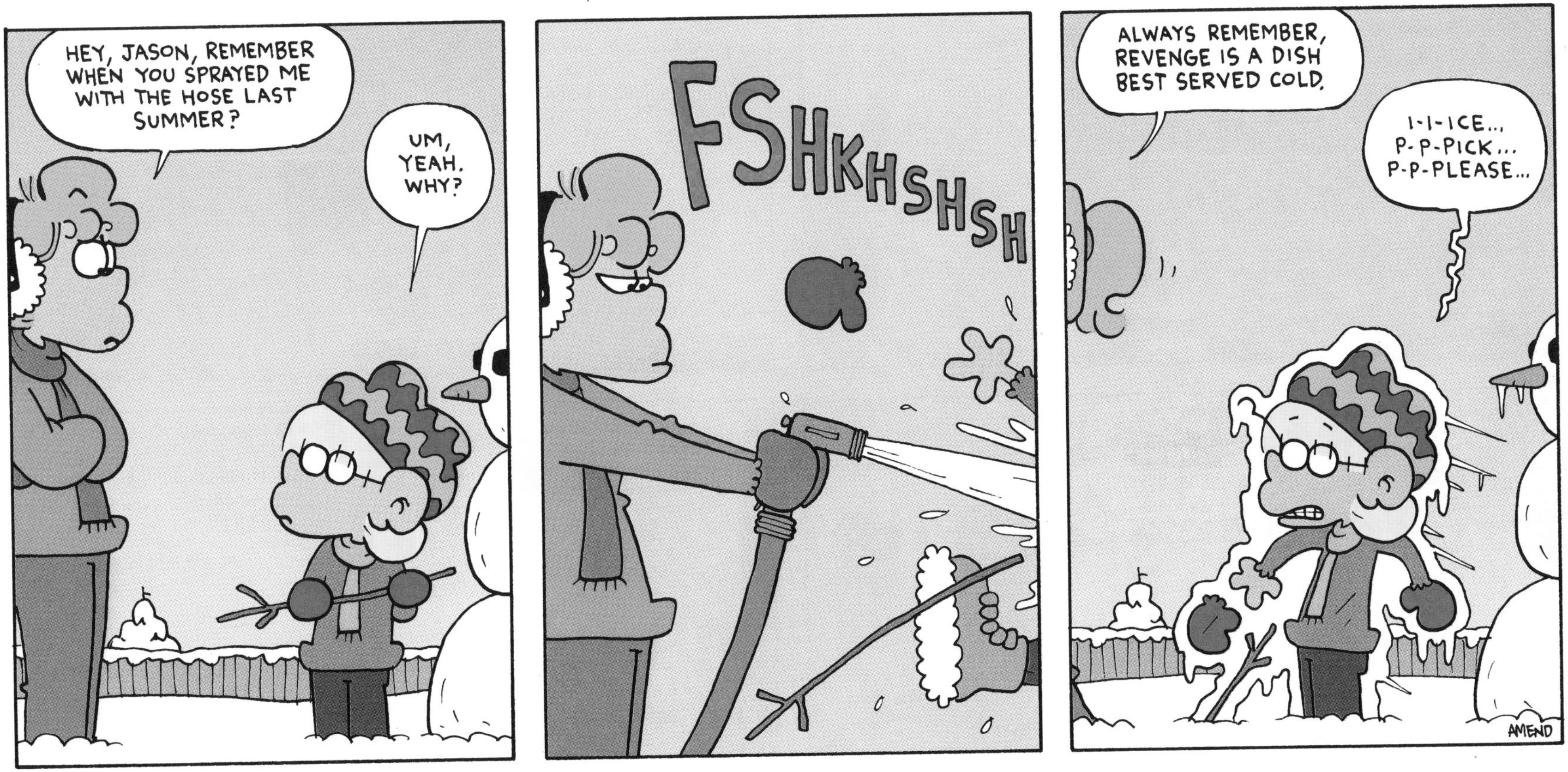
HEY, JASON, REMEMBER WHEN YOU SPRAYED ME WITH THE HOSE LAST SUMMER?
UM, YEAH. WHY?
FSHKHSHSH
ALWAYS REMEMBER, REVENGE IS A DISH BEST SERVED COLD.
I-I-ICE... P-P-PICK... P-P-PLEASE...
AMEND

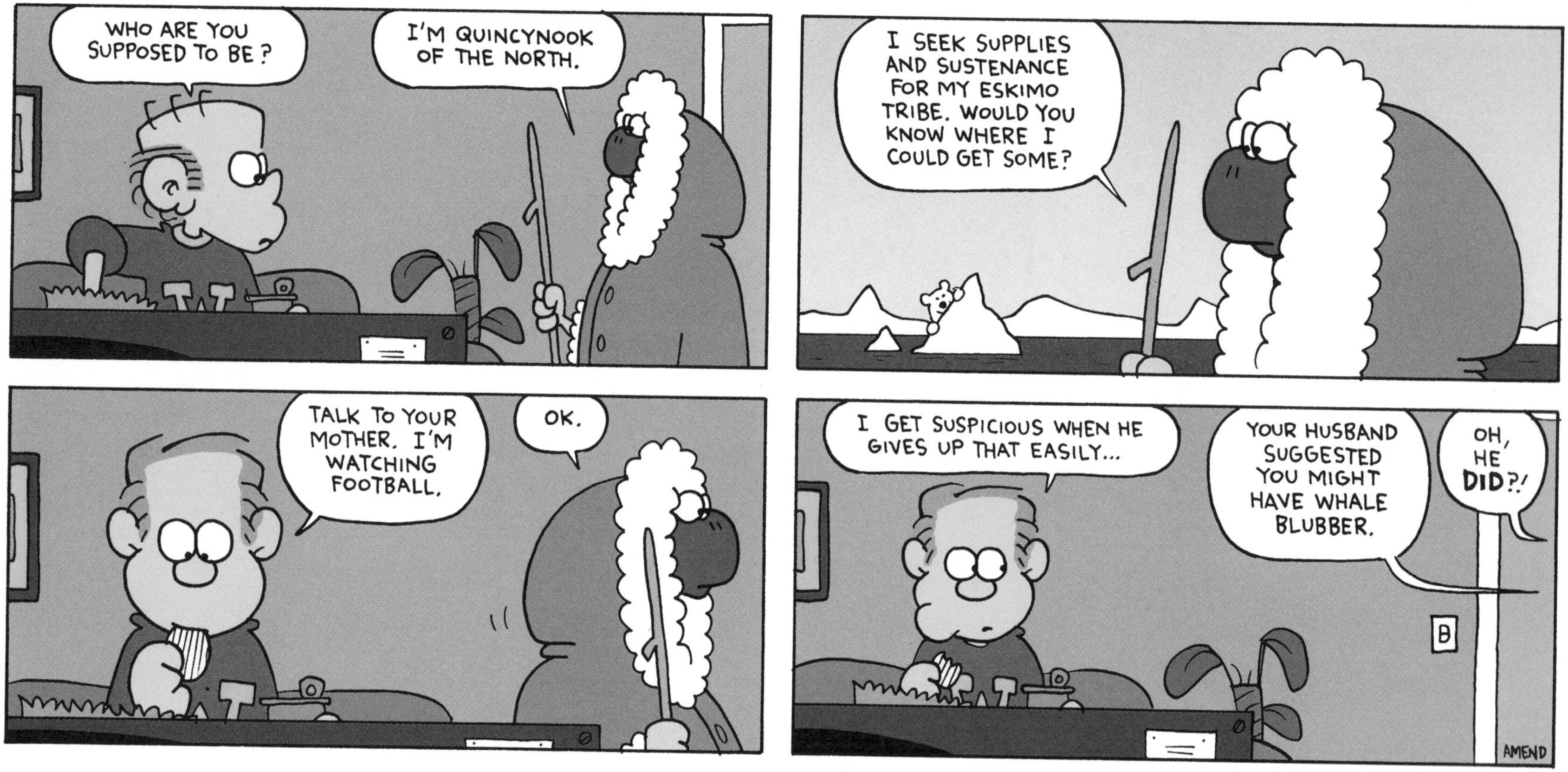
WHO ARE YOU SUPPOSED TO BE?
I'M QUINCYNOOK OF THE NORTH.
I SEEK SUPPLIES AND SUSTENANCE FOR MY ESKIMO TRIBE. WOULD YOU KNOW WHERE I COULD GET SOME?
TALK TO YOUR MOTHER. I'M WATCHING FOOTBALL.
OK.
I GET SUSPICIOUS WHEN HE GIVES UP THAT EASILY...
YOUR HUSBAND SUGGESTED YOU MIGHT HAVE WHALE BLUBBER.
OH, HE DID?!
AMEND

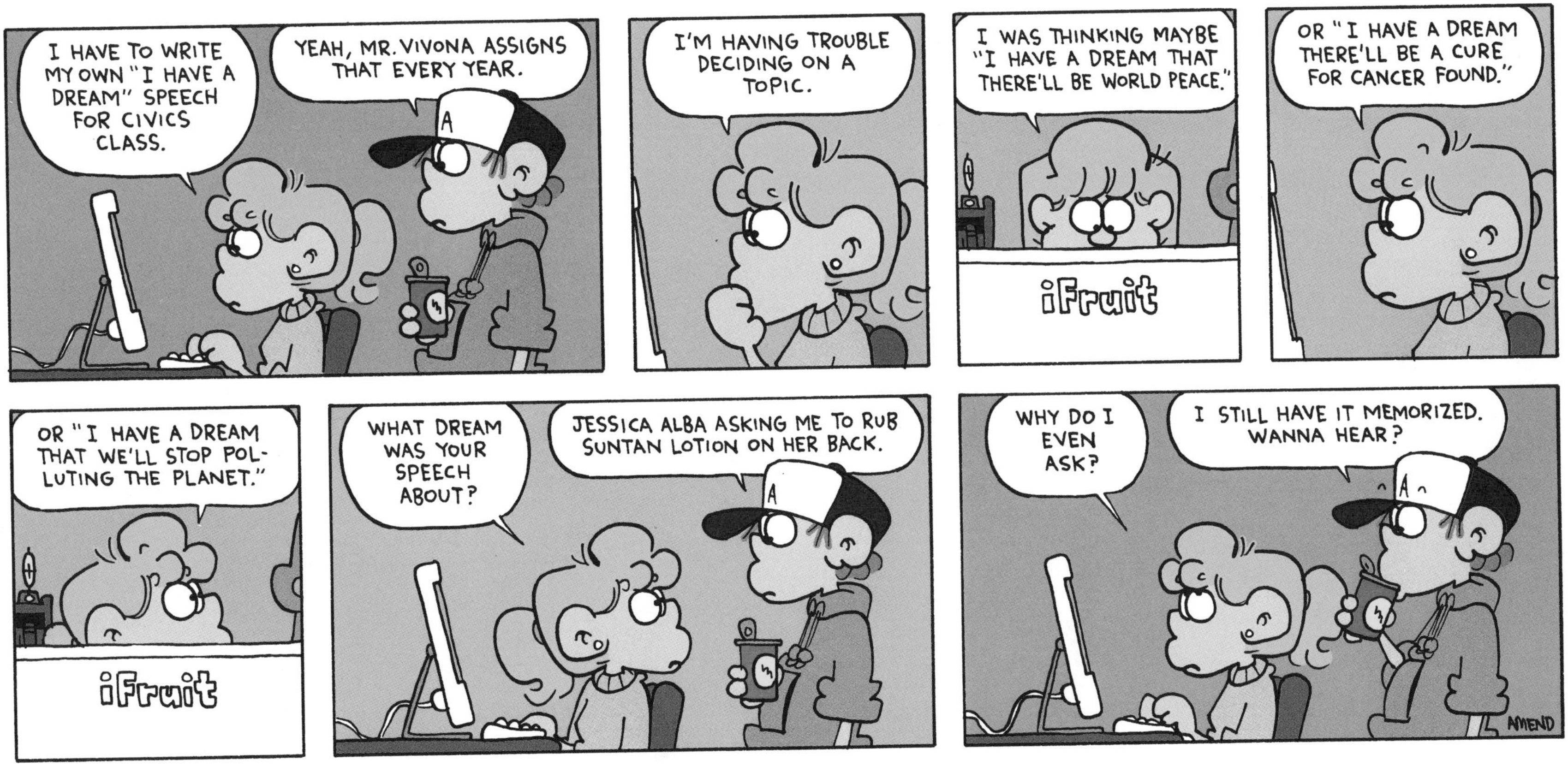
I HAVE TO WRITE MY OWN "I HAVE A DREAM" SPEECH FOR CIVICS CLASS.
YEAH, MR. VIVONA ASSIGNS THAT EVERY YEAR.
I'M HAVING TROUBLE DECIDING ON A TOPIC.
I WAS THINKING MAYBE "I HAVE A DREAM THAT THERE'LL BE WORLD PEACE."
iFruit
OR "I HAVE A DREAM THERE'LL BE A CURE FOR CANCER FOUND."
OR "I HAVE A DREAM THAT WE'LL STOP POL-LUTING THE PLANET."
iFruit
WHAT DREAM WAS YOUR SPEECH ABOUT?
JESSICA ALBA ASKING ME TO RUB SUNTAN LOTION ON HER BACK.
WHY DO I EVEN ASK?
I STILL HAVE IT MEMORIZED. WANNA HEAR?
AMEND

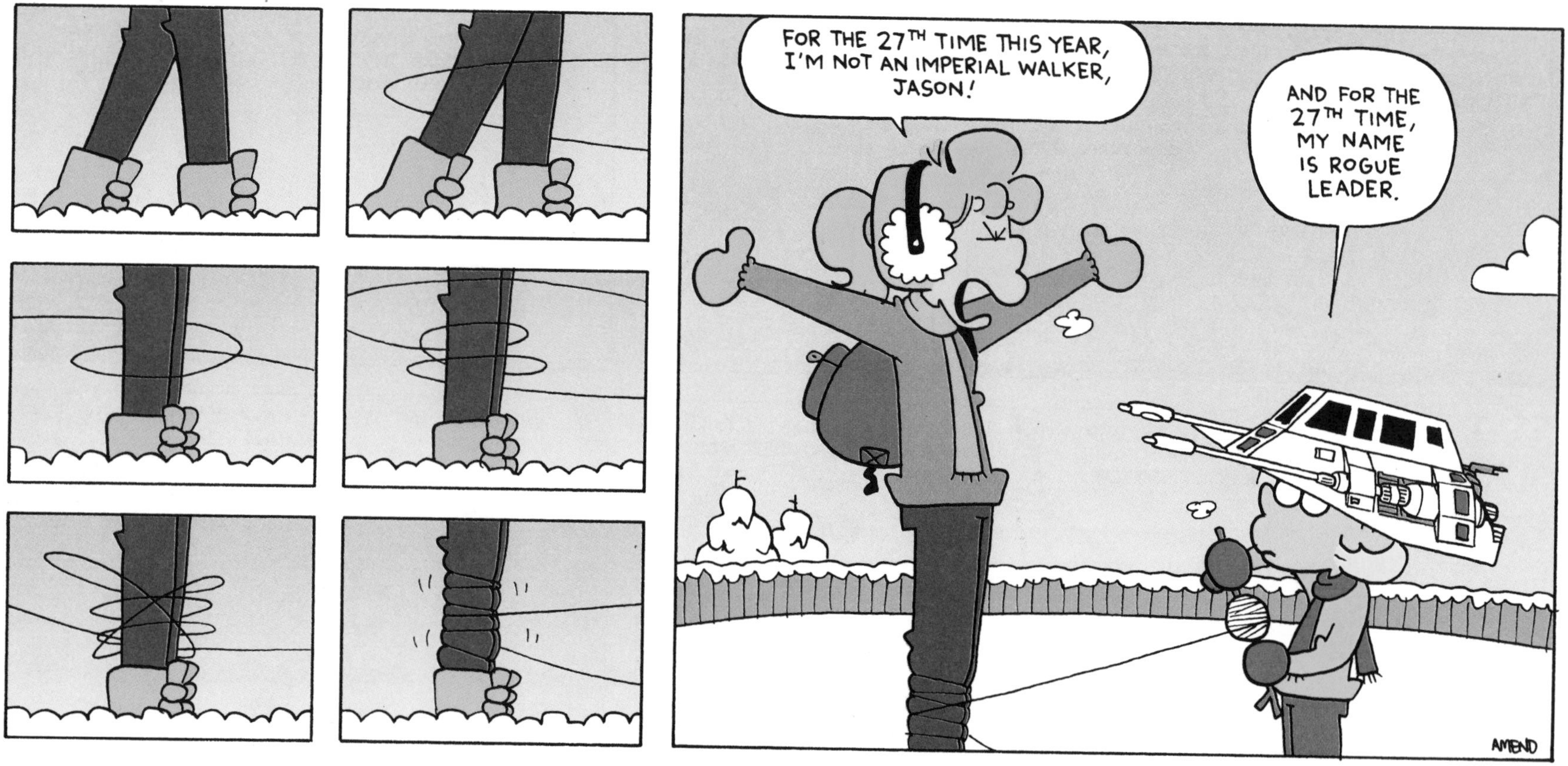
FOR THE 27TH TIME THIS YEAR, I'M NOT AN IMPERIAL WALKER, JASON!
AND FOR THE 27TH TIME, MY NAME IS ROGUE LEADER.
AMEND

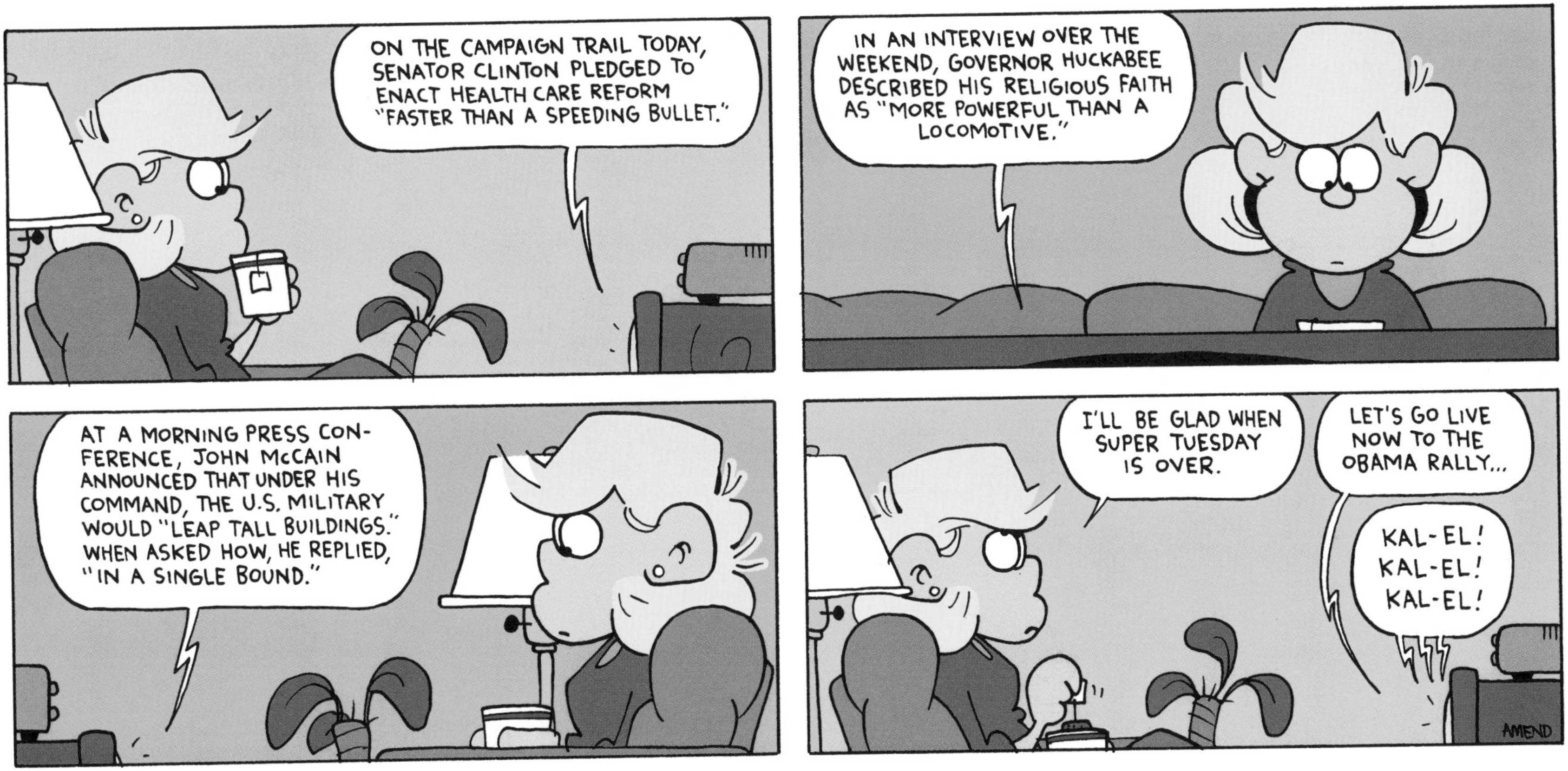
ON THE CAMPAIGN TRAIL TODAY, SENATOR CLINTON PLEDGED TO ENACT HEALTH CARE REFORM "FASTER THAN A SPEEDING BULLET."
IN AN INTERVIEW OVER THE WEEKEND, GOVERNOR HUCKABEE DESCRIBED HIS RELIGIOUS FAITH AS "MORE POWERFUL THAN A LOCOMOTIVE."
AT A MORNING PRESS CONFERENCE, JOHN McCAIN ANNOUNCED THAT UNDER HIS COMMAND, THE U.S. MILITARY WOULD "LEAP TALL BUILDINGS." WHEN ASKED HOW, HE REPLIED, "IN A SINGLE BOUND."
I'LL BE GLAD WHEN SUPER TUESDAY IS OVER.
LET'S GO LIVE NOW TO THE OBAMA RALLY...
KAL-EL! KAL-EL! KAL-EL!
AMEND

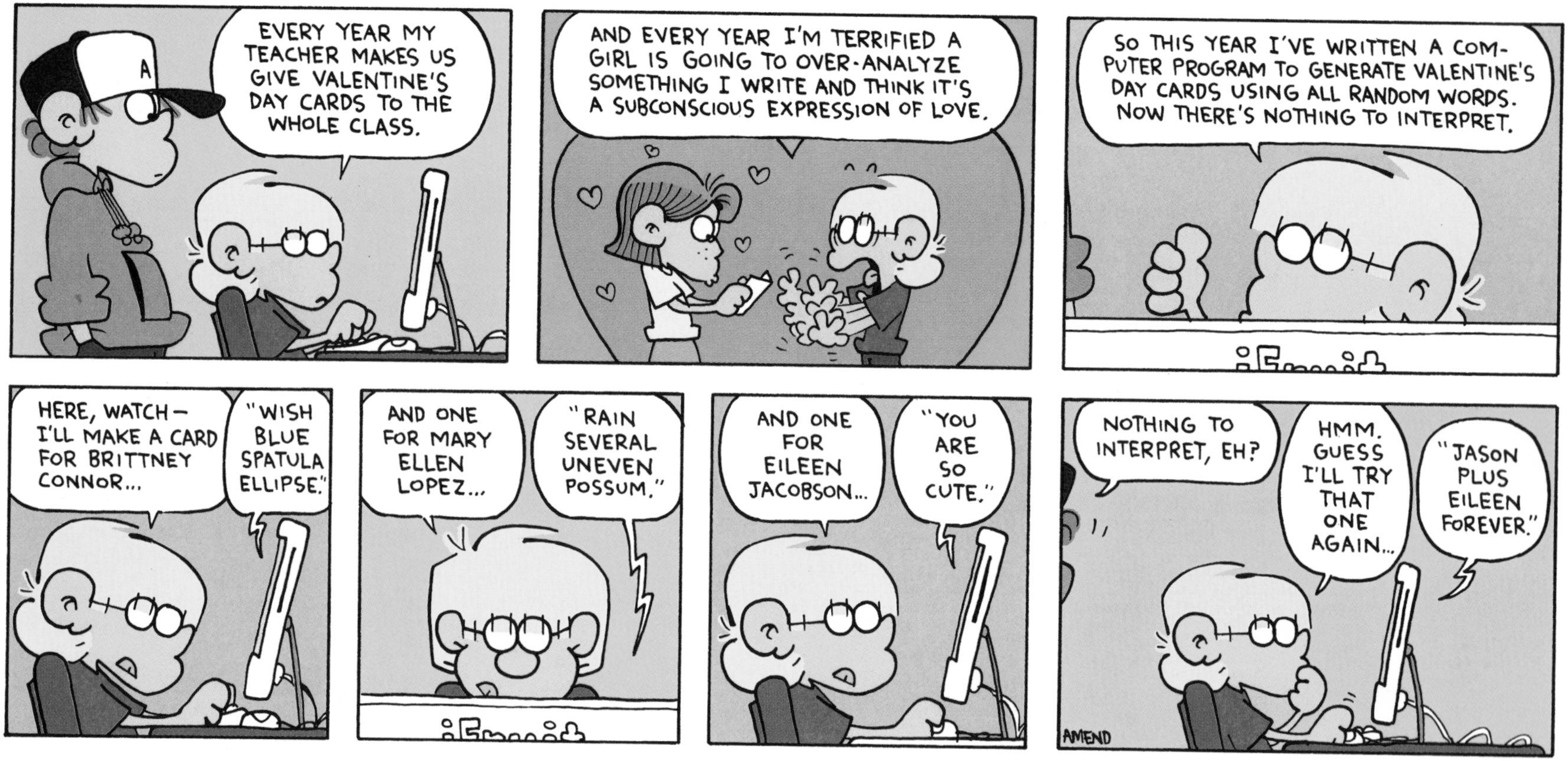
EVERY YEAR MY TEACHER MAKES US GIVE VALENTINE'S DAY CARDS TO THE WHOLE CLASS.
AND EVERY YEAR I'M TERRIFIED A GIRL IS GOING TO OVER-ANALYZE SOMETHING I WRITE AND THINK IT'S A SUBCONSCIOUS EXPRESSION OF LOVE.
SO THIS YEAR I'VE WRITTEN A COMPUTER PROGRAM TO GENERATE VALENTINE'S DAY CARDS USING ALL RANDOM WORDS. NOW THERE'S NOTHING TO INTERPRET.
HERE, WATCH— I'LL MAKE A CARD FOR BRITTNEY CONNOR...
"WISH BLUE SPATULA ELLIPSE."
AND ONE FOR MARY ELLEN LOPEZ...
"RAIN SEVERAL UNEVEN POSSUM."
AND ONE FOR EILEEN JACOBSON...
"YOU ARE SO CUTE."
NOTHING TO INTERPRET, EH?
HMM. GUESS I'LL TRY THAT ONE AGAIN...
"JASON PLUS EILEEN FOREVER."
AMEND

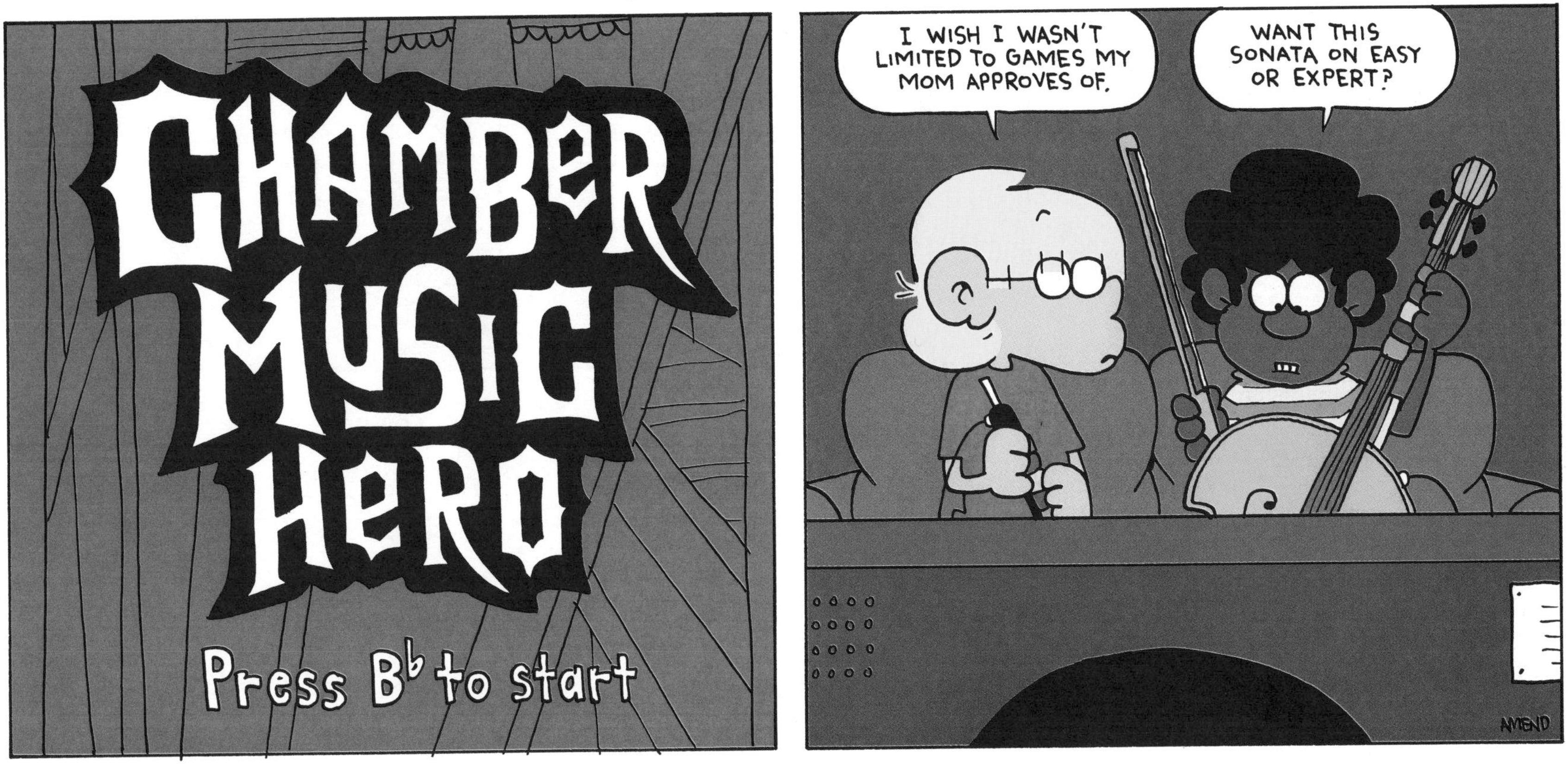
CHAMBER MUSIC HERO
Press B♭ to start
I WISH I WASN'T LIMITED TO GAMES MY MOM APPROVES OF.
WANT THIS SONATA ON EASY OR EXPERT?
AMEND

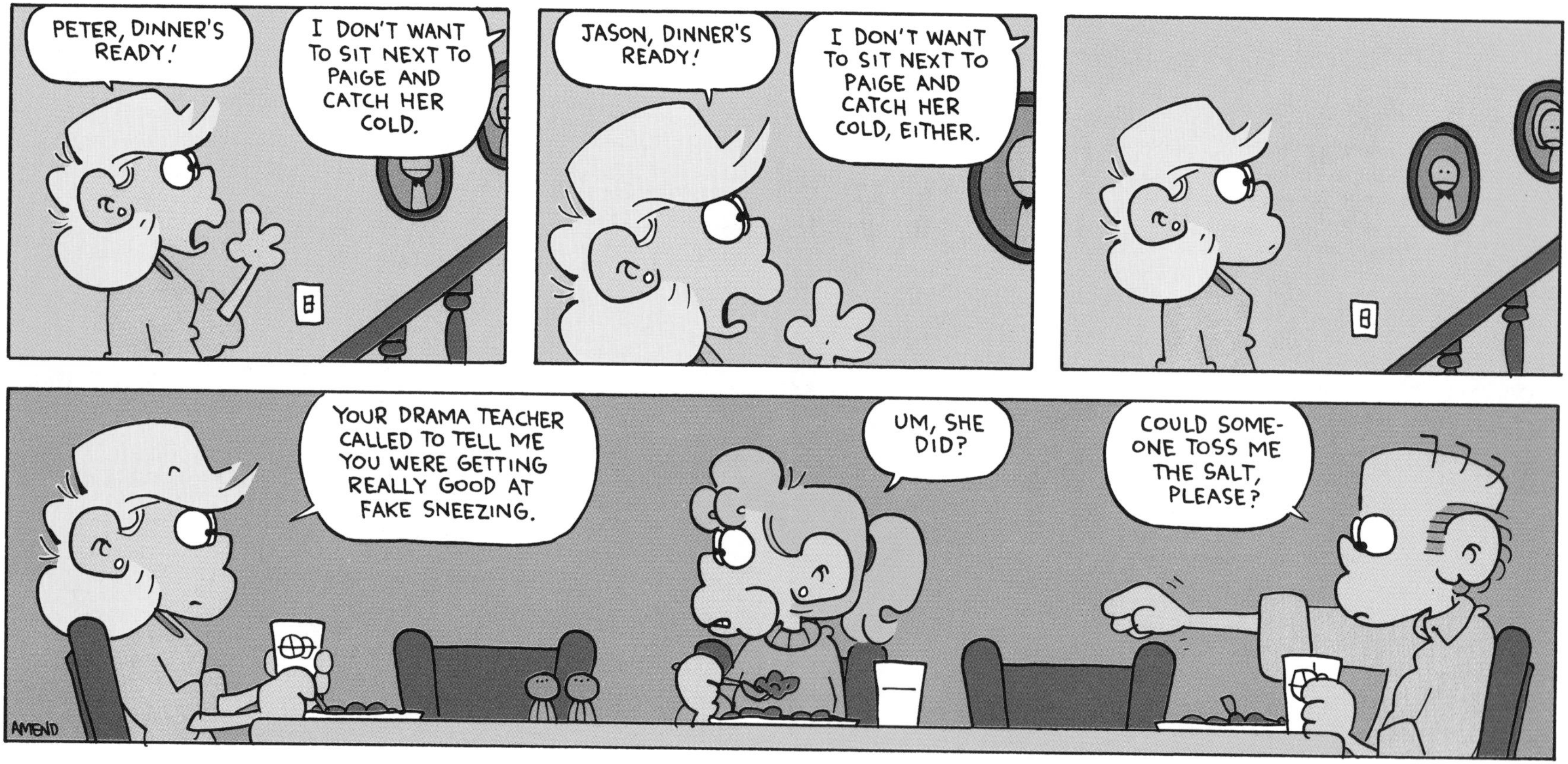
PETER, DINNER'S READY!
I DON'T WANT TO SIT NEXT TO PAIGE AND CATCH HER COLD.
JASON, DINNER'S READY!
I DON'T WANT TO SIT NEXT TO PAIGE AND CATCH HER COLD, EITHER.
YOUR DRAMA TEACHER CALLED TO TELL ME YOU WERE GETTING REALLY GOOD AT FAKE SNEEZING.
UM, SHE DID?
COULD SOME-ONE TOSS ME THE SALT, PLEASE?
AMEND

WHATCHA DOING?

TRYING TO FIND SHAPES IN, THE CLOUDS.

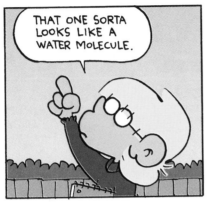

THAT ONE SORTA LOOKS LIKE A WATER MOLECULE.

AND THAT ONE KINDA LOOKS LIKE A STAR FLEET INSIGNIA.

AMEND

AND THAT ONE LOOKS A LOT LIKE A NUMBER 2½ PENCIL.

3-2

ORDINARILY, I'D CALL YOU A WEIRDO. HOWEVER...

67

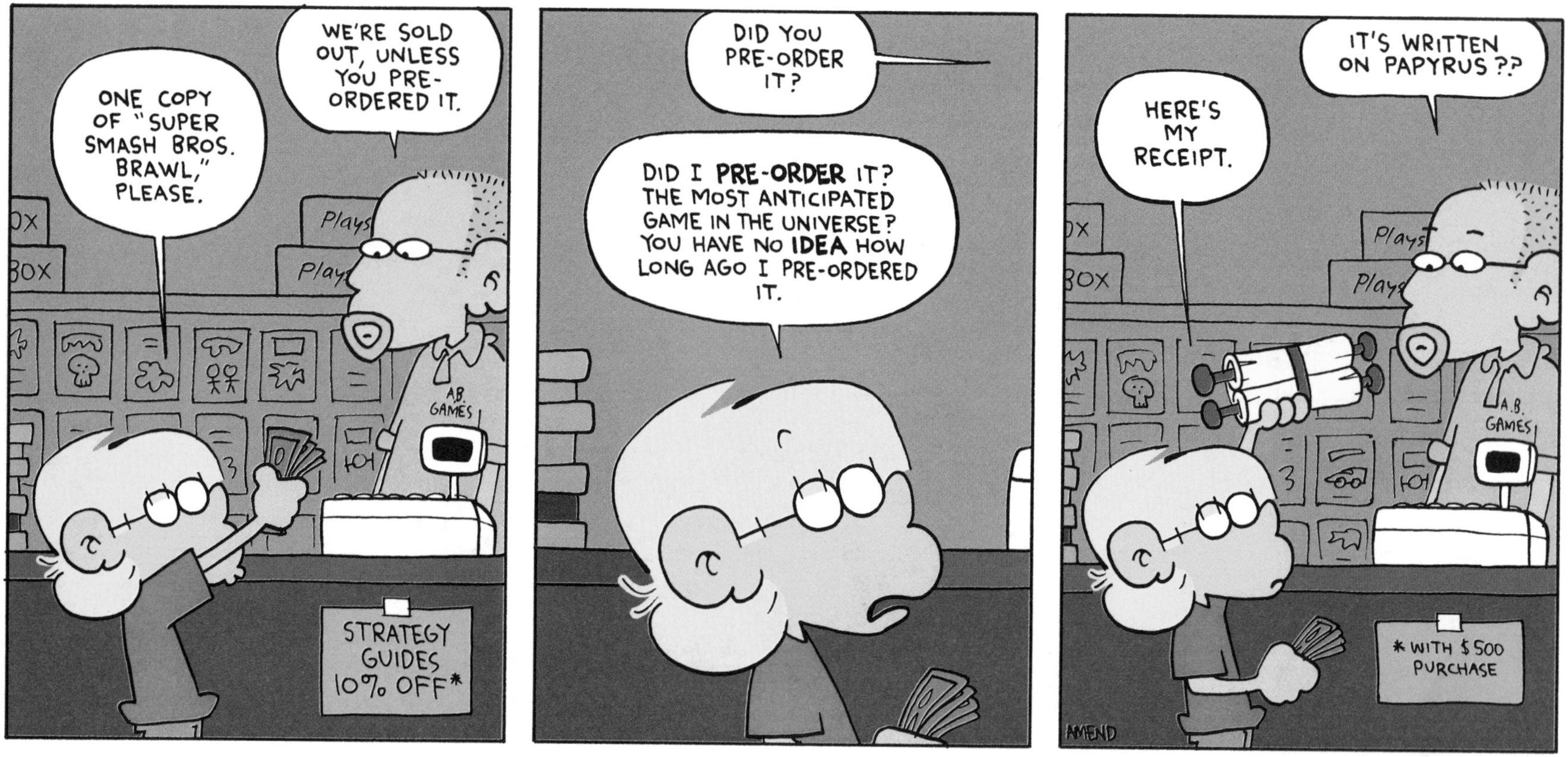
ONE COPY OF "SUPER SMASH BROS. BRAWL," PLEASE.
WE'RE SOLD OUT, UNLESS YOU PRE-ORDERED IT.
A.B. GAMES
STRATEGY GUIDES 10% OFF*
DID YOU PRE-ORDER IT?
DID I **PRE-ORDER** IT? THE MOST ANTICIPATED GAME IN THE UNIVERSE? YOU HAVE NO **IDEA** HOW LONG AGO I PRE-ORDERED IT.
HERE'S MY RECEIPT.
IT'S WRITTEN ON PAPYRUS??
A.B. GAMES
* WITH $500 PURCHASE
AMEND

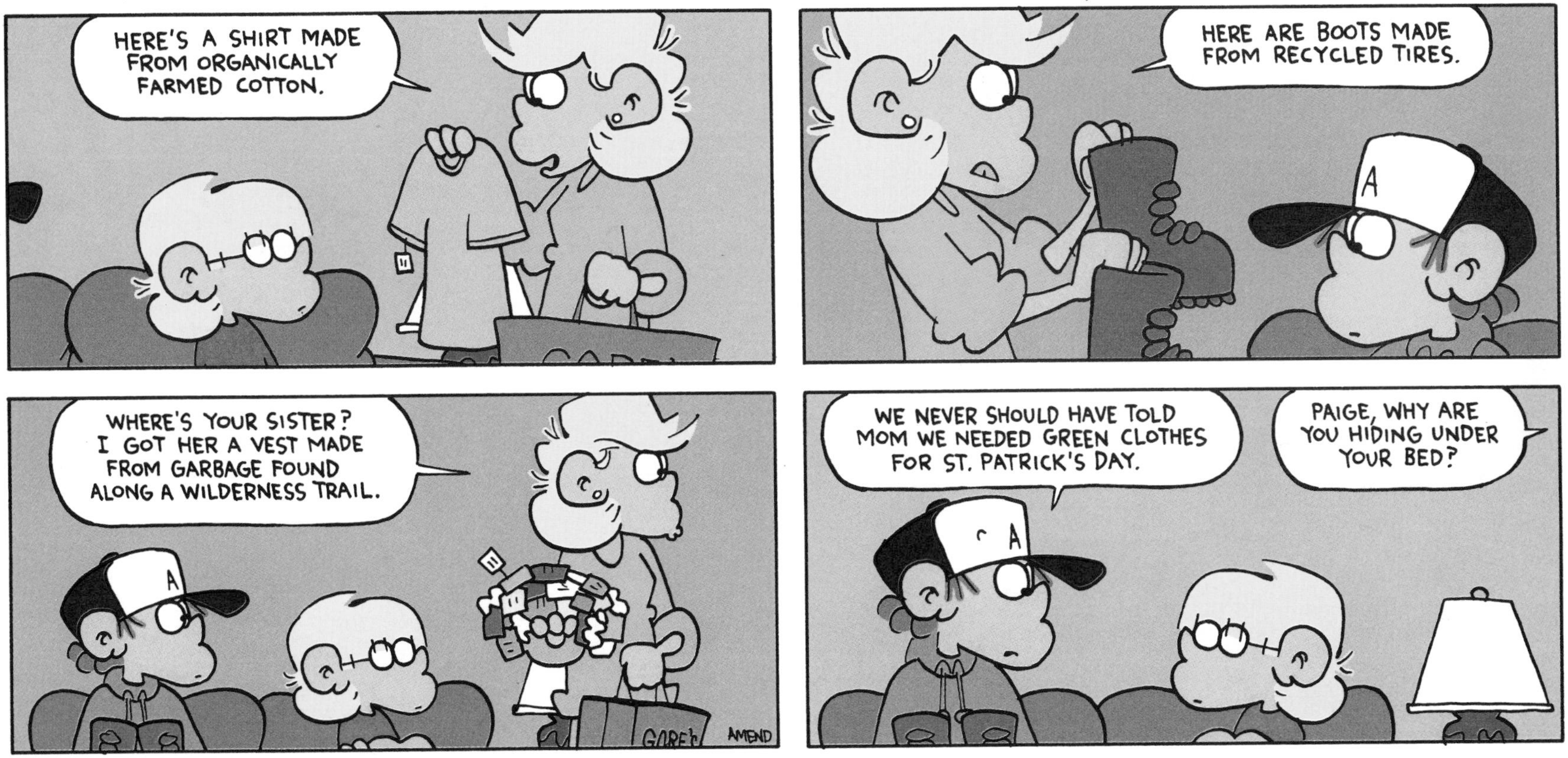
HERE'S A SHIRT MADE FROM ORGANICALLY FARMED COTTON.
HERE ARE BOOTS MADE FROM RECYCLED TIRES.
WHERE'S YOUR SISTER? I GOT HER A VEST MADE FROM GARBAGE FOUND ALONG A WILDERNESS TRAIL.
AMEND
WE NEVER SHOULD HAVE TOLD MOM WE NEEDED GREEN CLOTHES FOR ST. PATRICK'S DAY.
PAIGE, WHY ARE YOU HIDING UNDER YOUR BED?

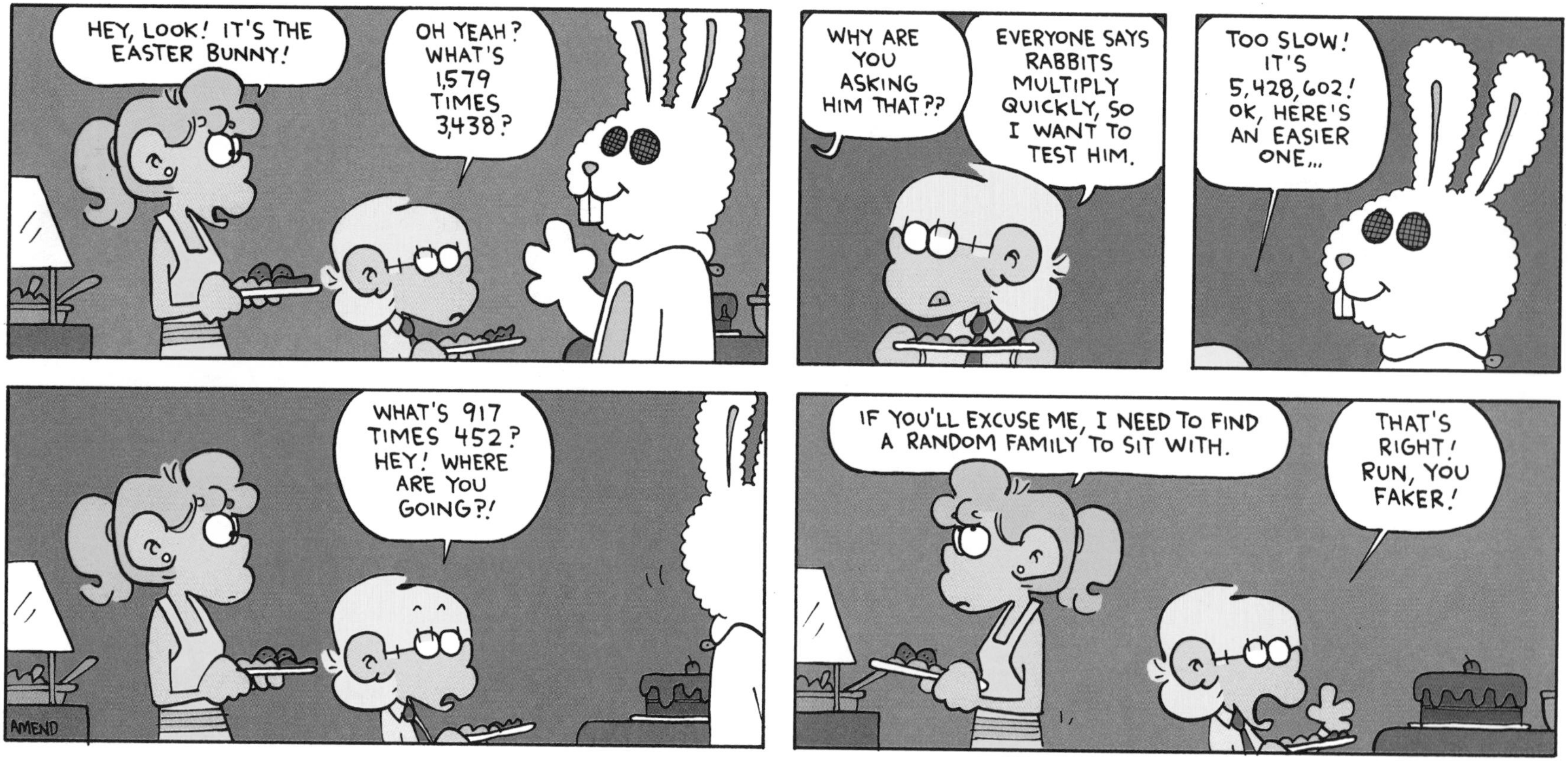
HEY, LOOK! IT'S THE EASTER BUNNY!
OH YEAH? WHAT'S 1,579 TIMES 3,438?
WHY ARE YOU ASKING HIM THAT??
EVERYONE SAYS RABBITS MULTIPLY QUICKLY, SO I WANT TO TEST HIM.
TOO SLOW! IT'S 5,428,602! OK, HERE'S AN EASIER ONE...
WHAT'S 917 TIMES 452? HEY! WHERE ARE YOU GOING?!
AMEND
IF YOU'LL EXCUSE ME, I NEED TO FIND A RANDOM FAMILY TO SIT WITH.
THAT'S RIGHT! RUN, YOU FAKER!

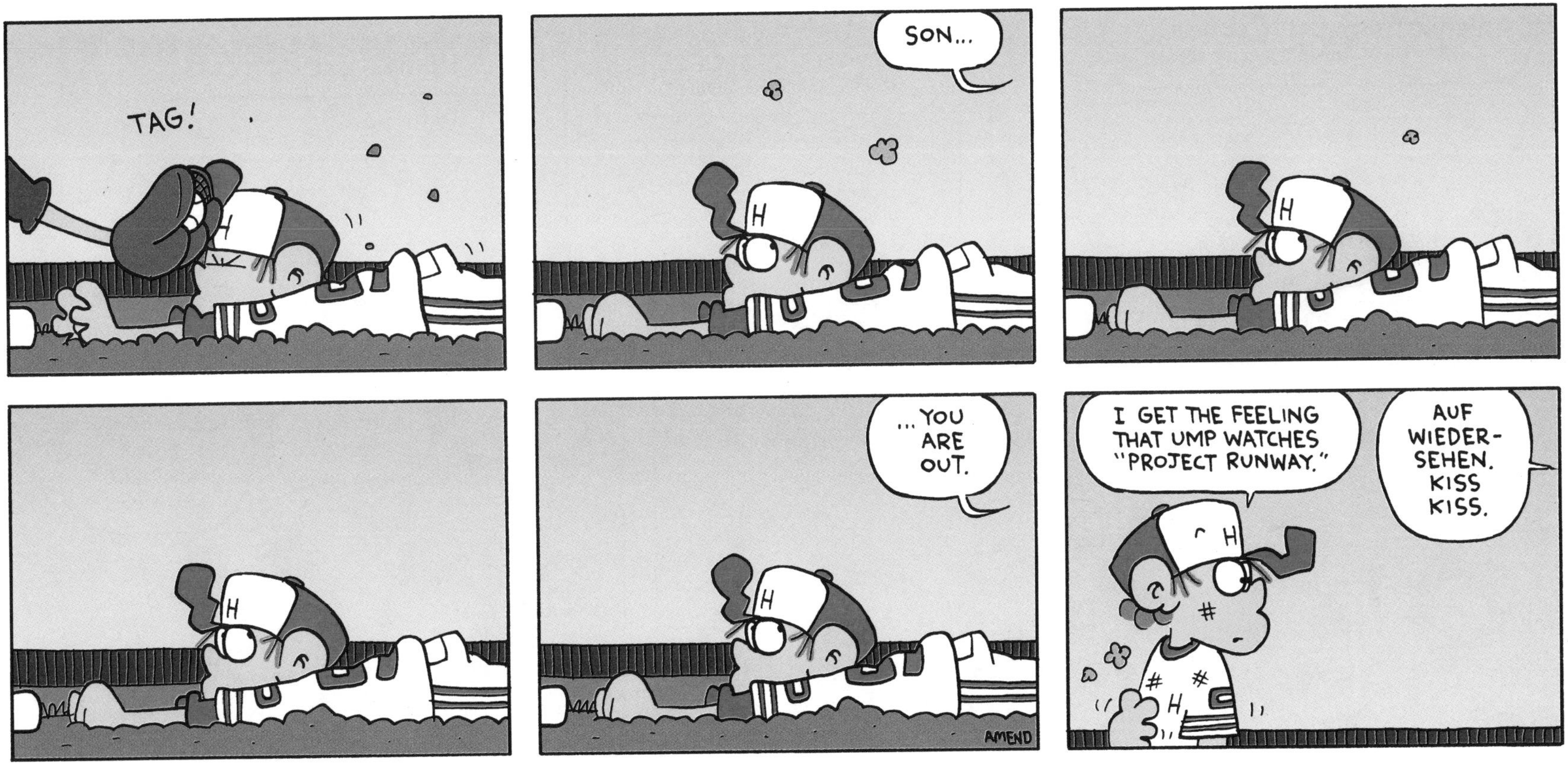
TAG!
SON...
...YOU ARE OUT.
I GET THE FEELING THAT UMP WATCHES "PROJECT RUNWAY."
AUF WIEDER-SEHEN. KISS KISS.
AMEND

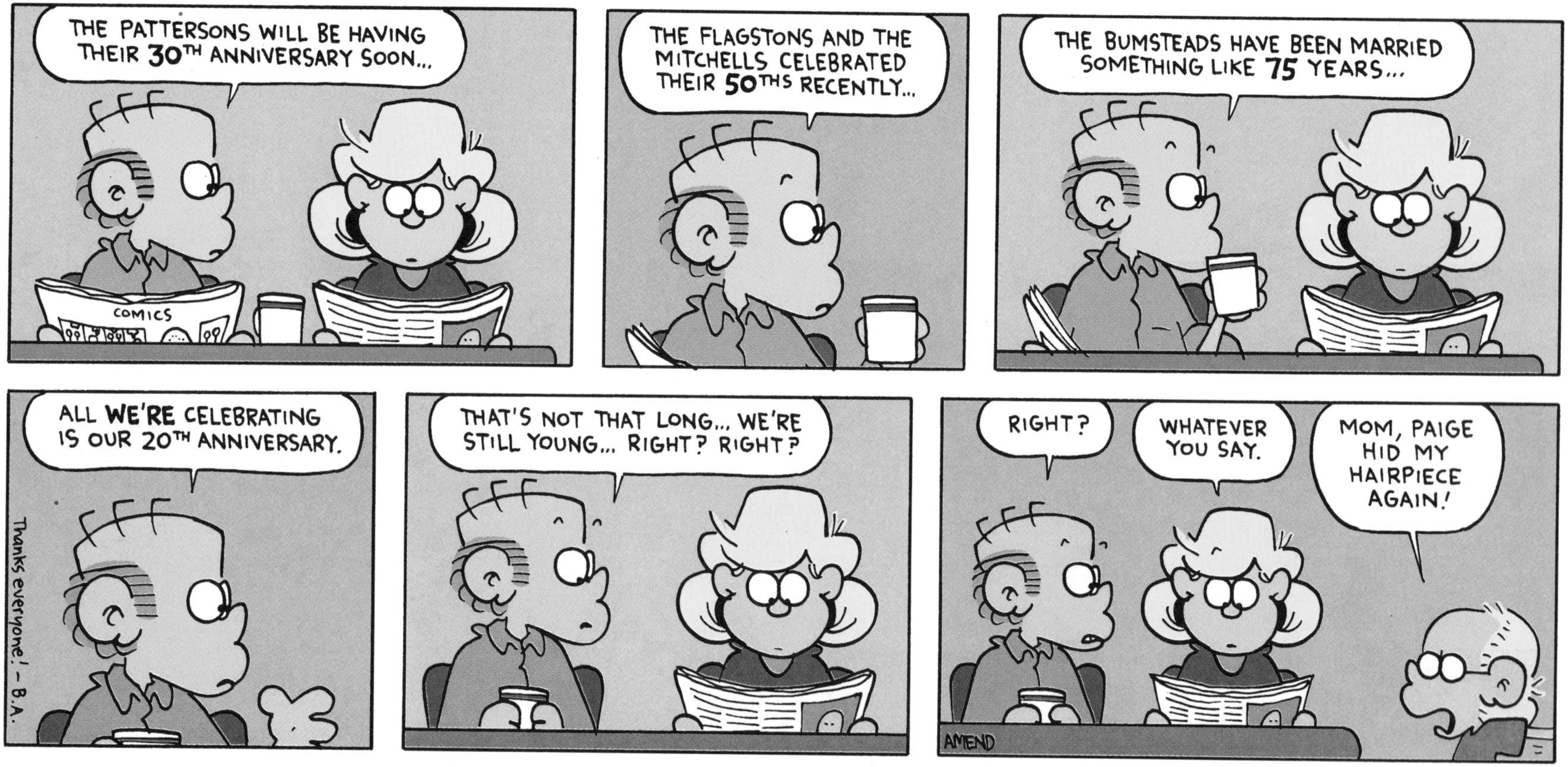
THE PATTERSONS WILL BE HAVING THEIR 30TH ANNIVERSARY SOON...
COMICS
THE FLAGSTONS AND THE MITCHELLS CELEBRATED THEIR 50THS RECENTLY...
THE BUMSTEADS HAVE BEEN MARRIED SOMETHING LIKE 75 YEARS...
ALL WE'RE CELEBRATING IS OUR 20TH ANNIVERSARY.
Thanks everyone! – B.A.
THAT'S NOT THAT LONG... WE'RE STILL YOUNG... RIGHT? RIGHT?
RIGHT?
WHATEVER YOU SAY.
MOM, PAIGE HID MY HAIRPIECE AGAIN!
AMEND

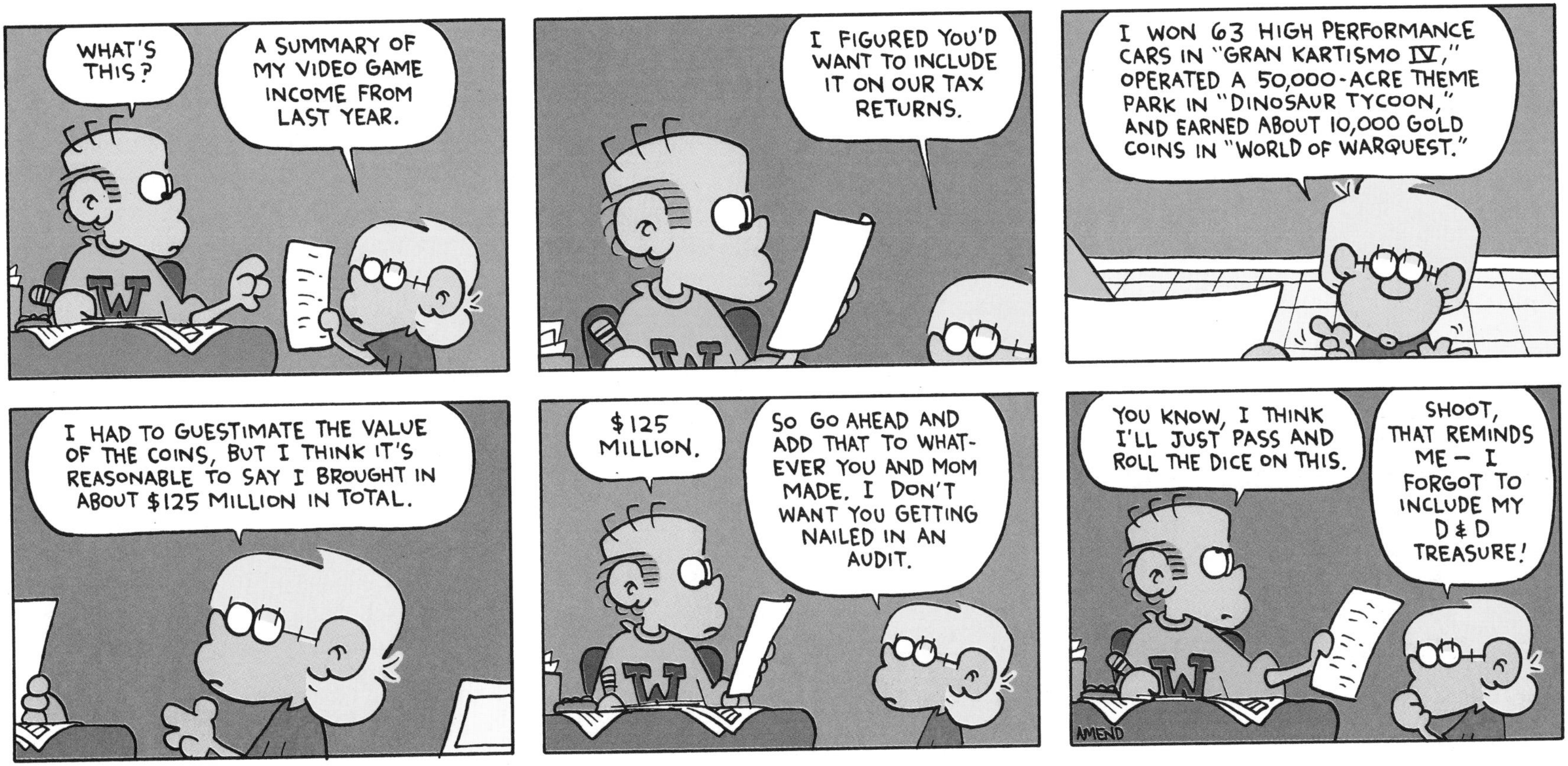
WHAT'S THIS?
A SUMMARY OF MY VIDEO GAME INCOME FROM LAST YEAR.
I FIGURED YOU'D WANT TO INCLUDE IT ON OUR TAX RETURNS.
I WON 63 HIGH PERFORMANCE CARS IN "GRAN KARTISMO IV," OPERATED A 50,000-ACRE THEME PARK IN "DINOSAUR TYCOON," AND EARNED ABOUT 10,000 GOLD COINS IN "WORLD OF WARQUEST."
I HAD TO GUESTIMATE THE VALUE OF THE COINS, BUT I THINK IT'S REASONABLE TO SAY I BROUGHT IN ABOUT $125 MILLION IN TOTAL.
$125 MILLION.
SO GO AHEAD AND ADD THAT TO WHATEVER YOU AND MOM MADE. I DON'T WANT YOU GETTING NAILED IN AN AUDIT.
YOU KNOW, I THINK I'LL JUST PASS AND ROLL THE DICE ON THIS.
SHOOT, THAT REMINDS ME — I FORGOT TO INCLUDE MY D & D TREASURE!
AMEND

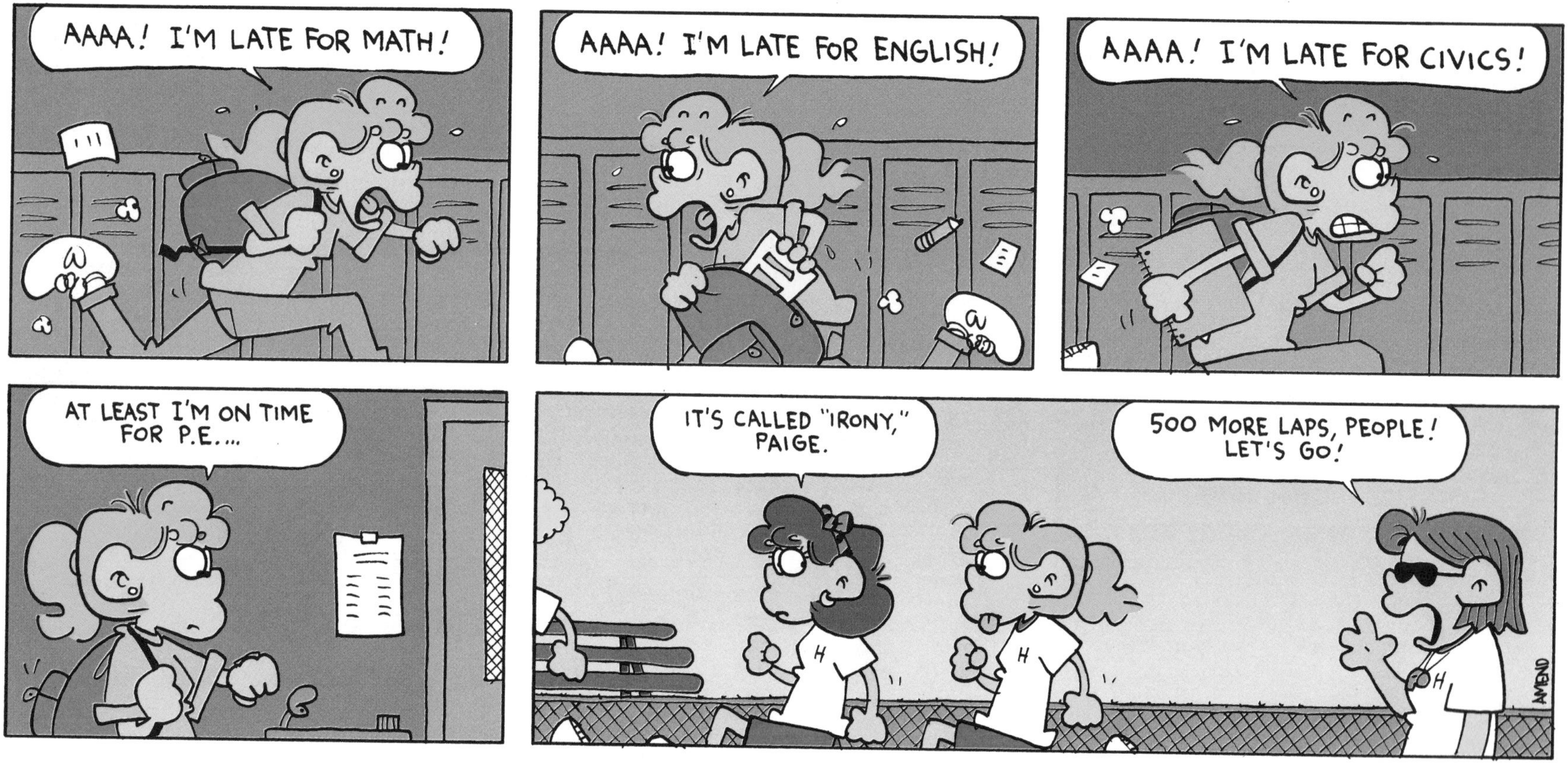
AAAA! I'M LATE FOR MATH!
AAAA! I'M LATE FOR ENGLISH!
AAAA! I'M LATE FOR CIVICS!
AT LEAST I'M ON TIME FOR P.E....
IT'S CALLED "IRONY," PAIGE.
500 MORE LAPS, PEOPLE! LET'S GO!
AMEND

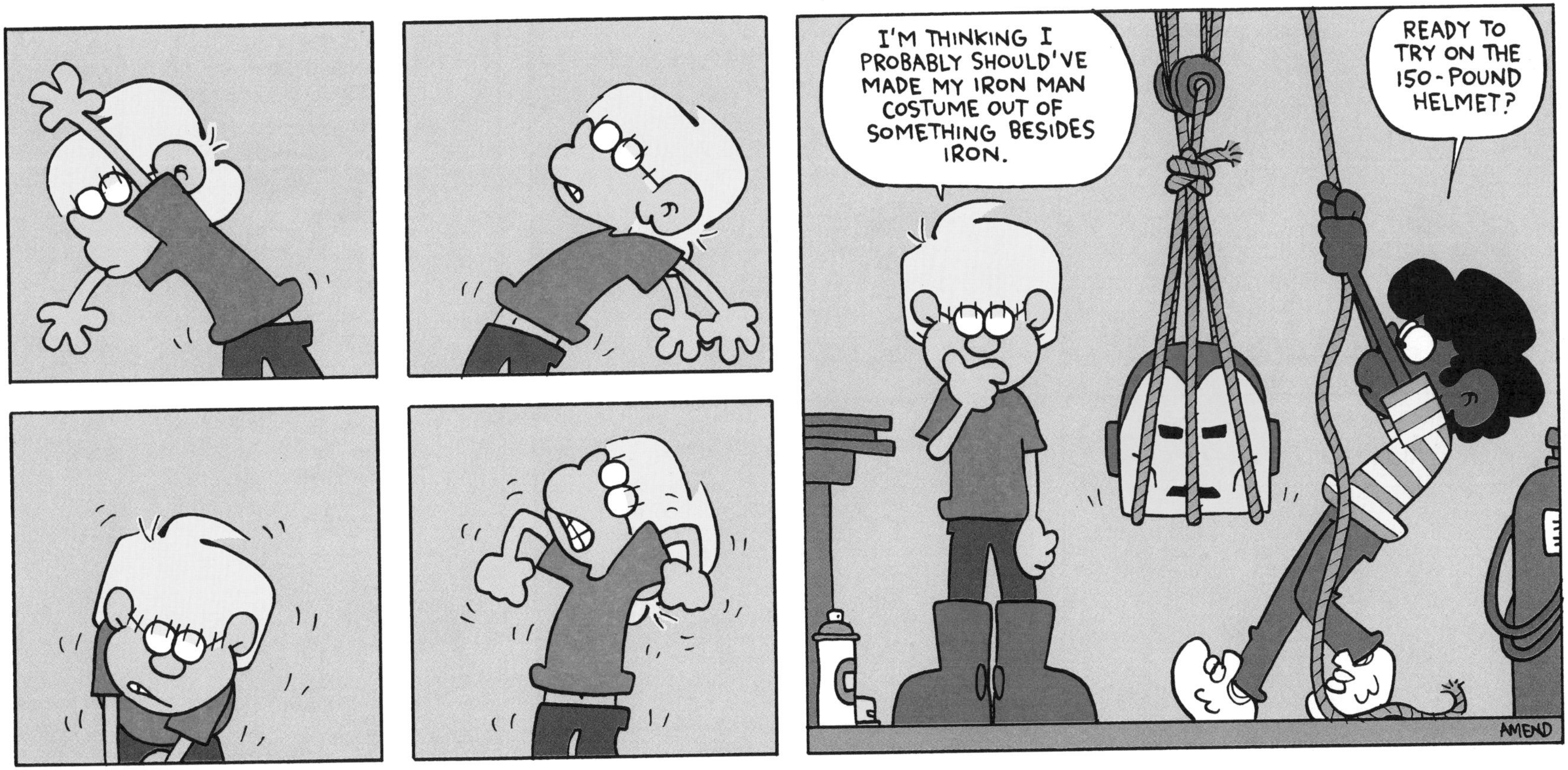
I'M THINKING I PROBABLY SHOULD'VE MADE MY IRON MAN COSTUME OUT OF SOMETHING BESIDES IRON.
READY TO TRY ON THE 150-POUND HELMET?
AMEND

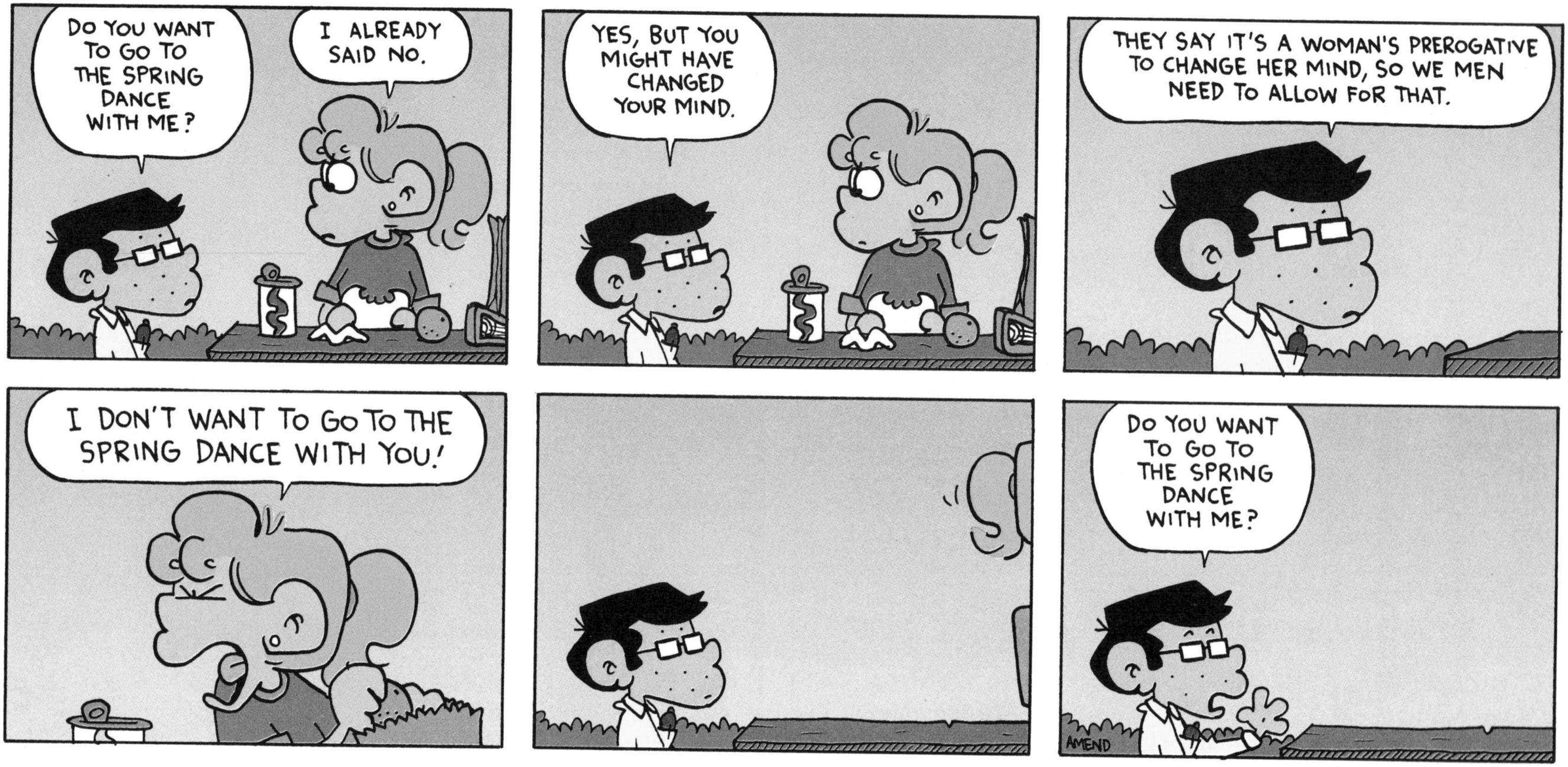
DO YOU WANT TO GO TO THE SPRING DANCE WITH ME?
I ALREADY SAID NO.
YES, BUT YOU MIGHT HAVE CHANGED YOUR MIND.
THEY SAY IT'S A WOMAN'S PREROGATIVE TO CHANGE HER MIND, SO WE MEN NEED TO ALLOW FOR THAT.
I DON'T WANT TO GO TO THE SPRING DANCE WITH YOU!
DO YOU WANT TO GO TO THE SPRING DANCE WITH ME?
AMEND

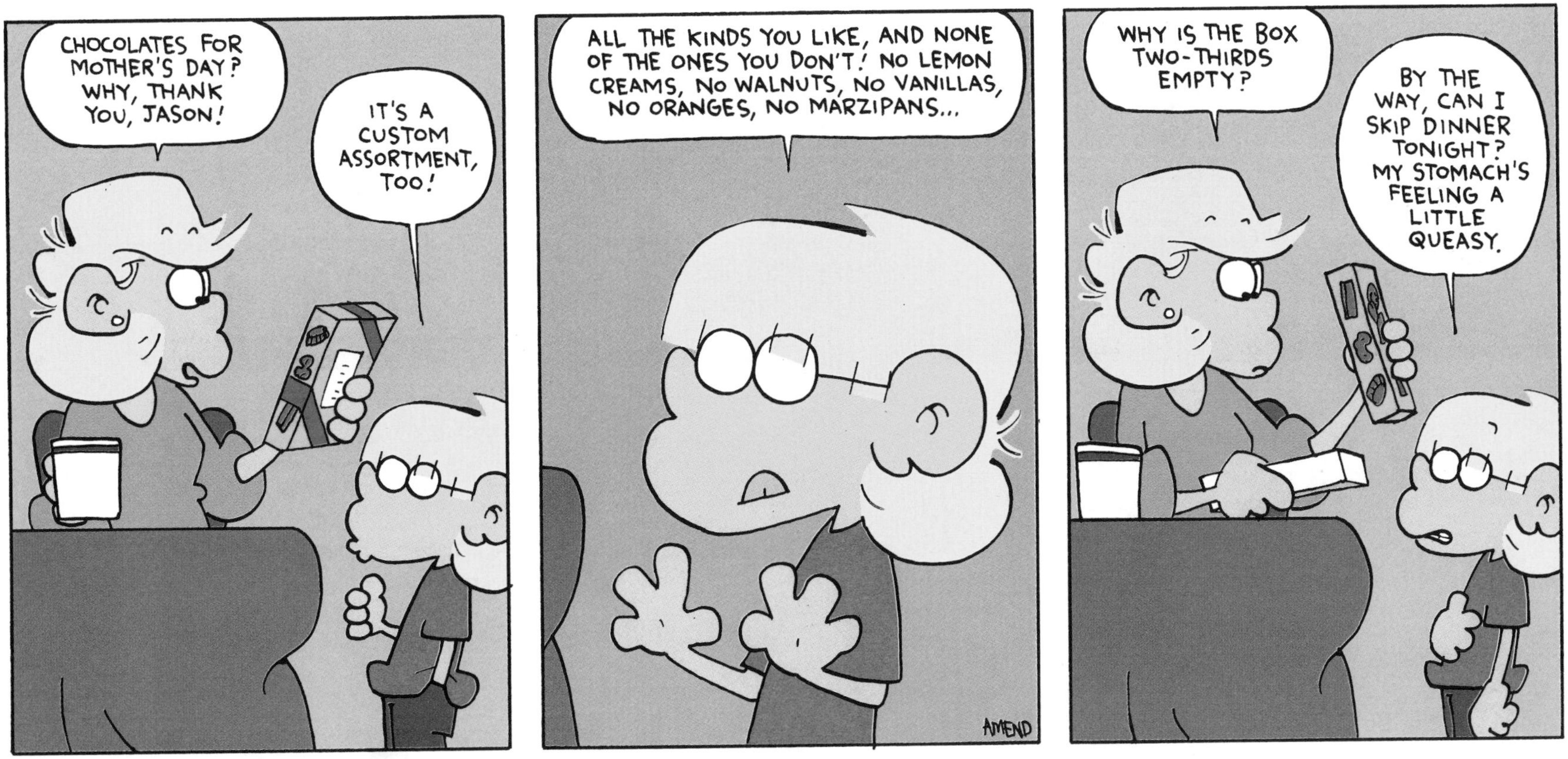
CHOCOLATES FOR MOTHER'S DAY? WHY, THANK YOU, JASON!
IT'S A CUSTOM ASSORTMENT, TOO!
ALL THE KINDS YOU LIKE, AND NONE OF THE ONES YOU DON'T! NO LEMON CREAMS, NO WALNUTS, NO VANILLAS, NO ORANGES, NO MARZIPANS...
AMEND
WHY IS THE BOX TWO-THIRDS EMPTY?
BY THE WAY, CAN I SKIP DINNER TONIGHT? MY STOMACH'S FEELING A LITTLE QUEASY.

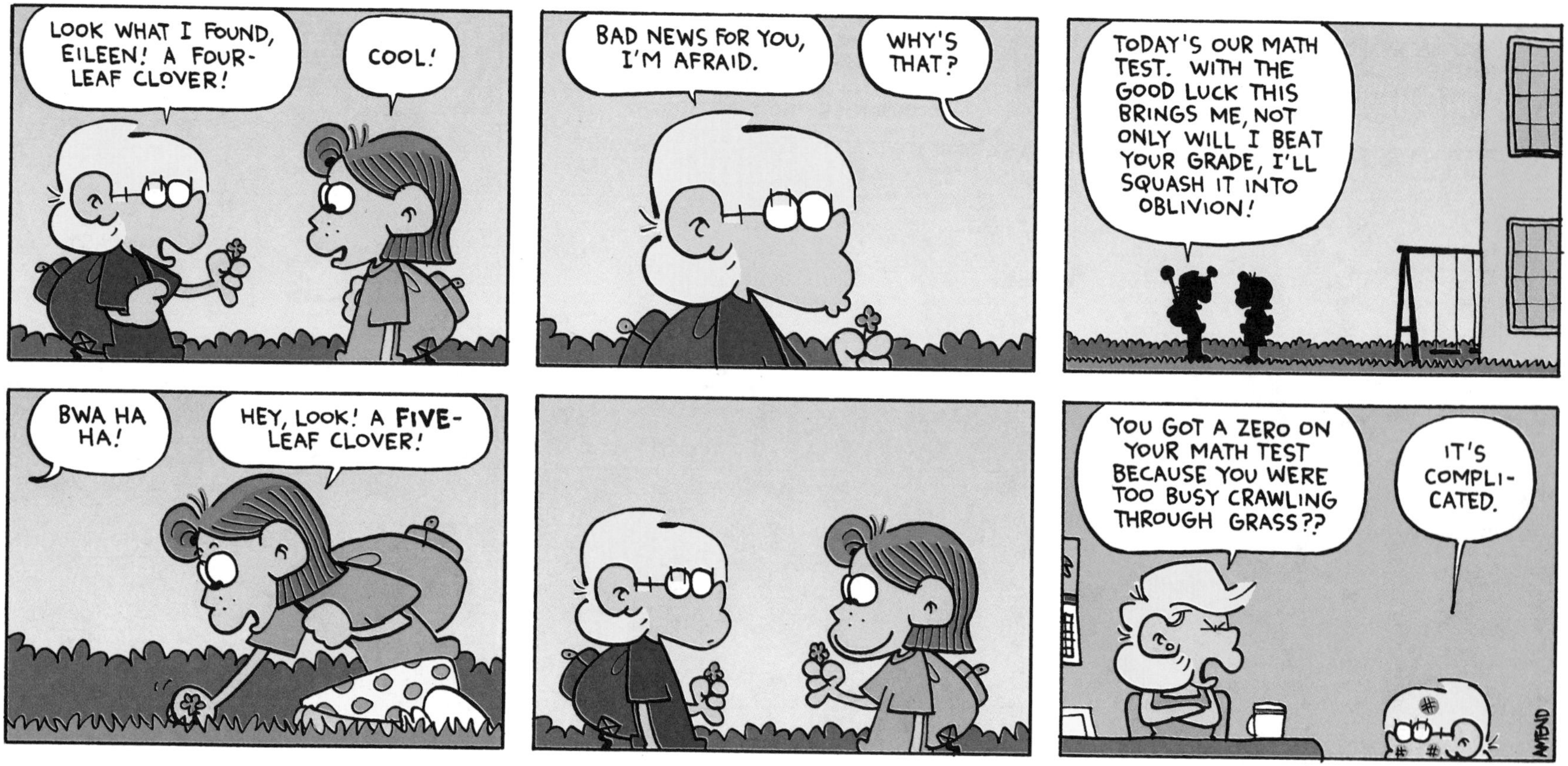
LOOK WHAT I FOUND, EILEEN! A FOUR-LEAF CLOVER!
COOL!
BAD NEWS FOR YOU, I'M AFRAID.
WHY'S THAT?
TODAY'S OUR MATH TEST. WITH THE GOOD LUCK THIS BRINGS ME, NOT ONLY WILL I BEAT YOUR GRADE, I'LL SQUASH IT INTO OBLIVION!
BWA HA HA!
HEY, LOOK! A **FIVE**-LEAF CLOVER!
YOU GOT A ZERO ON YOUR MATH TEST BECAUSE YOU WERE TOO BUSY CRAWLING THROUGH GRASS??
IT'S COMPLICATED.
AMEND

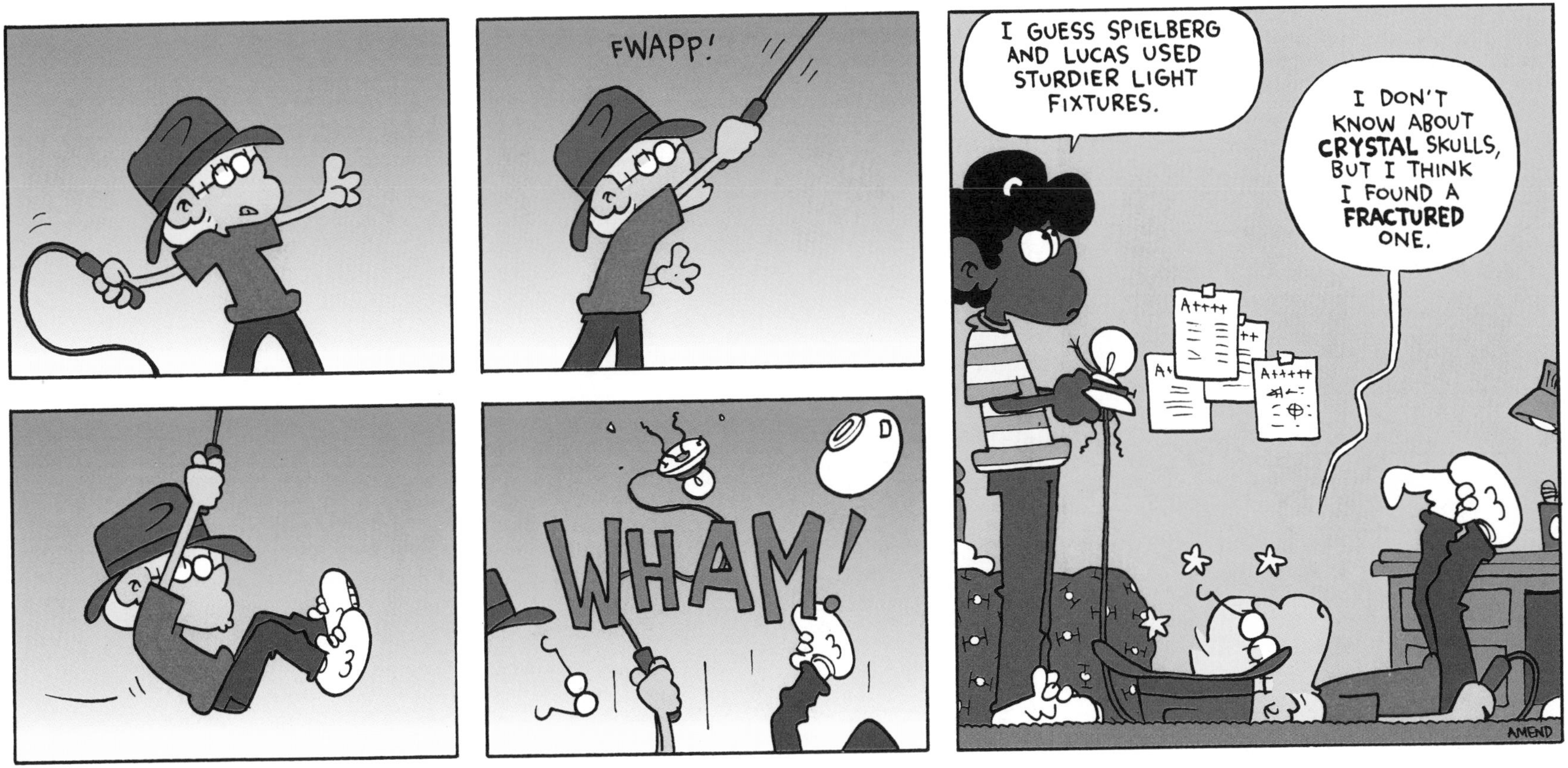
FWAPP!
WHAM!
I GUESS SPIELBERG AND LUCAS USED STURDIER LIGHT FIXTURES.
I DON'T KNOW ABOUT **CRYSTAL** SKULLS, BUT I THINK I FOUND A **FRACTURED** ONE.
AMEND

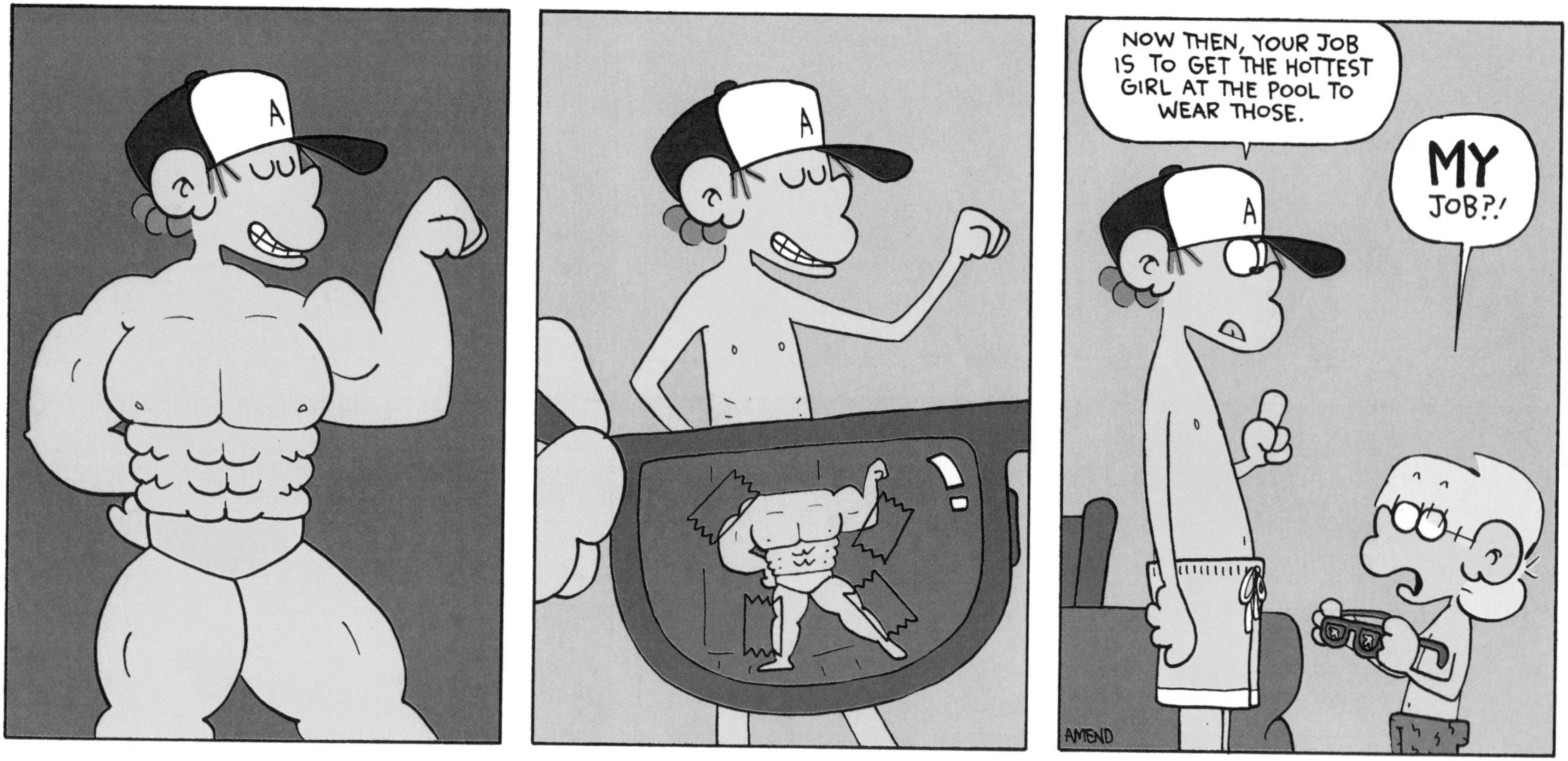
NOW THEN, YOUR JOB IS TO GET THE HOTTEST GIRL AT THE POOL TO WEAR THOSE.
MY JOB?!
AMEND

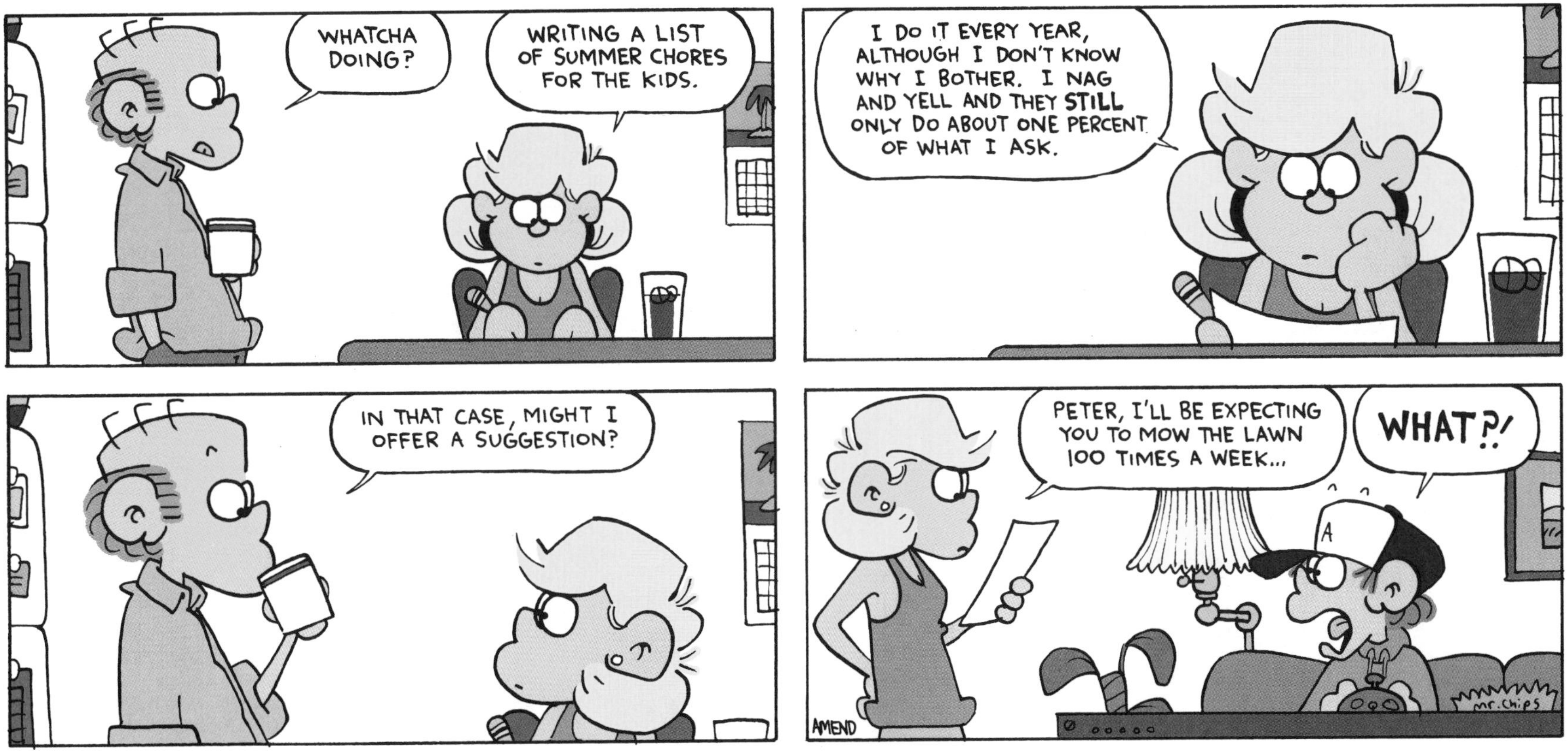
WHATCHA DOING?
WRITING A LIST OF SUMMER CHORES FOR THE KIDS.
I DO IT EVERY YEAR, ALTHOUGH I DON'T KNOW WHY I BOTHER. I NAG AND YELL AND THEY **STILL** ONLY DO ABOUT ONE PERCENT OF WHAT I ASK.
IN THAT CASE, MIGHT I OFFER A SUGGESTION?
PETER, I'LL BE EXPECTING YOU TO MOW THE LAWN 100 TIMES A WEEK...
WHAT?!
AMEND
mr. chips

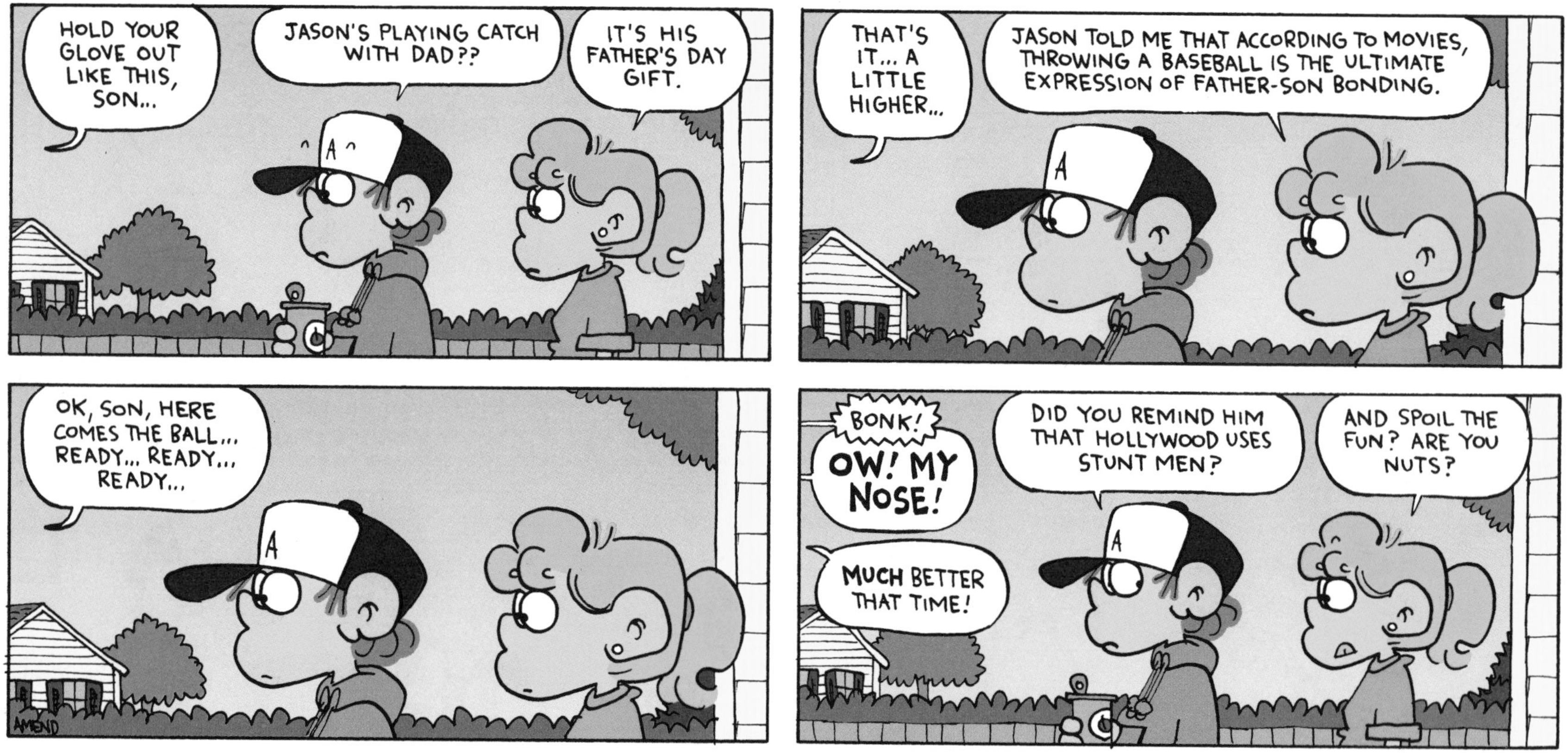
HOLD YOUR GLOVE OUT LIKE THIS, SON...
JASON'S PLAYING CATCH WITH DAD??
IT'S HIS FATHER'S DAY GIFT.
THAT'S IT... A LITTLE HIGHER...
JASON TOLD ME THAT ACCORDING TO MOVIES, THROWING A BASEBALL IS THE ULTIMATE EXPRESSION OF FATHER-SON BONDING.
OK, SON, HERE COMES THE BALL... READY... READY... READY...
AMEND
BONK!
OW! MY NOSE!
MUCH BETTER THAT TIME!
DID YOU REMIND HIM THAT HOLLYWOOD USES STUNT MEN?
AND SPOIL THE FUN? ARE YOU NUTS?

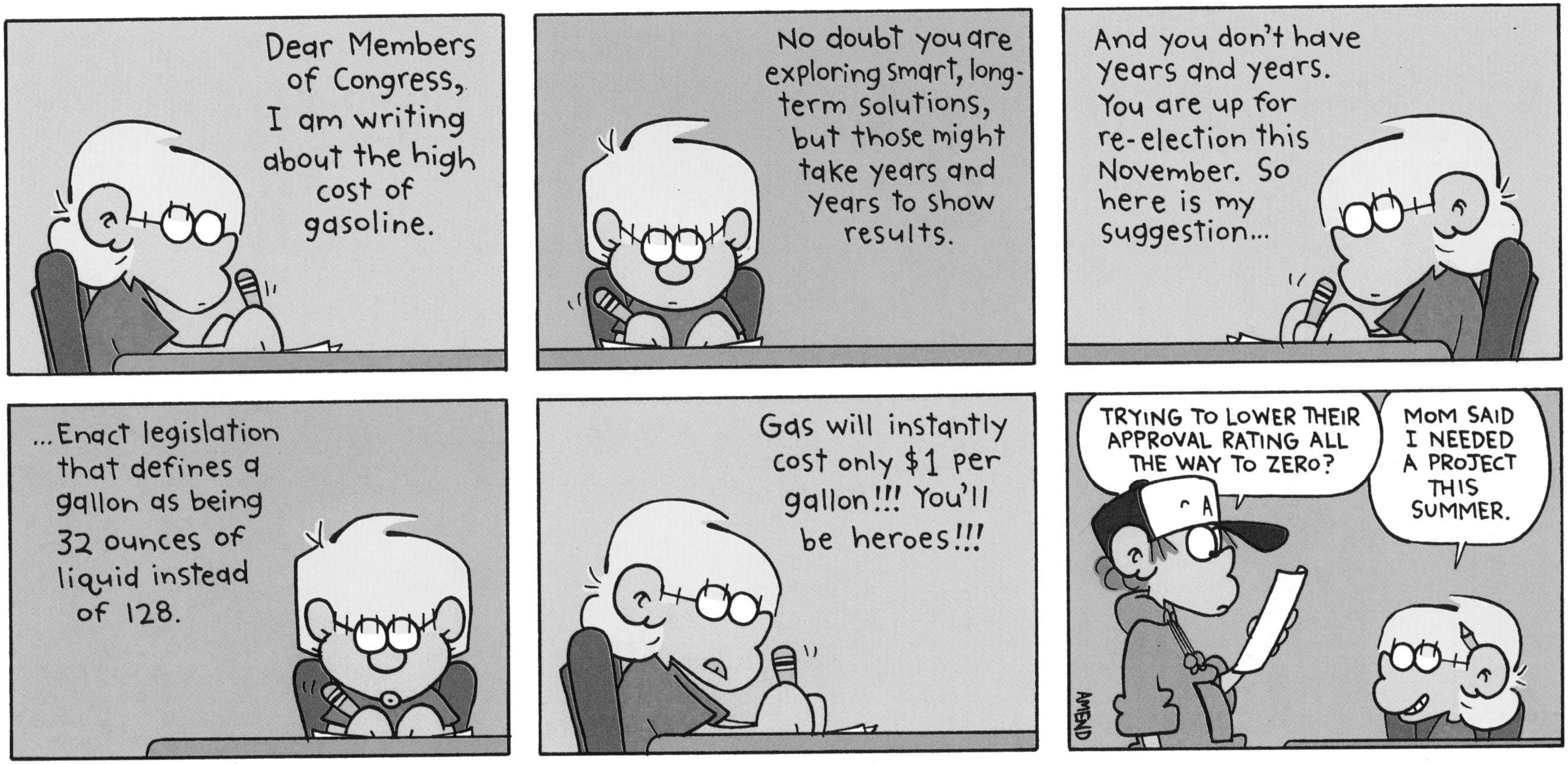
Dear Members of Congress, I am writing about the high cost of gasoline.
No doubt you are exploring smart, long-term solutions, but those might take years and years to show results.
And you don't have years and years. You are up for re-election this November. So here is my suggestion...
...Enact legislation that defines a gallon as being 32 ounces of liquid instead of 128.
Gas will instantly cost only $1 per gallon!!! You'll be heroes!!!
TRYING TO LOWER THEIR APPROVAL RATING ALL THE WAY TO ZERO?
MOM SAID I NEEDED A PROJECT THIS SUMMER.
AMEND

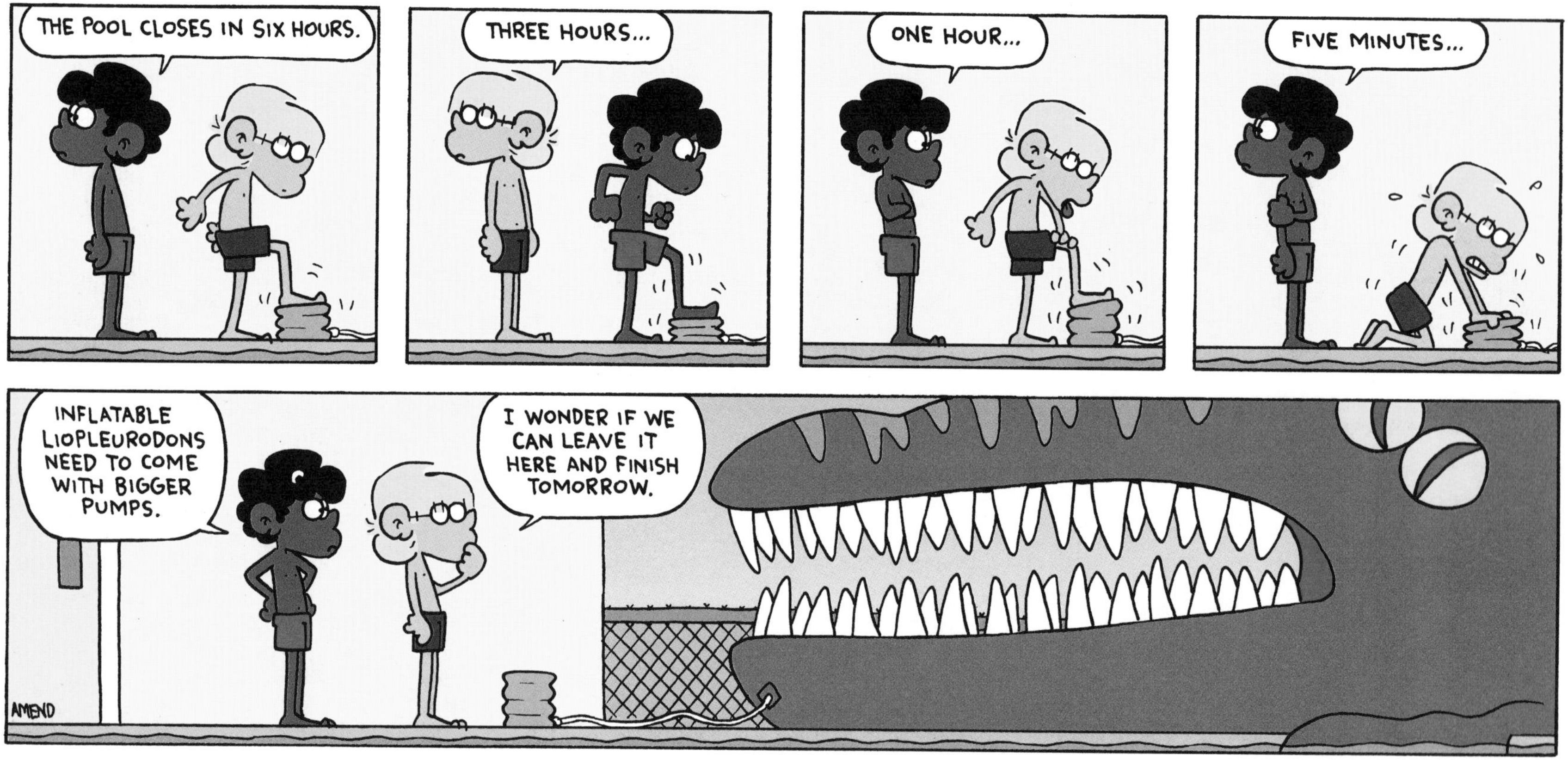
THE POOL CLOSES IN SIX HOURS.
THREE HOURS...
ONE HOUR...
FIVE MINUTES...
INFLATABLE LIOPLEURODONS NEED TO COME WITH BIGGER PUMPS.
I WONDER IF WE CAN LEAVE IT HERE AND FINISH TOMORROW.
AMEND

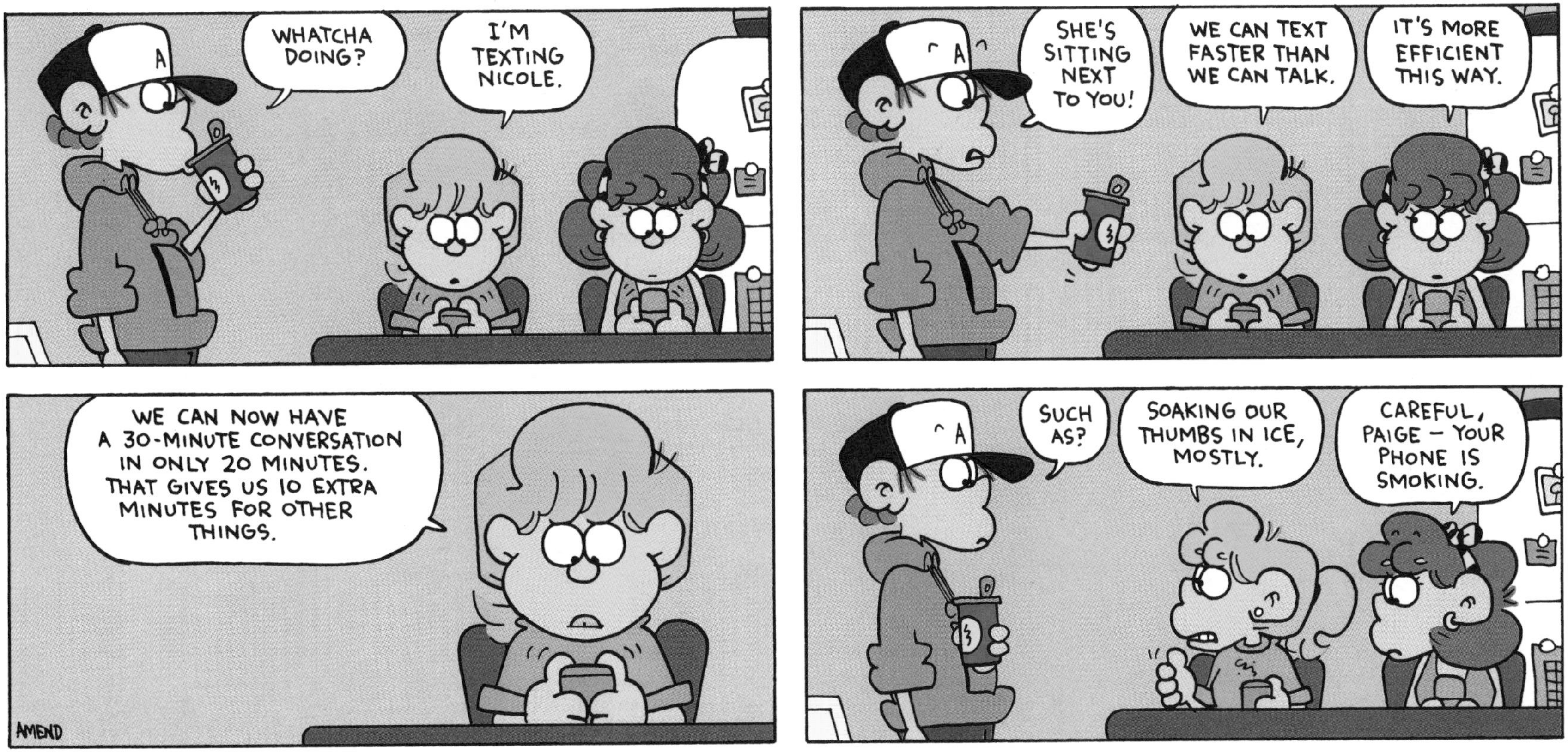
WHATCHA DOING?
I'M TEXTING NICOLE.
SHE'S SITTING NEXT TO YOU!
WE CAN TEXT FASTER THAN WE CAN TALK.
IT'S MORE EFFICIENT THIS WAY.
WE CAN NOW HAVE A 30-MINUTE CONVERSATION IN ONLY 20 MINUTES. THAT GIVES US 10 EXTRA MINUTES FOR OTHER THINGS.
AMEND
SUCH AS?
SOAKING OUR THUMBS IN ICE, MOSTLY.
CAREFUL, PAIGE – YOUR PHONE IS SMOKING.

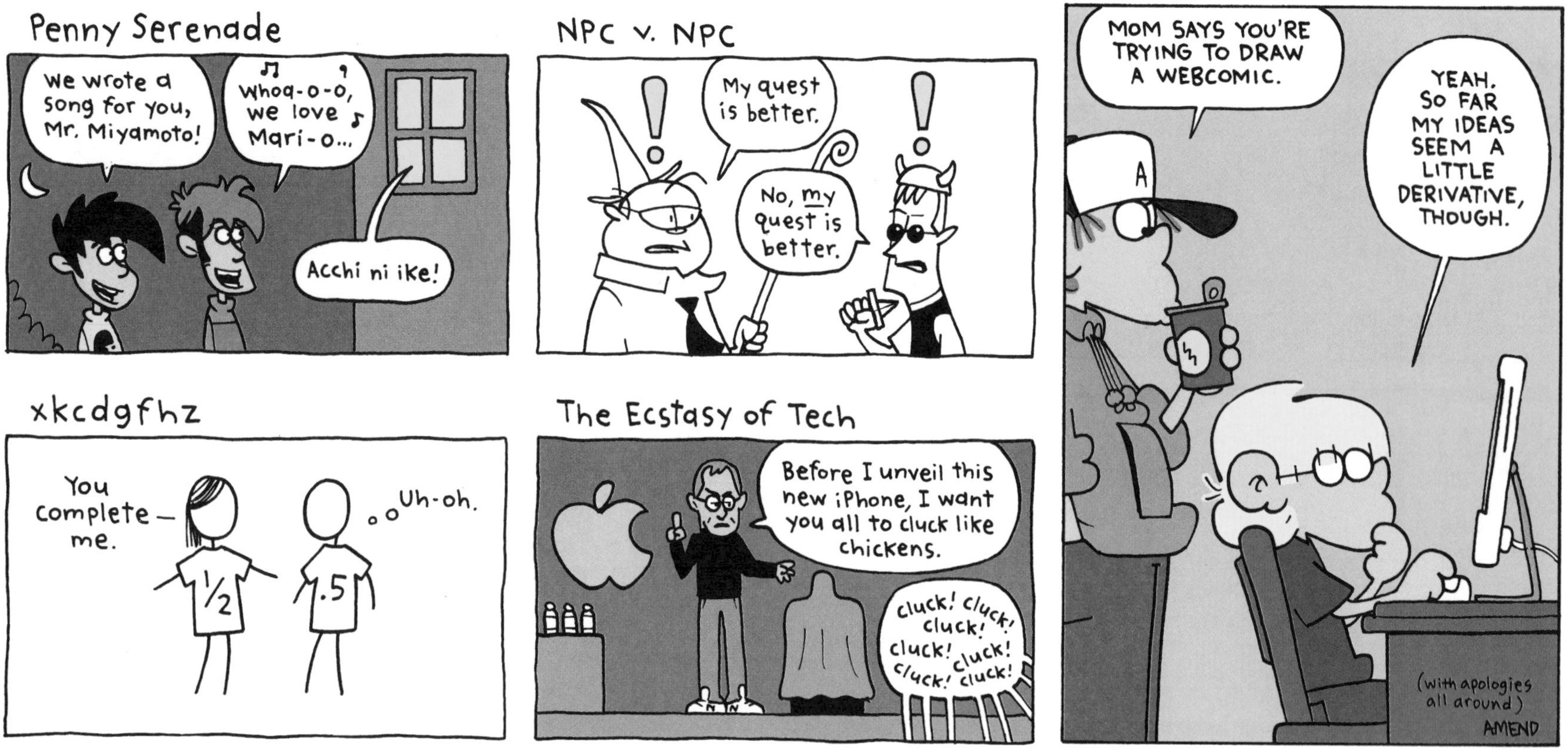
Penny Serenade
We wrote a song for you, Mr. Miyamoto!
Whoa-o-o, we love Mari-o...
Acchi ni ike!
NPC v. NPC
My quest is better.
No, my quest is better.
xkcdgfhz
You complete me.
Uh-oh.
1/2
.5
The Ecstasy of Tech
Before I unveil this new iPhone, I want you all to cluck like chickens.
cluck! cluck! cluck! cluck! cluck! cluck! cluck!
MOM SAYS YOU'RE TRYING TO DRAW A WEBCOMIC.
YEAH. SO FAR MY IDEAS SEEM A LITTLE DERIVATIVE, THOUGH.
(with apologies all around)
AMEND

JASON, I TOLD YOU NO SQUIRT GUNS IN THE HOUSE!

OH, REALLY?

THE 2ND AMENDMENT SAYS THAT I HAVE A RIGHT TO KEEP AND BEAR ARMS.

SQUIRTZOOKA 3000

AND THE SUPREME COURT AFFIRMED THAT RIGHT JUST LAST MONTH.

"DISTRICT OF COLUMBIA V. HELLER." SURELY YOU'RE AWARE OF IT. RIGHT? RIGHT?

GET IT OUT OF HERE! NOW!

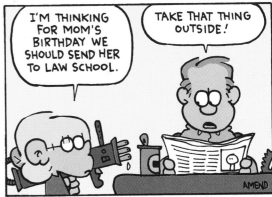

I'M THINKING FOR MOM'S BIRTHDAY WE SHOULD SEND HER TO LAW SCHOOL.

TAKE THAT THING OUTSIDE!

AMEND

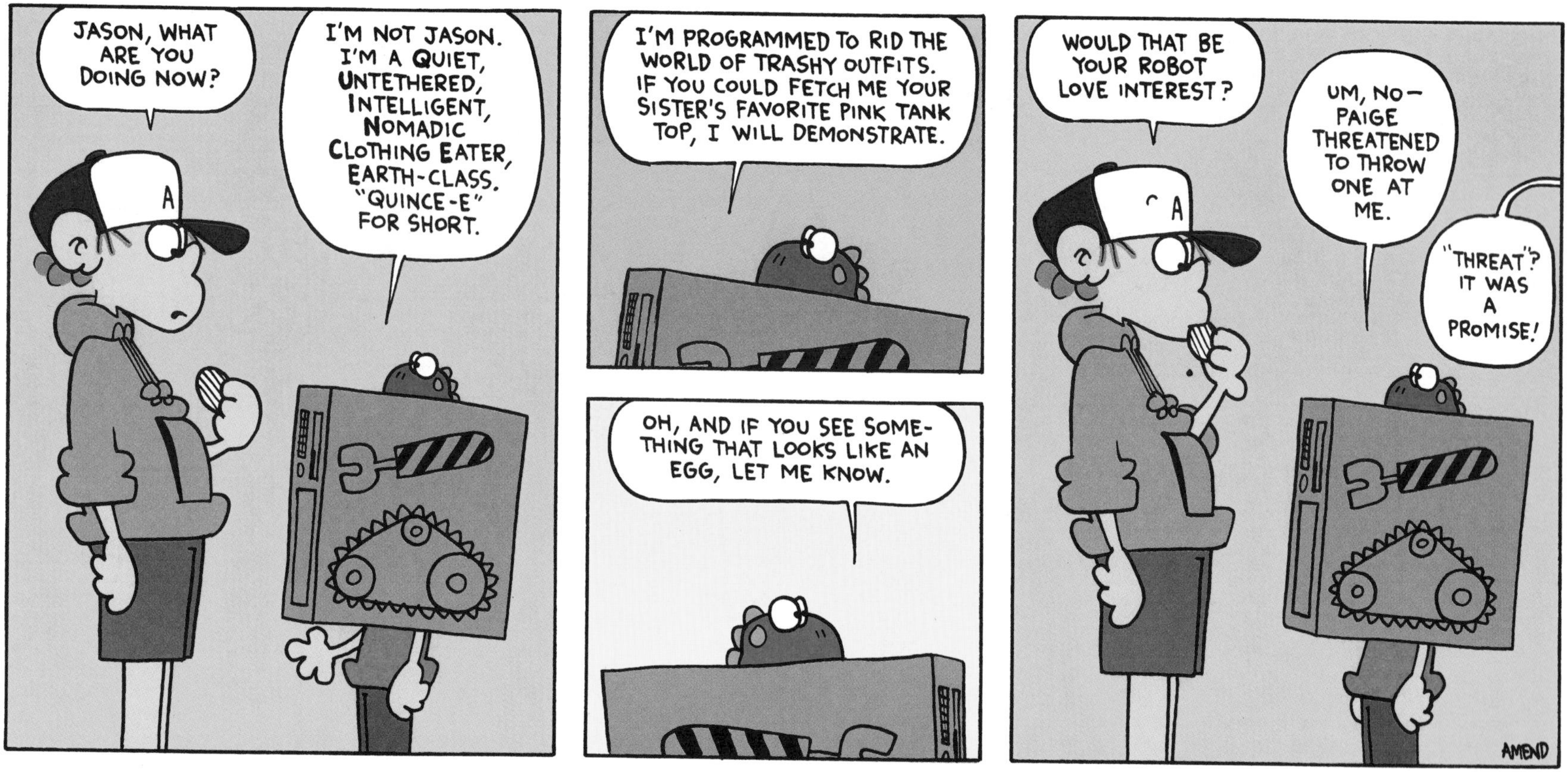
JASON, WHAT ARE YOU DOING NOW?
I'M NOT JASON. I'M A QUIET, UNTETHERED, INTELLIGENT, NOMADIC CLOTHING EATER, EARTH-CLASS. "QUINCE-E" FOR SHORT.
I'M PROGRAMMED TO RID THE WORLD OF TRASHY OUTFITS. IF YOU COULD FETCH ME YOUR SISTER'S FAVORITE PINK TANK TOP, I WILL DEMONSTRATE.
OH, AND IF YOU SEE SOMETHING THAT LOOKS LIKE AN EGG, LET ME KNOW.
WOULD THAT BE YOUR ROBOT LOVE INTEREST?
UM, NO—PAIGE THREATENED TO THROW ONE AT ME.
"THREAT"? IT WAS A PROMISE!
AMEND

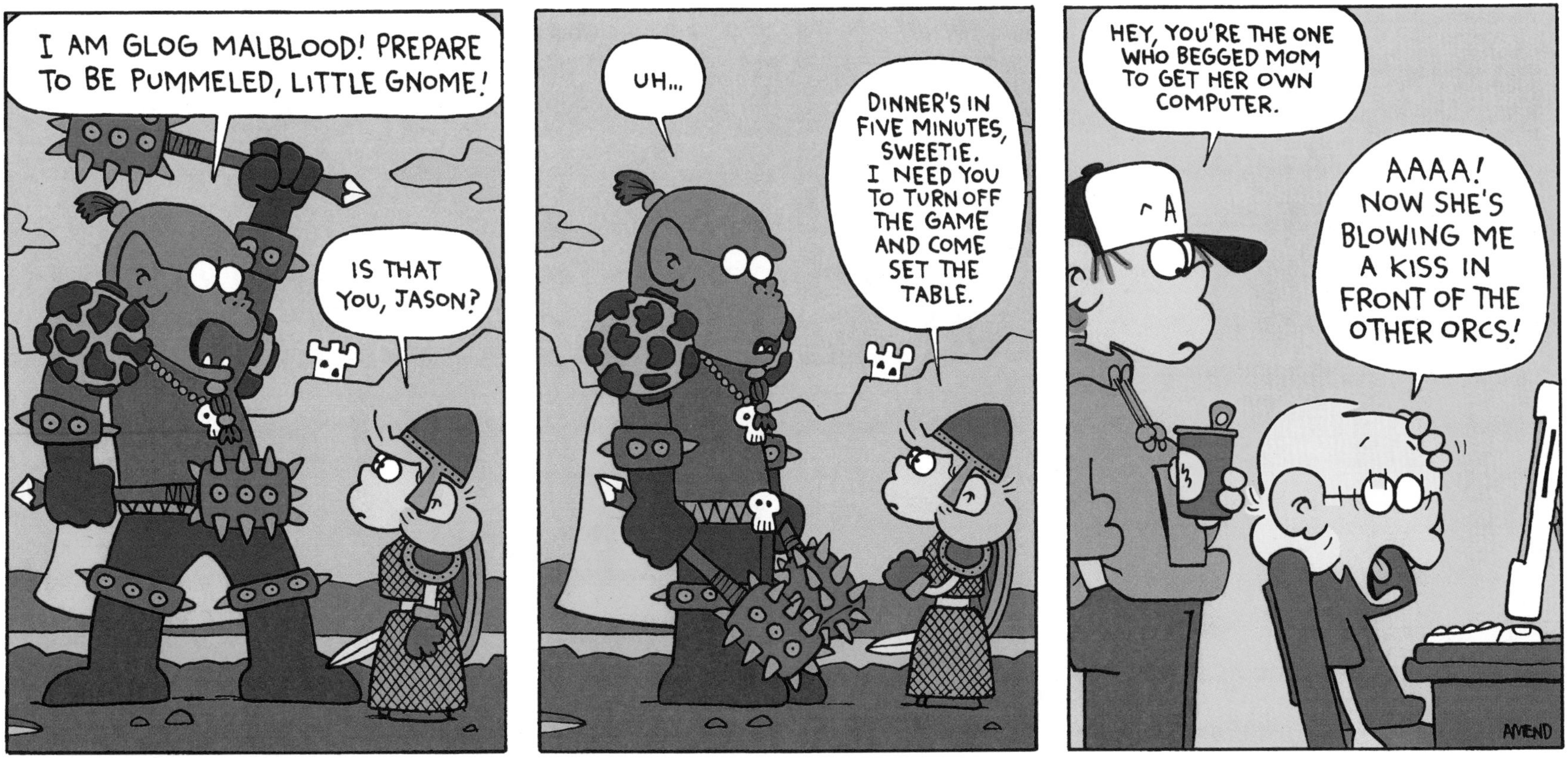
I AM GLOG MALBLOOD! PREPARE TO BE PUMMELED, LITTLE GNOME!
IS THAT YOU, JASON?
UH...
DINNER'S IN FIVE MINUTES, SWEETIE. I NEED YOU TO TURN OFF THE GAME AND COME SET THE TABLE.
HEY, YOU'RE THE ONE WHO BEGGED MOM TO GET HER OWN COMPUTER.
AAAA! NOW SHE'S BLOWING ME A KISS IN FRONT OF THE OTHER ORCS!
AMEND

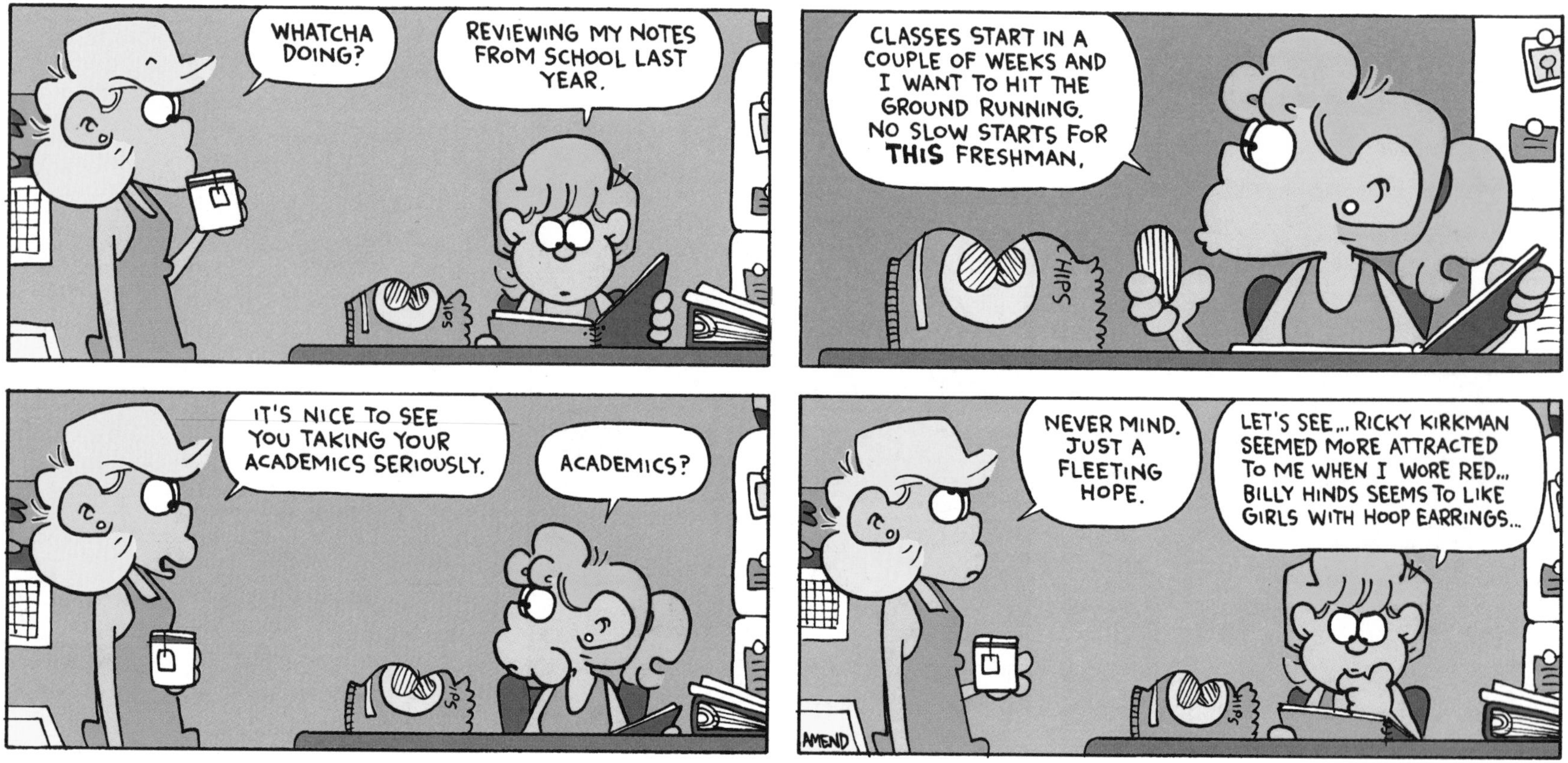
WHATCHA DOING?
REVIEWING MY NOTES FROM SCHOOL LAST YEAR.
CLASSES START IN A COUPLE OF WEEKS AND I WANT TO HIT THE GROUND RUNNING. NO SLOW STARTS FOR **THIS** FRESHMAN.
CHIPS
IT'S NICE TO SEE YOU TAKING YOUR ACADEMICS SERIOUSLY.
ACADEMICS?
NEVER MIND. JUST A FLEETING HOPE.
LET'S SEE... RICKY KIRKMAN SEEMED MORE ATTRACTED TO ME WHEN I WORE RED... BILLY HINDS SEEMS TO LIKE GIRLS WITH HOOP EARRINGS...
AMEND

I'M LOOKING FOR SOMETHING ALONG THE LINES OF A SELF-TANNING LOTION.

OH, YES. THOSE ARE ON AISLE FOUR.

ACTUALLY, WHAT I WANT IS AN UN-TANNING LOTION.

"UN-TANNING"?

SOMETHING THAT'LL MAKE ME LOOK GOOD AND PALE.

MY MOM MADE ME PLAY OUTSIDE THIS WEEK AND NOW MY SKIN HAS A FAINT HEALTHY COLOR.

AMEND

SCHOOL STARTS IN A FEW DAYS, AND IF PEOPLE THINK I STEPPED AWAY FROM MY COMPUTER FOR EVEN A NANOSECOND THIS SUMMER, I'LL LOSE HARD-EARNED GEEK CRED.

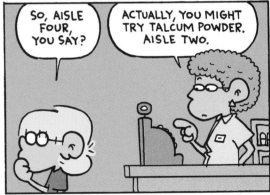

SO, AISLE FOUR, YOU SAY?

ACTUALLY, YOU MIGHT TRY TALCUM POWDER. AISLE TWO.

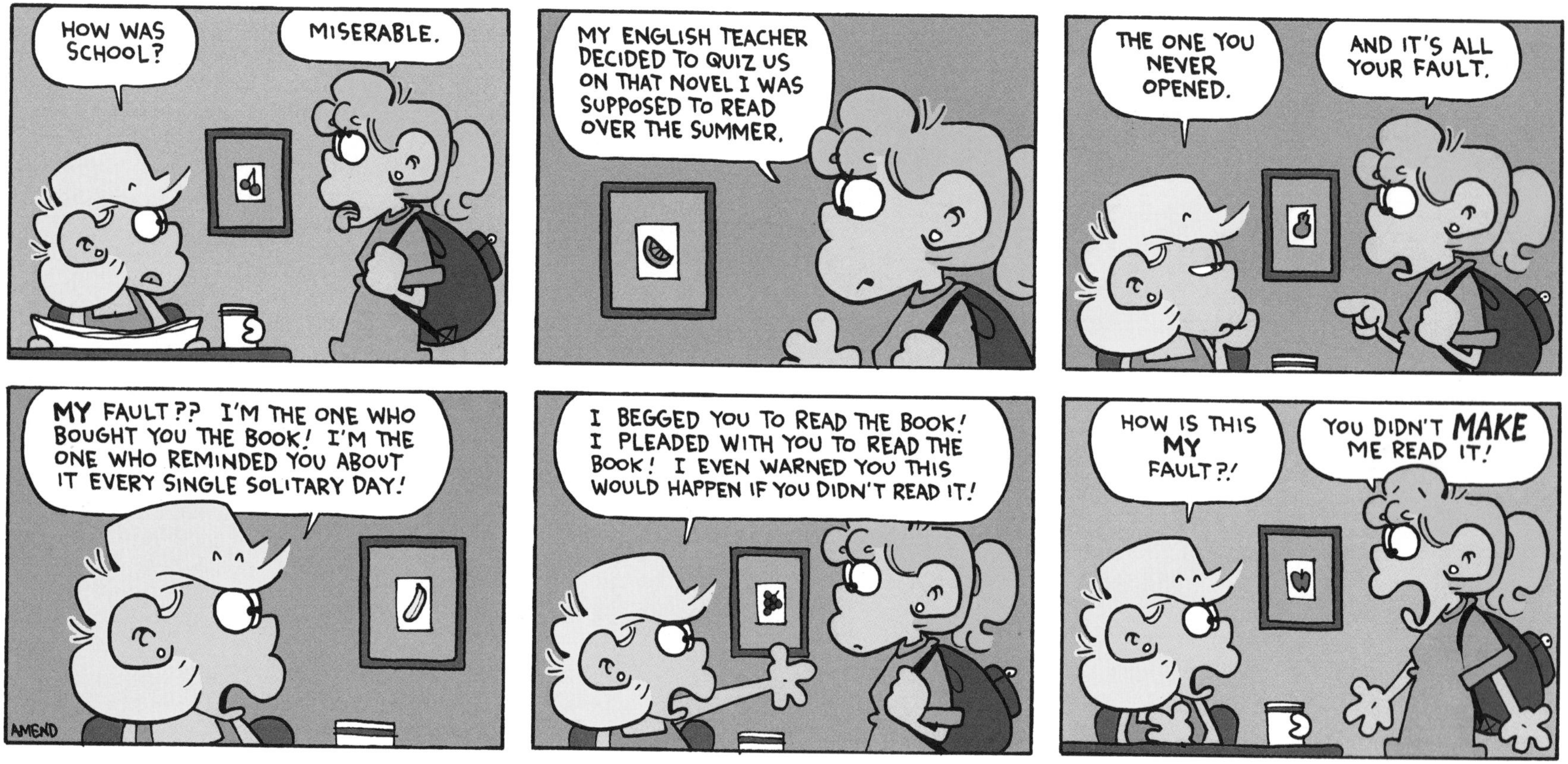
HOW WAS SCHOOL?
MISERABLE.
MY ENGLISH TEACHER DECIDED TO QUIZ US ON THAT NOVEL I WAS SUPPOSED TO READ OVER THE SUMMER.
THE ONE YOU NEVER OPENED.
AND IT'S ALL YOUR FAULT.
MY FAULT?? I'M THE ONE WHO BOUGHT YOU THE BOOK! I'M THE ONE WHO REMINDED YOU ABOUT IT EVERY SINGLE SOLITARY DAY!
AMEND
I BEGGED YOU TO READ THE BOOK! I PLEADED WITH YOU TO READ THE BOOK! I EVEN WARNED YOU THIS WOULD HAPPEN IF YOU DIDN'T READ IT!
HOW IS THIS MY FAULT?!
YOU DIDN'T MAKE ME READ IT!

SQUIRT
SQUIRT
SQUIRT
SQUIRT
SQUIRT
FOOM!
NASA'S ON THE PHONE. APPARENTLY, YOU OWE THEM SOME MONEY.
AGAIN??
AMEND

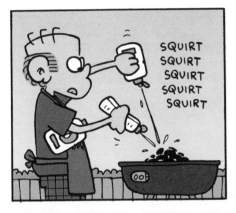

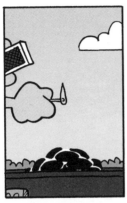

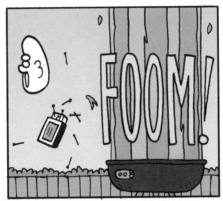

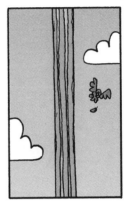

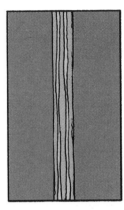

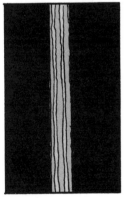

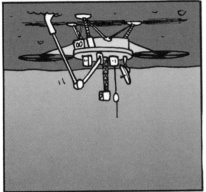

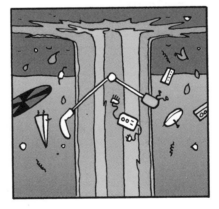

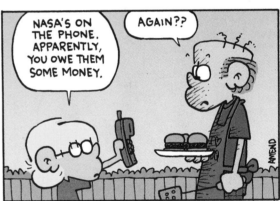

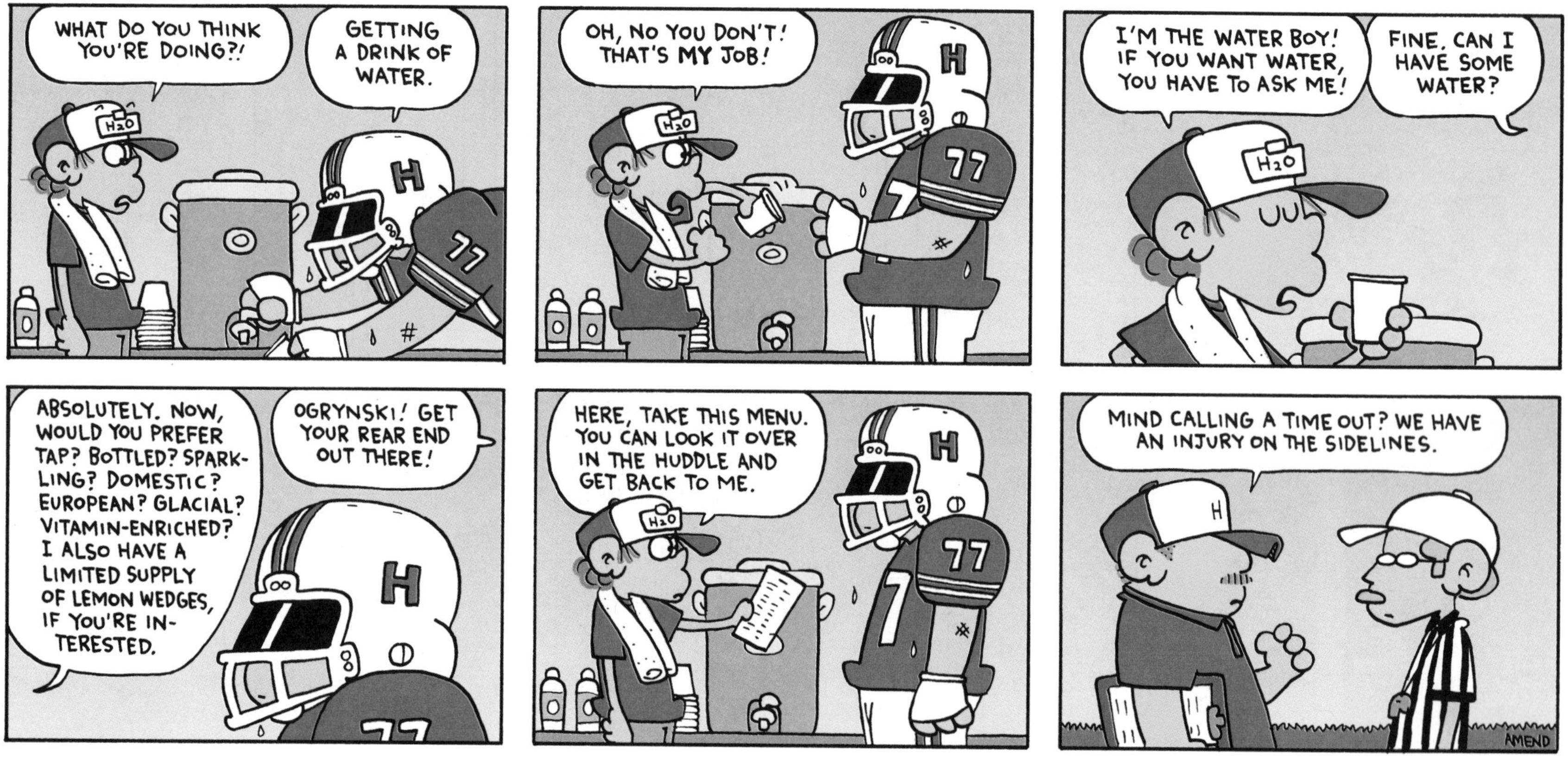
WHAT DO YOU THINK YOU'RE DOING?!
GETTING A DRINK OF WATER.
OH, NO YOU DON'T! THAT'S **MY** JOB!
I'M THE WATER BOY! IF YOU WANT WATER, YOU HAVE TO ASK ME!
FINE. CAN I HAVE SOME WATER?
ABSOLUTELY. NOW, WOULD YOU PREFER TAP? BOTTLED? SPARKLING? DOMESTIC? EUROPEAN? GLACIAL? VITAMIN-ENRICHED? I ALSO HAVE A LIMITED SUPPLY OF LEMON WEDGES, IF YOU'RE INTERESTED.
OGRYNSKI! GET YOUR REAR END OUT THERE!
HERE, TAKE THIS MENU. YOU CAN LOOK IT OVER IN THE HUDDLE AND GET BACK TO ME.
MIND CALLING A TIME OUT? WE HAVE AN INJURY ON THE SIDELINES.
AMEND

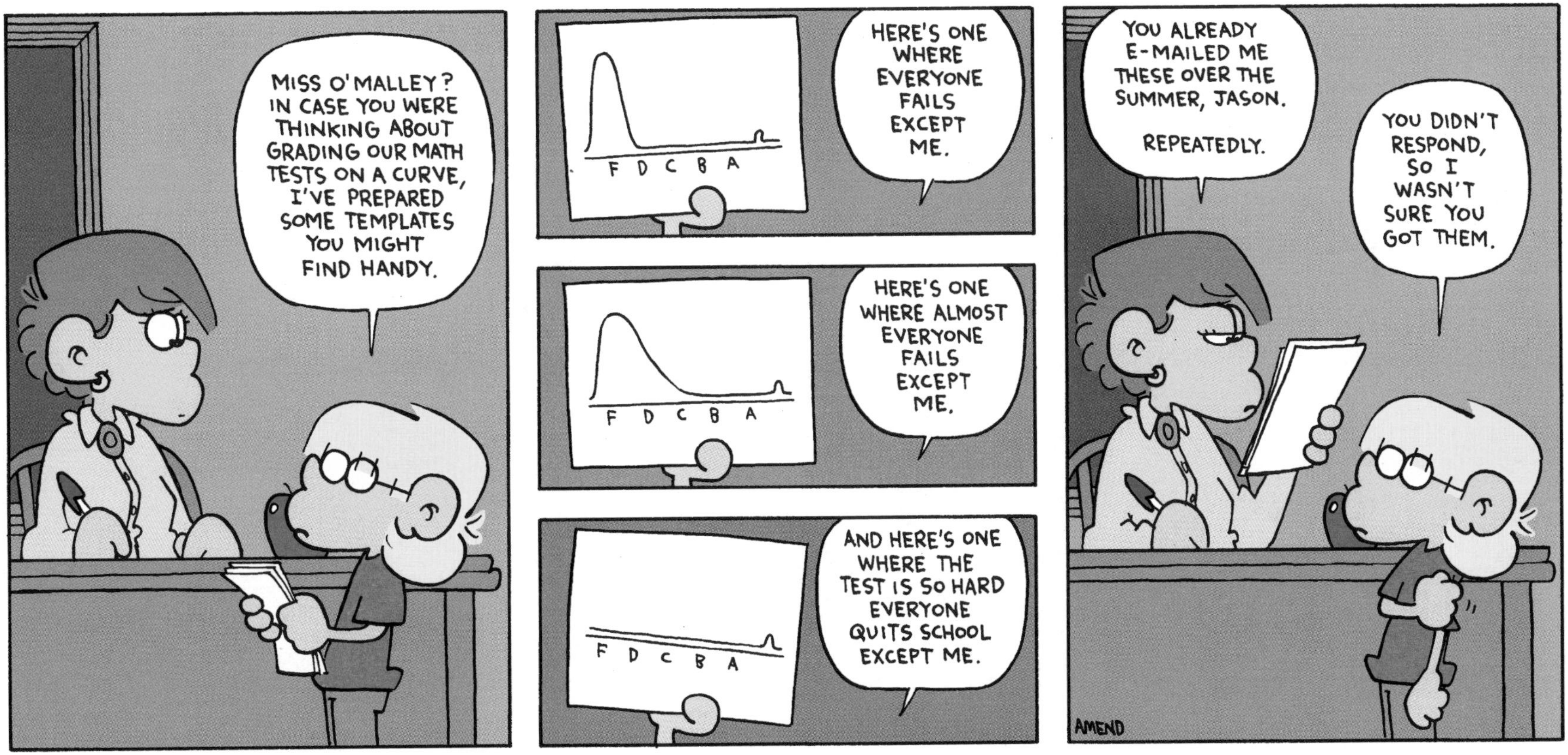
MISS O'MALLEY? IN CASE YOU WERE THINKING ABOUT GRADING OUR MATH TESTS ON A CURVE, I'VE PREPARED SOME TEMPLATES YOU MIGHT FIND HANDY.
F D C B A
HERE'S ONE WHERE EVERYONE FAILS EXCEPT ME.
F D C B A
HERE'S ONE WHERE ALMOST EVERYONE FAILS EXCEPT ME.
F D C B A
AND HERE'S ONE WHERE THE TEST IS SO HARD EVERYONE QUITS SCHOOL EXCEPT ME.
YOU ALREADY E-MAILED ME THESE OVER THE SUMMER, JASON.
REPEATEDLY.
YOU DIDN'T RESPOND, SO I WASN'T SURE YOU GOT THEM.
AMEND

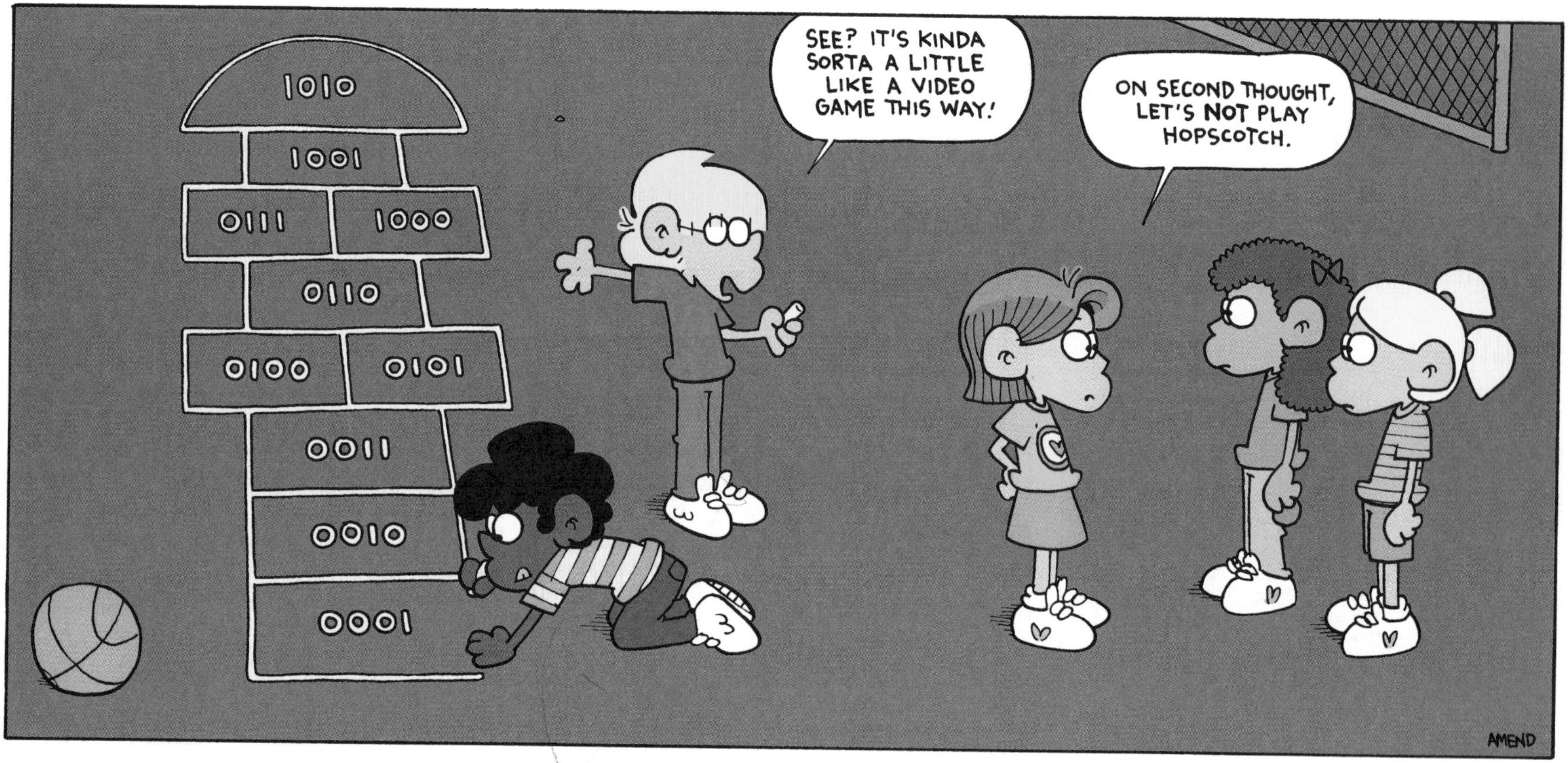
1010
1001
0111
1000
0110
0100
0101
0011
0010
0001
SEE? IT'S KINDA SORTA A LITTLE LIKE A VIDEO GAME THIS WAY!
ON SECOND THOUGHT, LET'S NOT PLAY HOPSCOTCH.
AMEND

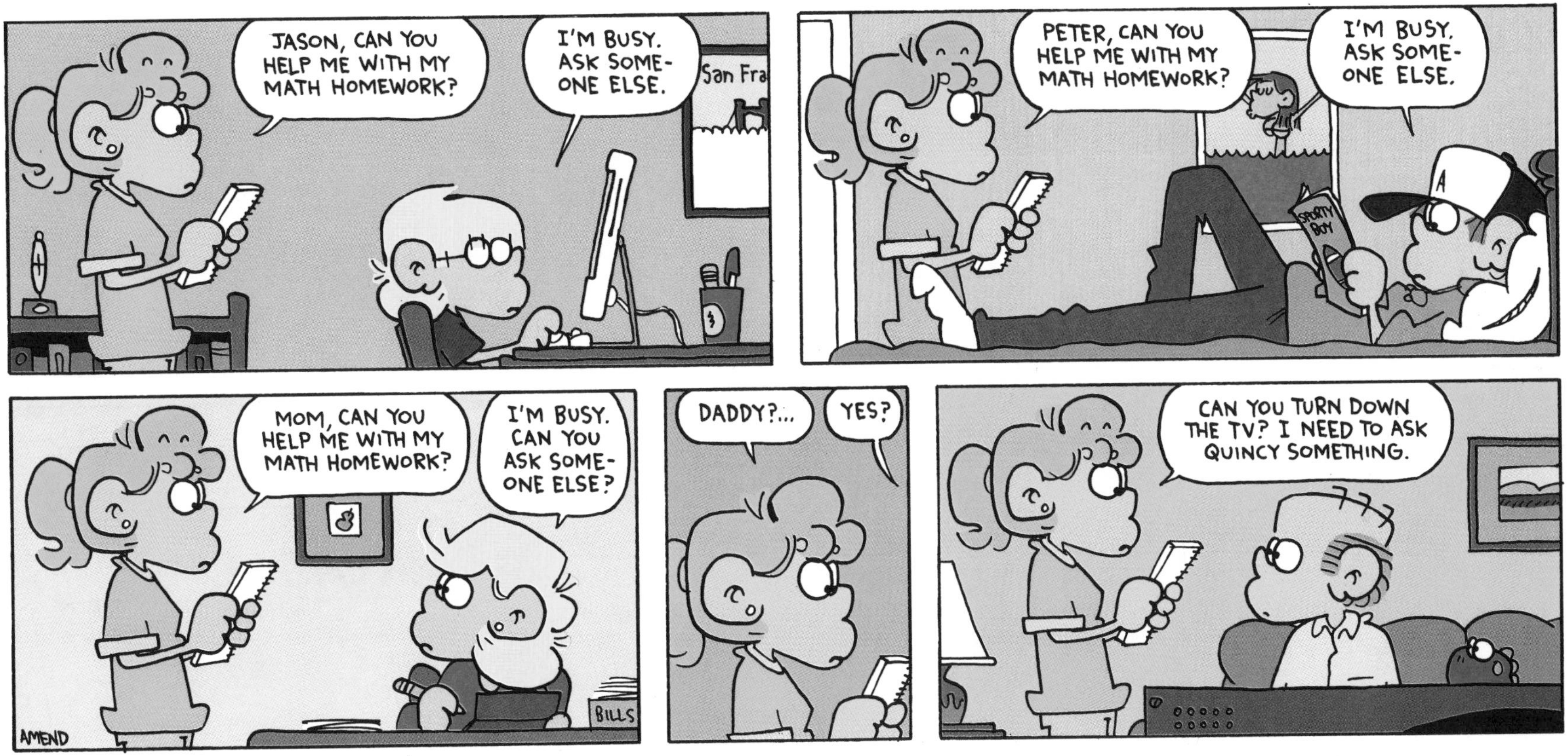
JASON, CAN YOU HELP ME WITH MY MATH HOMEWORK?
I'M BUSY. ASK SOME-ONE ELSE.
San Fra
PETER, CAN YOU HELP ME WITH MY MATH HOMEWORK?
I'M BUSY. ASK SOME-ONE ELSE.
SPORTY BOY
MOM, CAN YOU HELP ME WITH MY MATH HOMEWORK?
I'M BUSY. CAN YOU ASK SOME-ONE ELSE?
BILLS
AMEND
DADDY?...
YES?
CAN YOU TURN DOWN THE TV? I NEED TO ASK QUINCY SOMETHING.

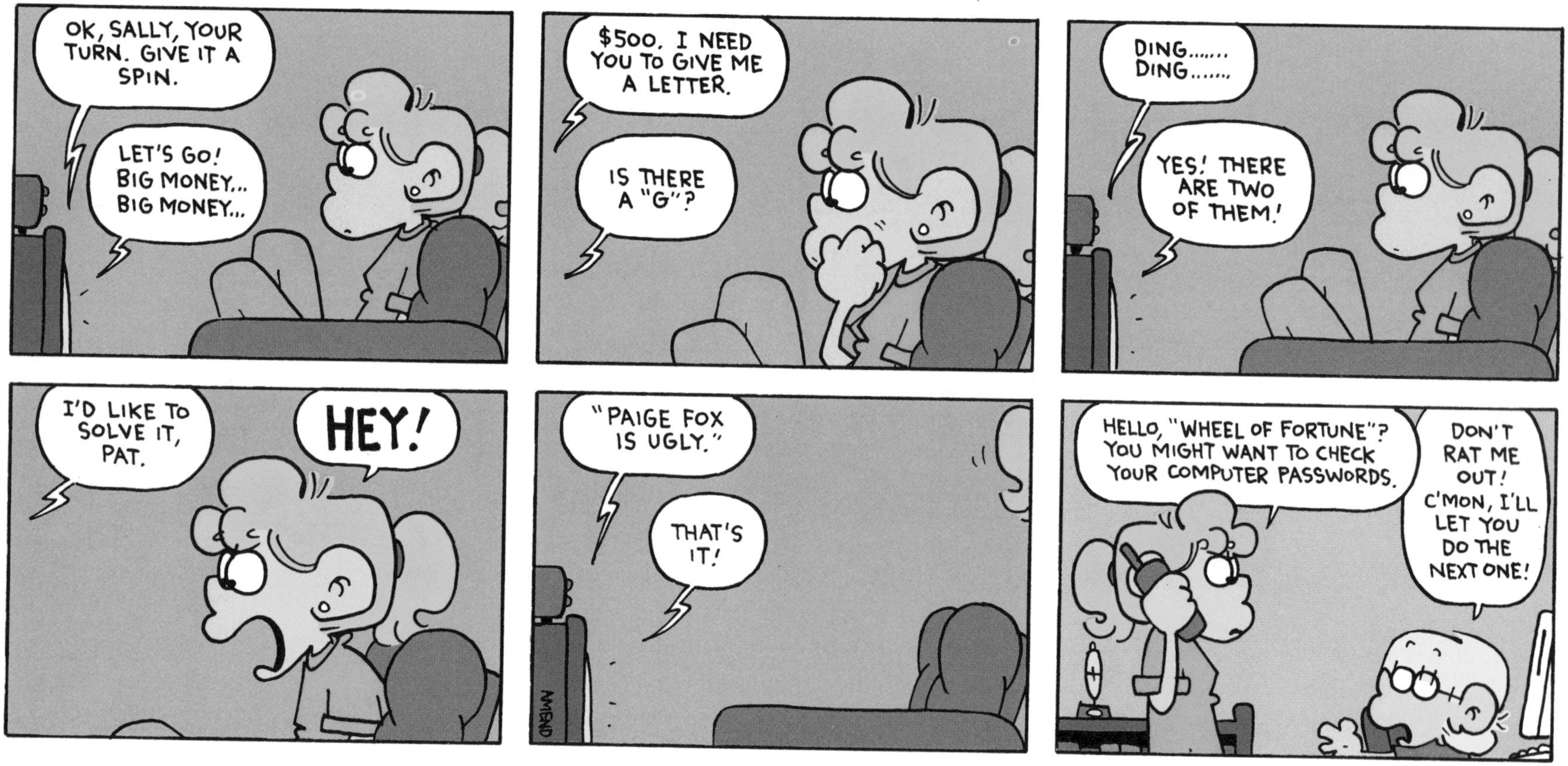

OK, SALLY, YOUR TURN. GIVE IT A SPIN.
LET'S GO! BIG MONEY... BIG MONEY...
$500. I NEED YOU TO GIVE ME A LETTER.
IS THERE A "G"?
DING....... DING.......
YES! THERE ARE TWO OF THEM!
I'D LIKE TO SOLVE IT, PAT.
HEY!
"PAIGE FOX IS UGLY."
THAT'S IT!
AMEND
HELLO, "WHEEL OF FORTUNE"? YOU MIGHT WANT TO CHECK YOUR COMPUTER PASSWORDS.
DON'T RAT ME OUT! C'MON, I'LL LET YOU DO THE NEXT ONE!

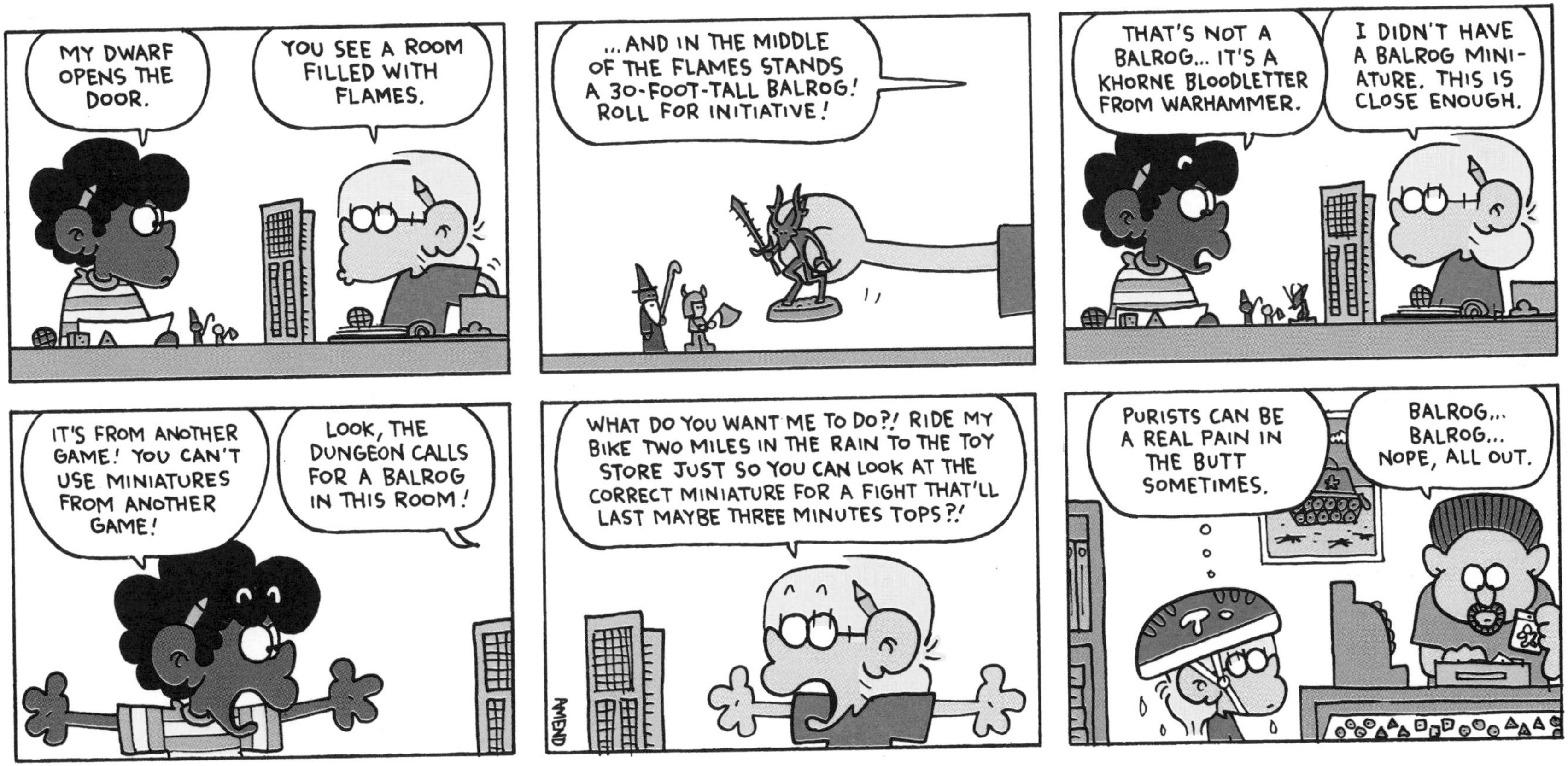
MY DWARF OPENS THE DOOR.
YOU SEE A ROOM FILLED WITH FLAMES.
...AND IN THE MIDDLE OF THE FLAMES STANDS A 30-FOOT-TALL BALROG! ROLL FOR INITIATIVE!
THAT'S NOT A BALROG... IT'S A KHORNE BLOODLETTER FROM WARHAMMER.
I DIDN'T HAVE A BALROG MINI-ATURE. THIS IS CLOSE ENOUGH.
IT'S FROM ANOTHER GAME! YOU CAN'T USE MINIATURES FROM ANOTHER GAME!
LOOK, THE DUNGEON CALLS FOR A BALROG IN THIS ROOM!
WHAT DO YOU WANT ME TO DO?! RIDE MY BIKE TWO MILES IN THE RAIN TO THE TOY STORE JUST SO YOU CAN LOOK AT THE CORRECT MINIATURE FOR A FIGHT THAT'LL LAST MAYBE THREE MINUTES TOPS?!
AMEND
PURISTS CAN BE A REAL PAIN IN THE BUTT SOMETIMES.
BALROG... BALROG... NOPE, ALL OUT.

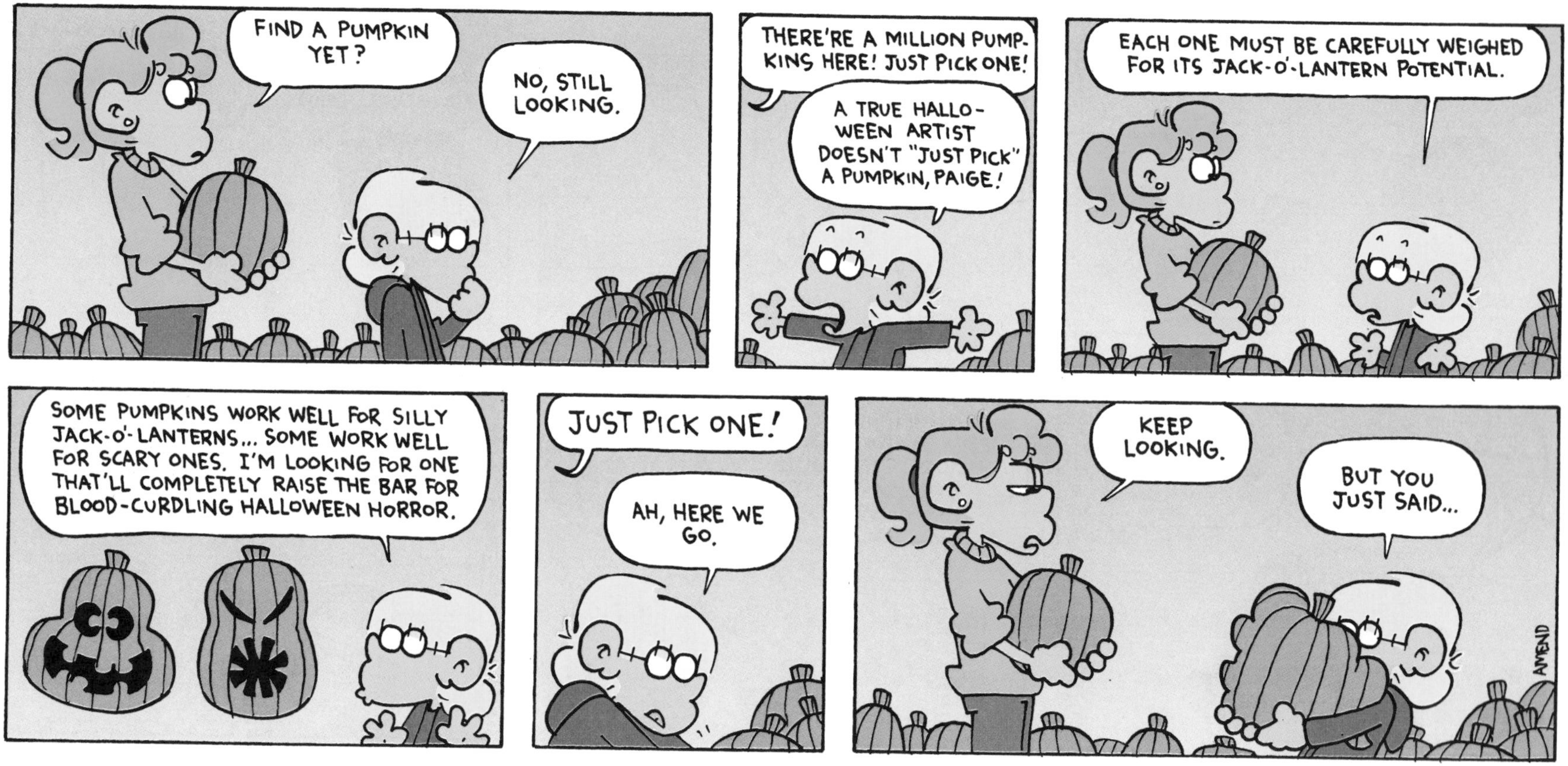
FIND A PUMPKIN YET?
NO, STILL LOOKING.
THERE'RE A MILLION PUMPKINS HERE! JUST PICK ONE!
A TRUE HALLOWEEN ARTIST DOESN'T "JUST PICK" A PUMPKIN, PAIGE!
EACH ONE MUST BE CAREFULLY WEIGHED FOR ITS JACK-O'-LANTERN POTENTIAL.
SOME PUMPKINS WORK WELL FOR SILLY JACK-O'-LANTERNS... SOME WORK WELL FOR SCARY ONES. I'M LOOKING FOR ONE THAT'LL COMPLETELY RAISE THE BAR FOR BLOOD-CURDLING HALLOWEEN HORROR.
JUST PICK ONE!
AH, HERE WE GO.
KEEP LOOKING.
BUT YOU JUST SAID...
AMEND

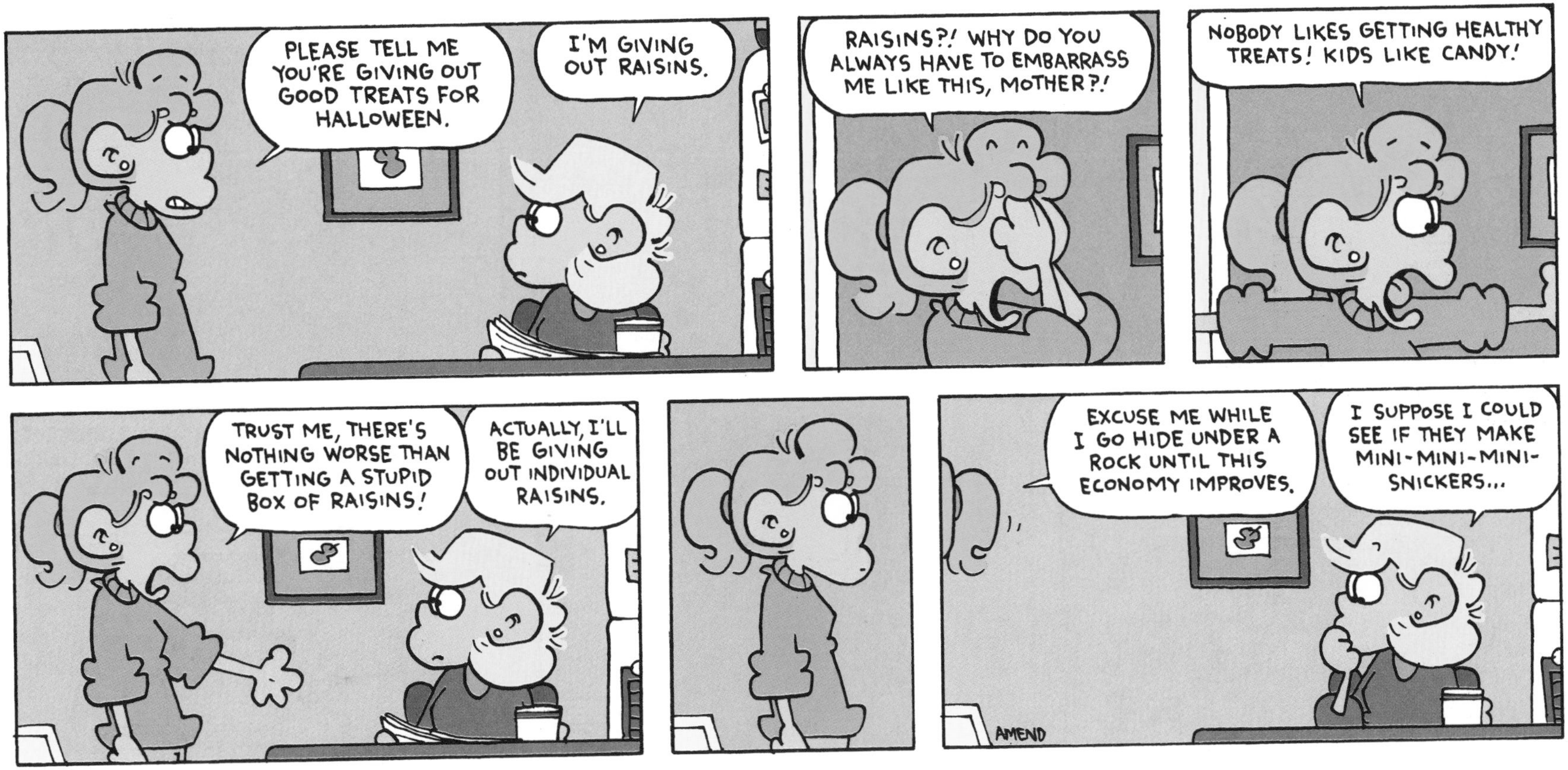
PLEASE TELL ME YOU'RE GIVING OUT GOOD TREATS FOR HALLOWEEN.
I'M GIVING OUT RAISINS.
RAISINS?! WHY DO YOU ALWAYS HAVE TO EMBARRASS ME LIKE THIS, MOTHER?!
NOBODY LIKES GETTING HEALTHY TREATS! KIDS LIKE CANDY!
TRUST ME, THERE'S NOTHING WORSE THAN GETTING A STUPID BOX OF RAISINS!
ACTUALLY, I'LL BE GIVING OUT INDIVIDUAL RAISINS.
EXCUSE ME WHILE I GO HIDE UNDER A ROCK UNTIL THIS ECONOMY IMPROVES.
I SUPPOSE I COULD SEE IF THEY MAKE MINI-MINI-MINI-SNICKERS...
AMEND

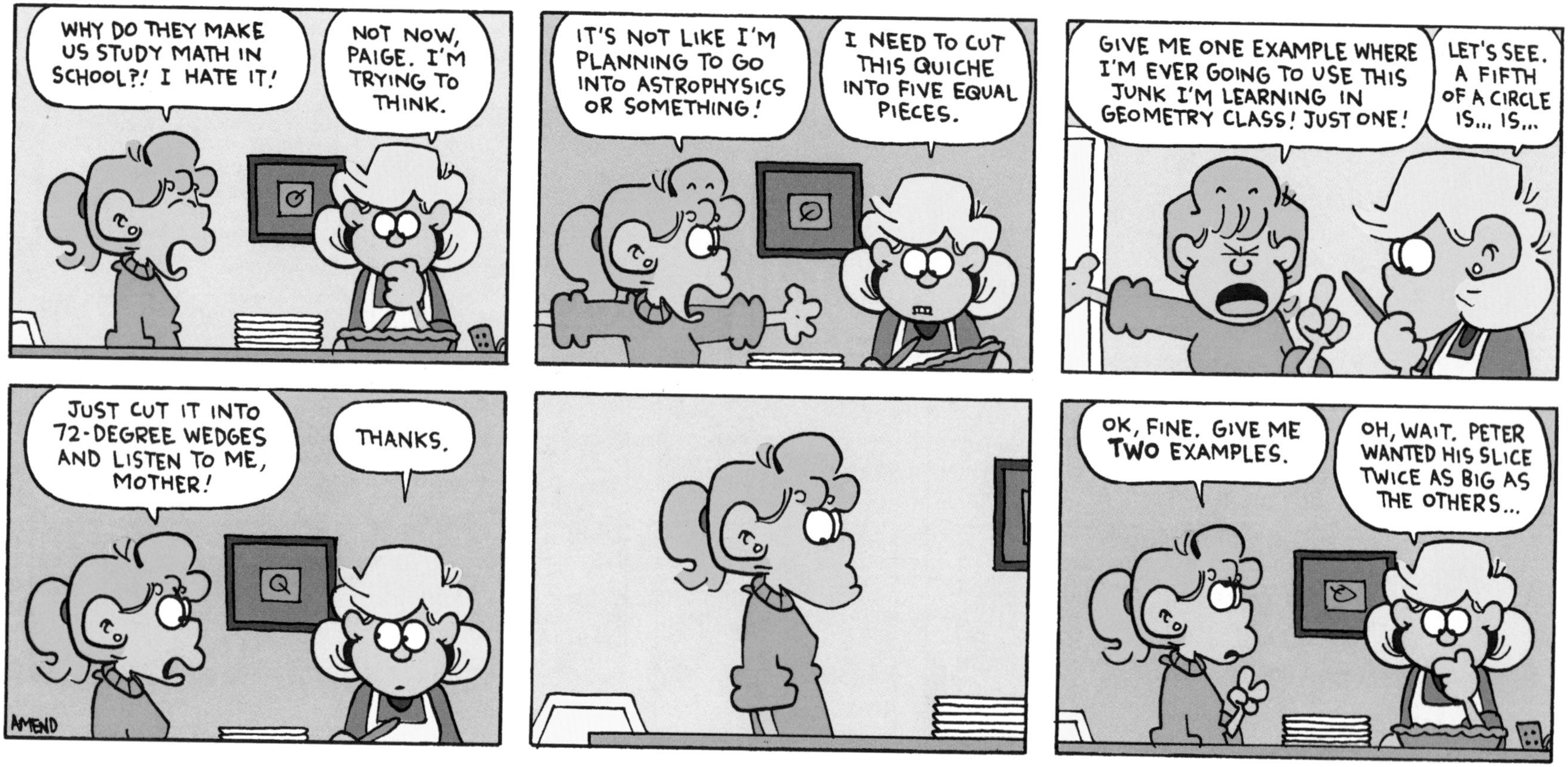
WHY DO THEY MAKE US STUDY MATH IN SCHOOL?! I HATE IT!
NOT NOW, PAIGE. I'M TRYING TO THINK.
IT'S NOT LIKE I'M PLANNING TO GO INTO ASTROPHYSICS OR SOMETHING!
I NEED TO CUT THIS QUICHE INTO FIVE EQUAL PIECES.
GIVE ME ONE EXAMPLE WHERE I'M EVER GOING TO USE THIS JUNK I'M LEARNING IN GEOMETRY CLASS! JUST ONE!
LET'S SEE. A FIFTH OF A CIRCLE IS... IS...
JUST CUT IT INTO 72-DEGREE WEDGES AND LISTEN TO ME, MOTHER!
THANKS.
AMEND
OK, FINE. GIVE ME TWO EXAMPLES.
OH, WAIT. PETER WANTED HIS SLICE TWICE AS BIG AS THE OTHERS...

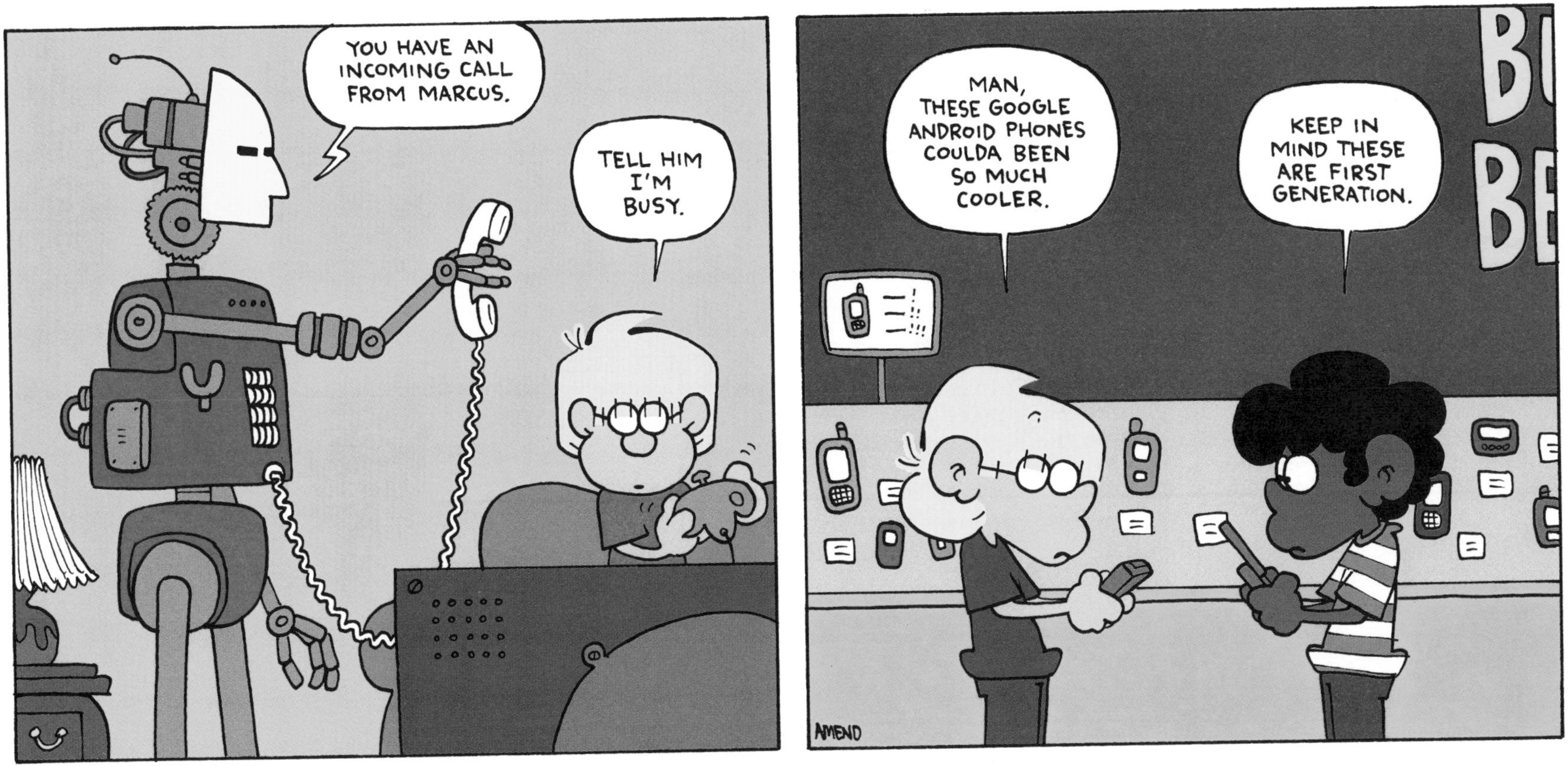
YOU HAVE AN INCOMING CALL FROM MARCUS.
TELL HIM I'M BUSY.
MAN, THESE GOOGLE ANDROID PHONES COULDA BEEN SO MUCH COOLER.
KEEP IN MIND THESE ARE FIRST GENERATION.
AMEND

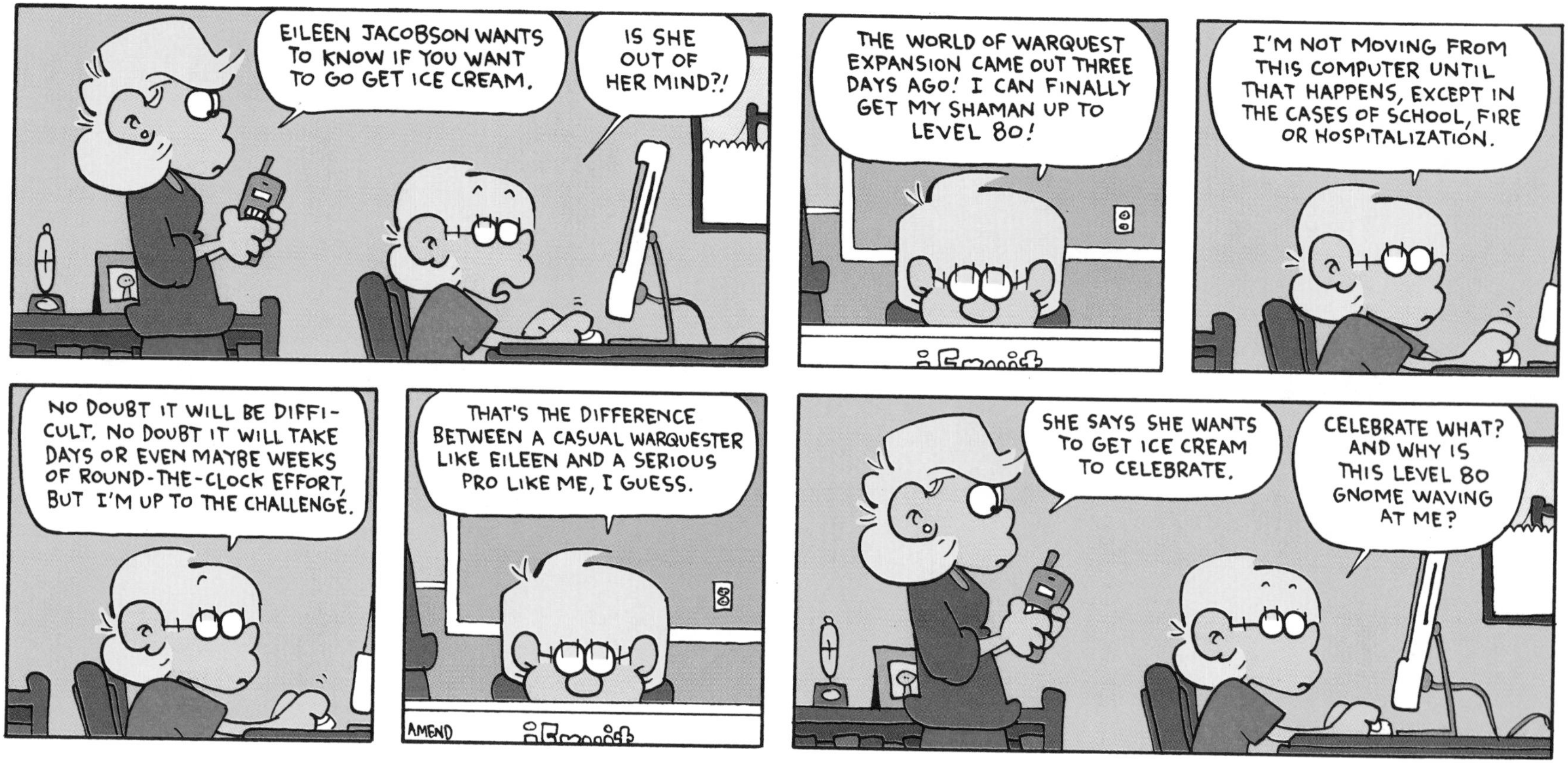
EILEEN JACOBSON WANTS TO KNOW IF YOU WANT TO GO GET ICE CREAM.
IS SHE OUT OF HER MIND?!
THE WORLD OF WARQUEST EXPANSION CAME OUT THREE DAYS AGO! I CAN FINALLY GET MY SHAMAN UP TO LEVEL 80!
I'M NOT MOVING FROM THIS COMPUTER UNTIL THAT HAPPENS, EXCEPT IN THE CASES OF SCHOOL, FIRE OR HOSPITALIZATION.
NO DOUBT IT WILL BE DIFFI-CULT. NO DOUBT IT WILL TAKE DAYS OR EVEN MAYBE WEEKS OF ROUND-THE-CLOCK EFFORT, BUT I'M UP TO THE CHALLENGE.
THAT'S THE DIFFERENCE BETWEEN A CASUAL WARQUESTER LIKE EILEEN AND A SERIOUS PRO LIKE ME, I GUESS.
AMEND
SHE SAYS SHE WANTS TO GET ICE CREAM TO CELEBRATE.
CELEBRATE WHAT? AND WHY IS THIS LEVEL 80 GNOME WAVING AT ME?

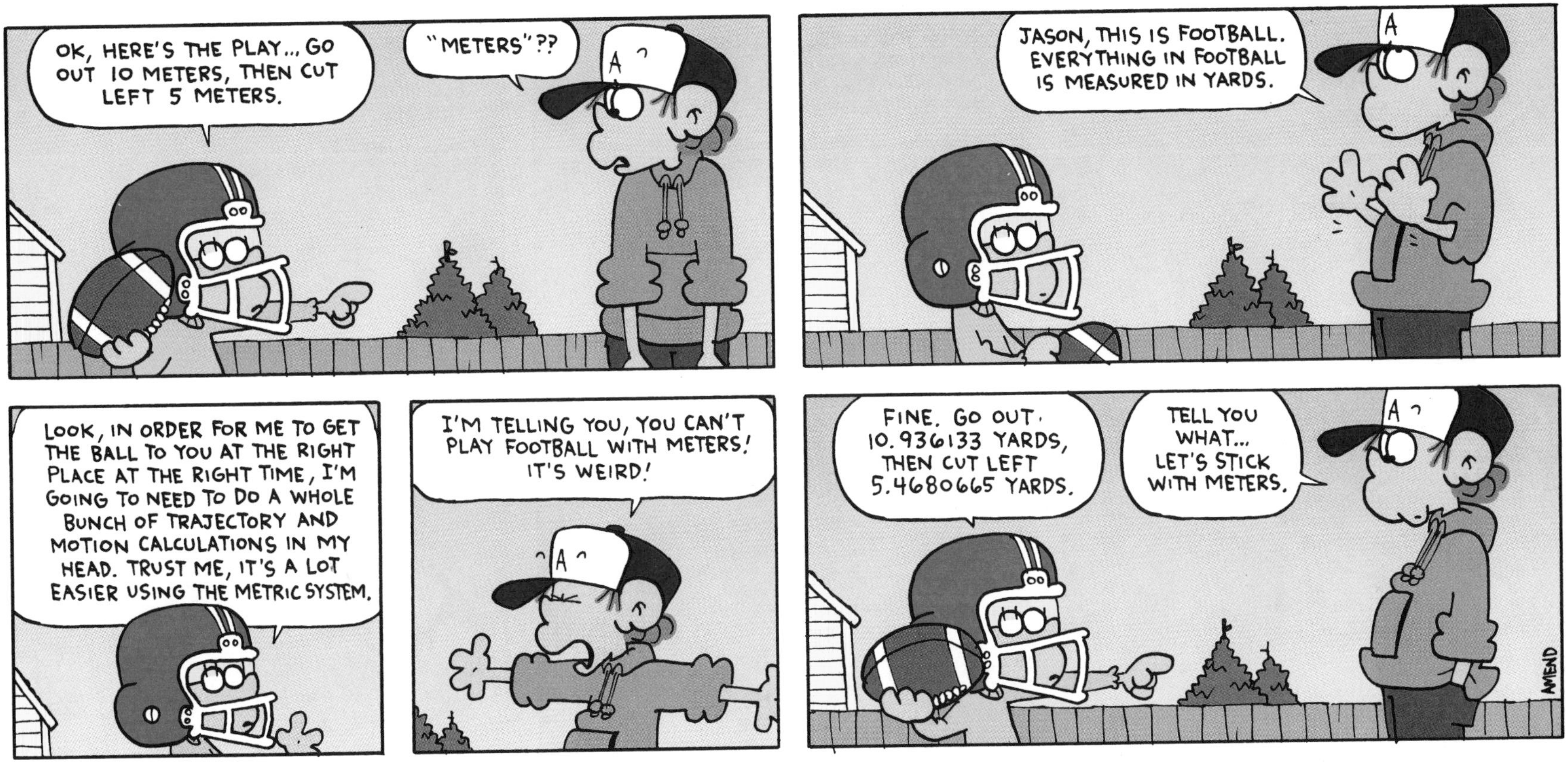
OK, HERE'S THE PLAY... GO OUT 10 METERS, THEN CUT LEFT 5 METERS.
"METERS"??
JASON, THIS IS FOOTBALL. EVERYTHING IN FOOTBALL IS MEASURED IN YARDS.
LOOK, IN ORDER FOR ME TO GET THE BALL TO YOU AT THE RIGHT PLACE AT THE RIGHT TIME, I'M GOING TO NEED TO DO A WHOLE BUNCH OF TRAJECTORY AND MOTION CALCULATIONS IN MY HEAD. TRUST ME, IT'S A LOT EASIER USING THE METRIC SYSTEM.
I'M TELLING YOU, YOU CAN'T PLAY FOOTBALL WITH METERS! IT'S WEIRD!
FINE. GO OUT 10.936133 YARDS, THEN CUT LEFT 5.4680665 YARDS.
TELL YOU WHAT... LET'S STICK WITH METERS.
AMEND

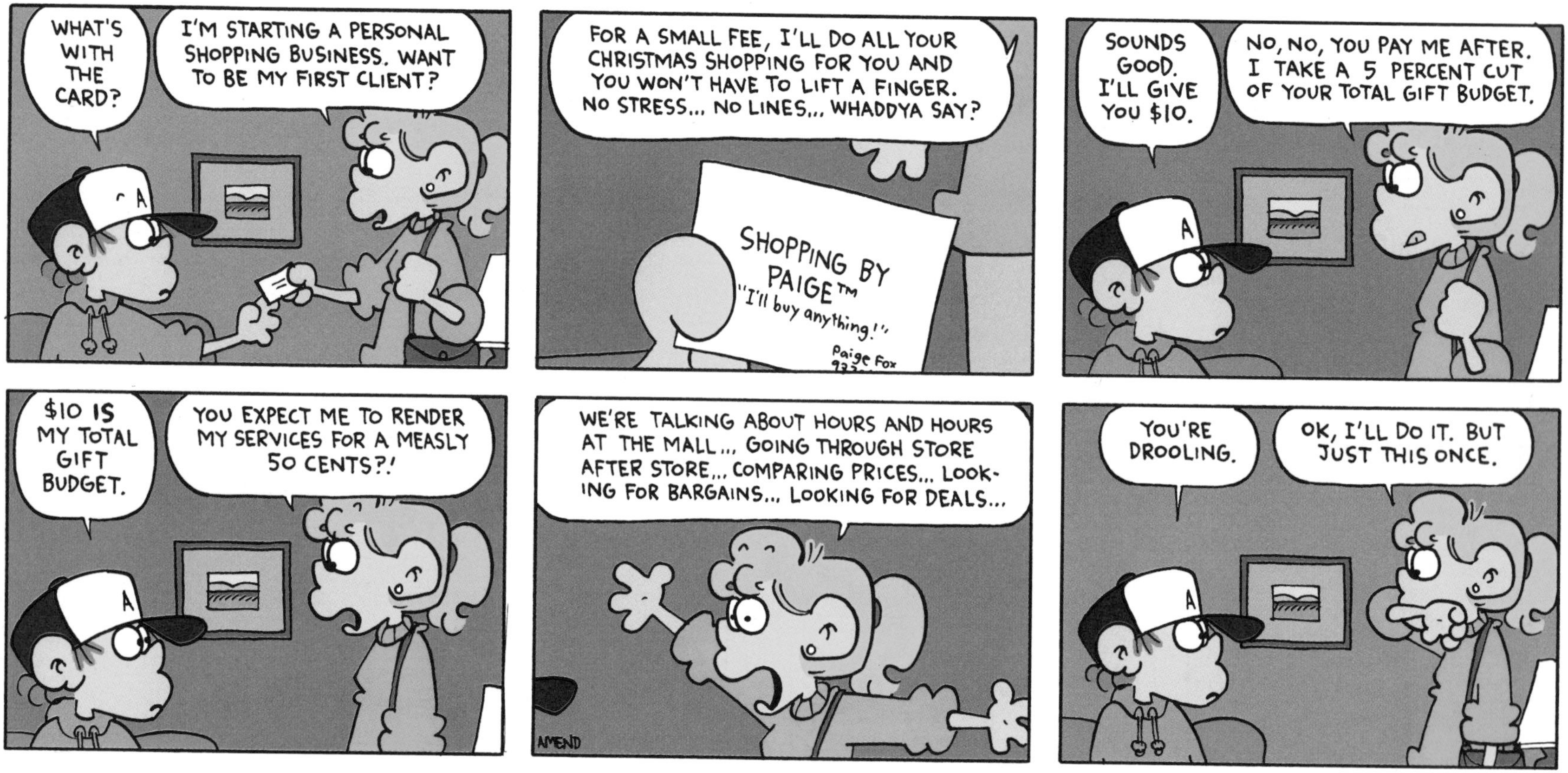
WHAT'S WITH THE CARD?
I'M STARTING A PERSONAL SHOPPING BUSINESS. WANT TO BE MY FIRST CLIENT?
FOR A SMALL FEE, I'LL DO ALL YOUR CHRISTMAS SHOPPING FOR YOU AND YOU WON'T HAVE TO LIFT A FINGER. NO STRESS... NO LINES... WHADDYA SAY?
SHOPPING BY PAIGE™
"I'll buy anything!"
Paige Fox
SOUNDS GOOD. I'LL GIVE YOU $10.
NO, NO, YOU PAY ME AFTER. I TAKE A 5 PERCENT CUT OF YOUR TOTAL GIFT BUDGET.
$10 IS MY TOTAL GIFT BUDGET.
YOU EXPECT ME TO RENDER MY SERVICES FOR A MEASLY 50 CENTS?!
WE'RE TALKING ABOUT HOURS AND HOURS AT THE MALL... GOING THROUGH STORE AFTER STORE... COMPARING PRICES... LOOKING FOR BARGAINS... LOOKING FOR DEALS...
AMEND
YOU'RE DROOLING.
OK, I'LL DO IT. BUT JUST THIS ONCE.

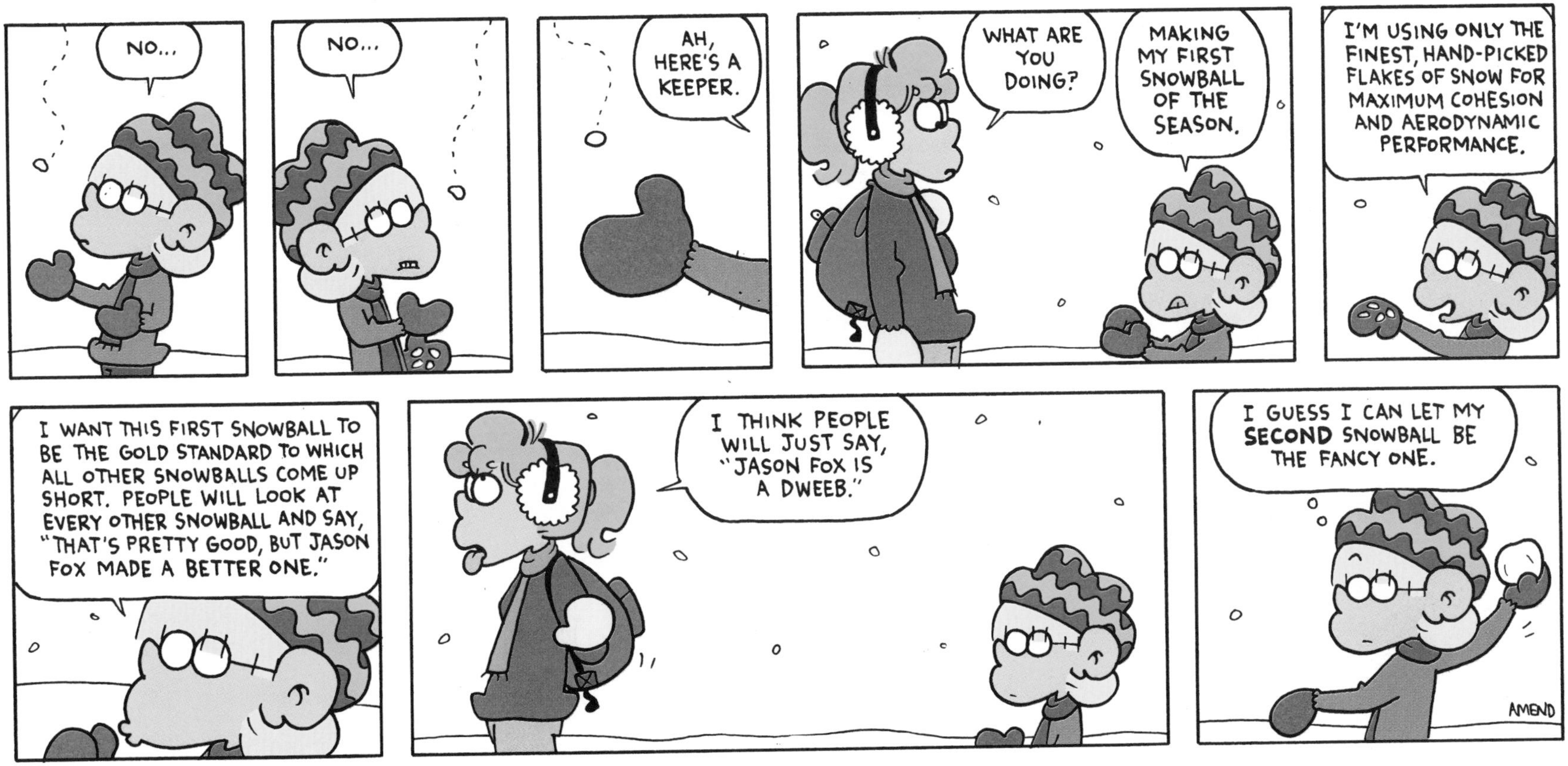
NO...
NO...
AH, HERE'S A KEEPER.
WHAT ARE YOU DOING?
MAKING MY FIRST SNOWBALL OF THE SEASON.
I'M USING ONLY THE FINEST, HAND-PICKED FLAKES OF SNOW FOR MAXIMUM COHESION AND AERODYNAMIC PERFORMANCE.
I WANT THIS FIRST SNOWBALL TO BE THE GOLD STANDARD TO WHICH ALL OTHER SNOWBALLS COME UP SHORT. PEOPLE WILL LOOK AT EVERY OTHER SNOWBALL AND SAY, "THAT'S PRETTY GOOD, BUT JASON FOX MADE A BETTER ONE."
I THINK PEOPLE WILL JUST SAY, "JASON FOX IS A DWEEB."
I GUESS I CAN LET MY **SECOND** SNOWBALL BE THE FANCY ONE.
AMEND

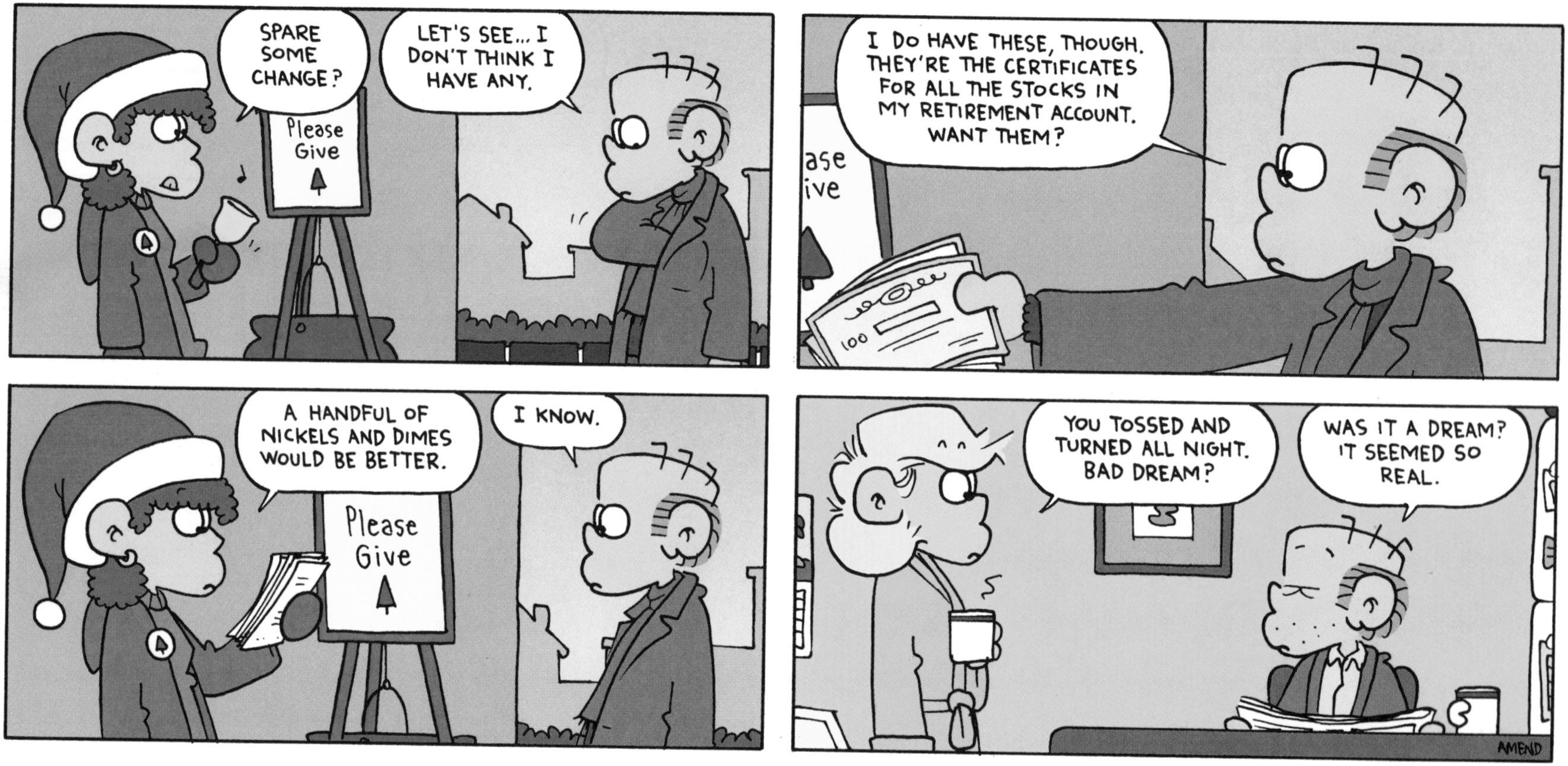

SPARE SOME CHANGE?
Please Give
LET'S SEE... I DON'T THINK I HAVE ANY.
I DO HAVE THESE, THOUGH. THEY'RE THE CERTIFICATES FOR ALL THE STOCKS IN MY RETIREMENT ACCOUNT. WANT THEM?
100
A HANDFUL OF NICKELS AND DIMES WOULD BE BETTER.
I KNOW.
Please Give
YOU TOSSED AND TURNED ALL NIGHT. BAD DREAM?
WAS IT A DREAM? IT SEEMED SO REAL.
AMEND

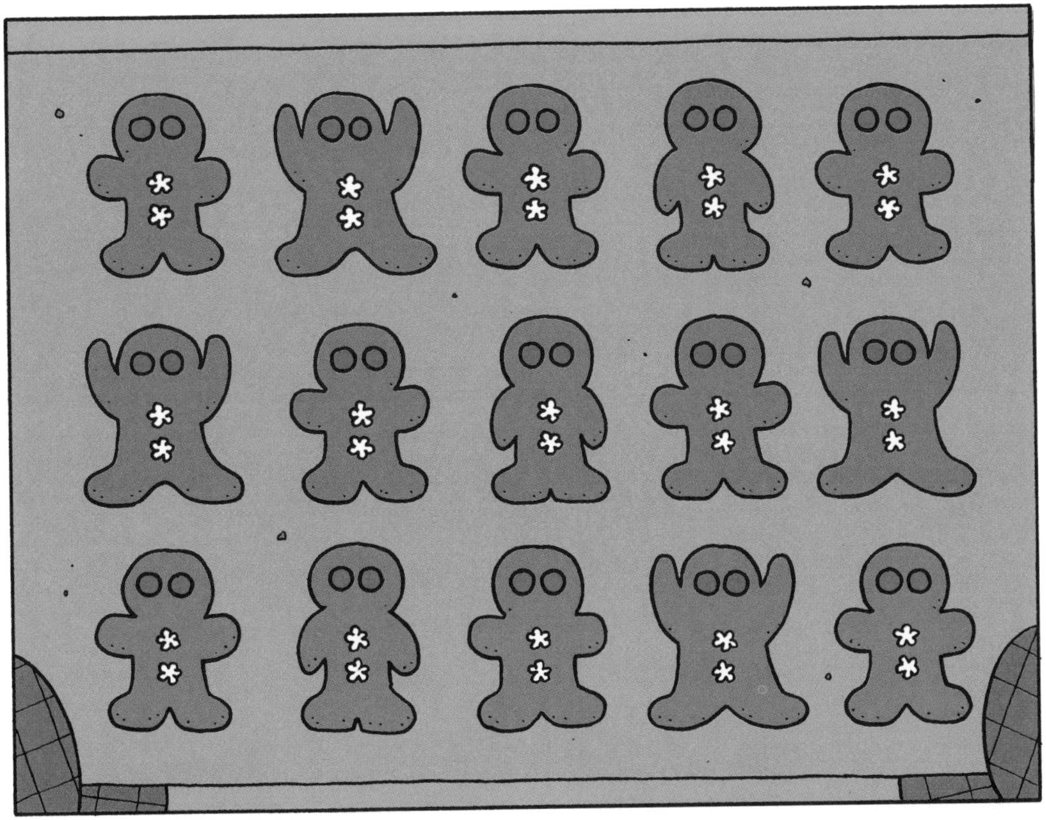

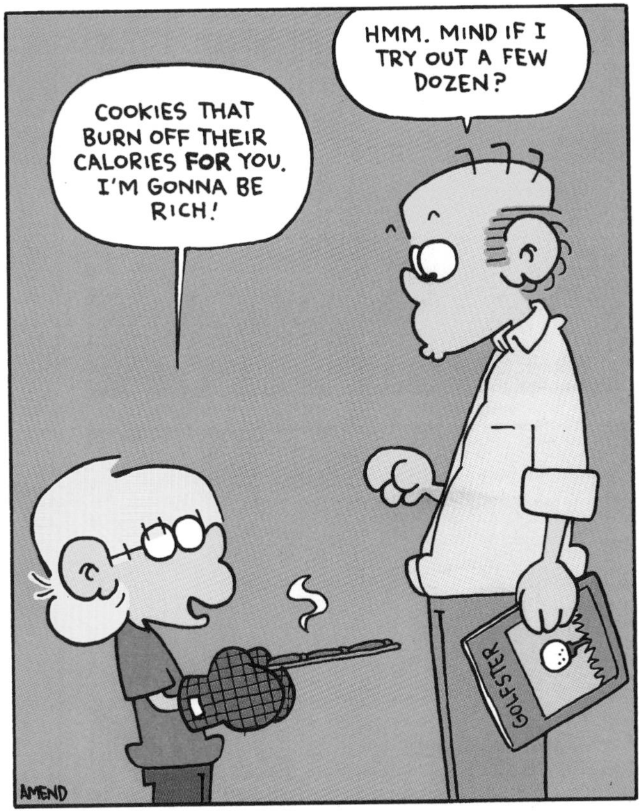
COOKIES THAT BURN OFF THEIR CALORIES FOR YOU. I'M GONNA BE RICH!
HMM. MIND IF I TRY OUT A FEW DOZEN?
GOLFSTER
AMEND

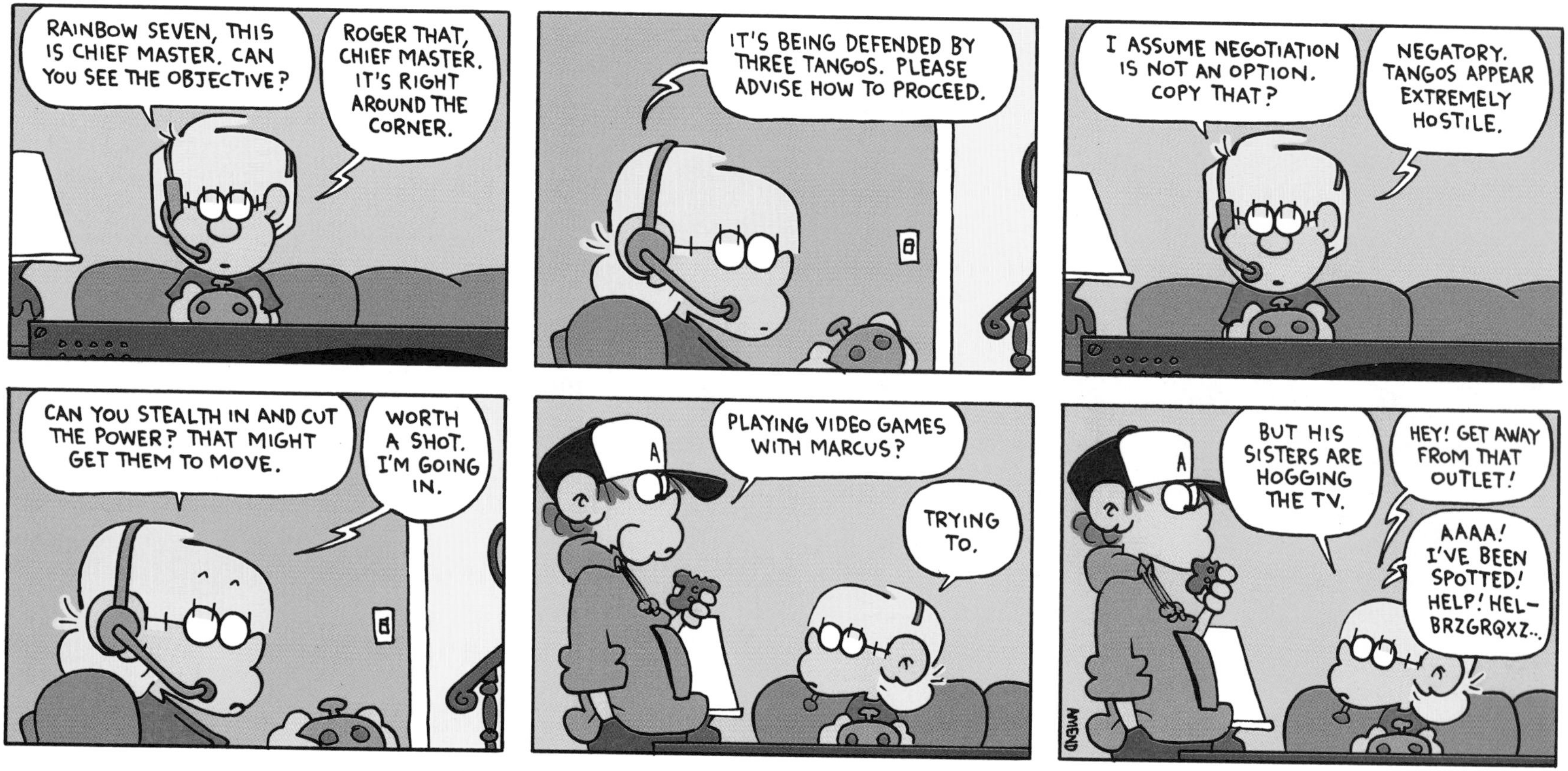
RAINBOW SEVEN, THIS IS CHIEF MASTER. CAN YOU SEE THE OBJECTIVE?
ROGER THAT, CHIEF MASTER. IT'S RIGHT AROUND THE CORNER.
IT'S BEING DEFENDED BY THREE TANGOS. PLEASE ADVISE HOW TO PROCEED.
I ASSUME NEGOTIATION IS NOT AN OPTION. COPY THAT?
NEGATORY. TANGOS APPEAR EXTREMELY HOSTILE.
CAN YOU STEALTH IN AND CUT THE POWER? THAT MIGHT GET THEM TO MOVE.
WORTH A SHOT. I'M GOING IN.
PLAYING VIDEO GAMES WITH MARCUS?
TRYING TO.
BUT HIS SISTERS ARE HOGGING THE TV.
HEY! GET AWAY FROM THAT OUTLET!
AAAA! I'VE BEEN SPOTTED! HELP! HEL-BRZGRQXZ..
AMEND

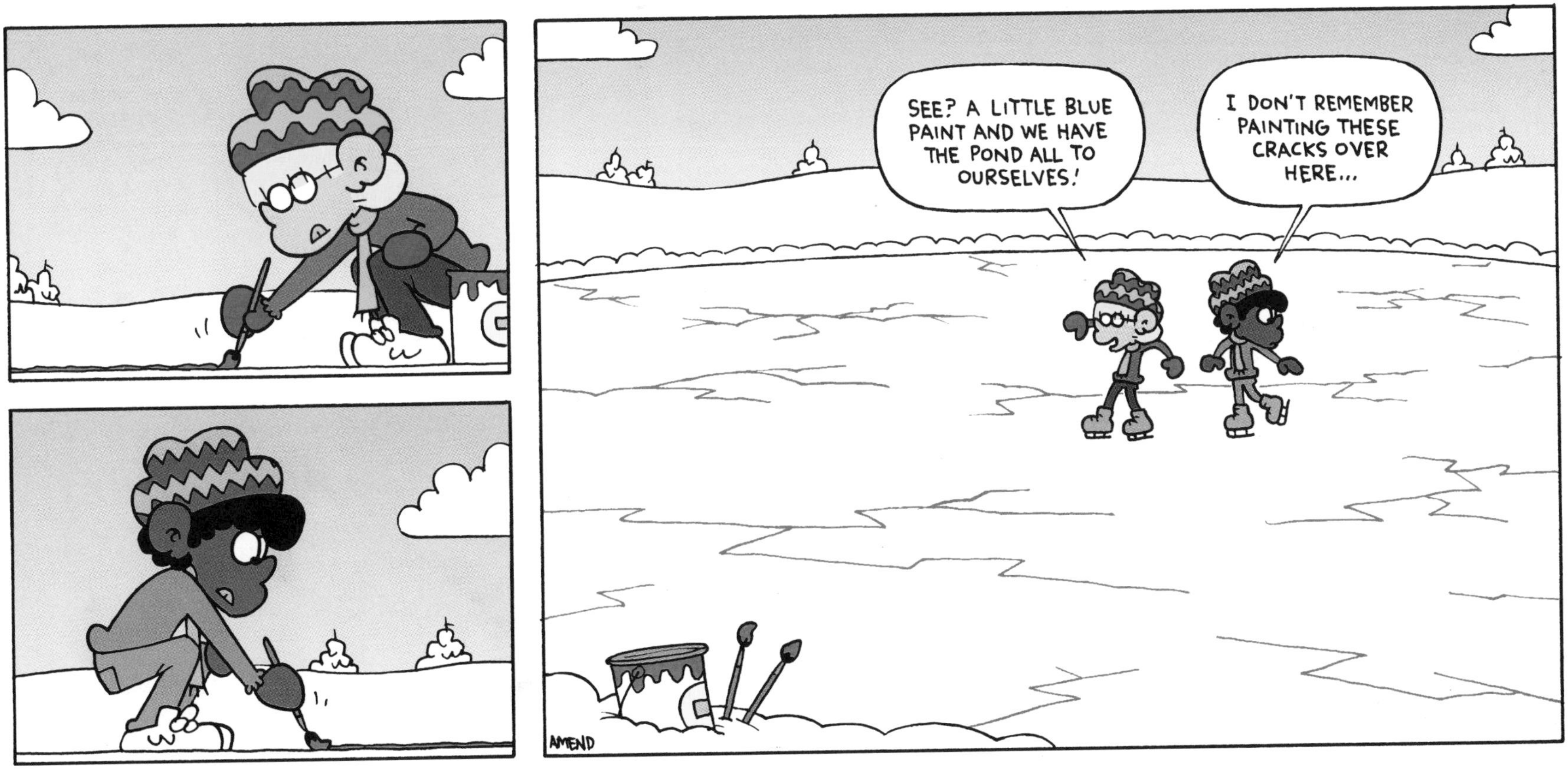
SEE? A LITTLE BLUE PAINT AND WE HAVE THE POND ALL TO OURSELVES!
I DON'T REMEMBER PAINTING THESE CRACKS OVER HERE...
AMEND

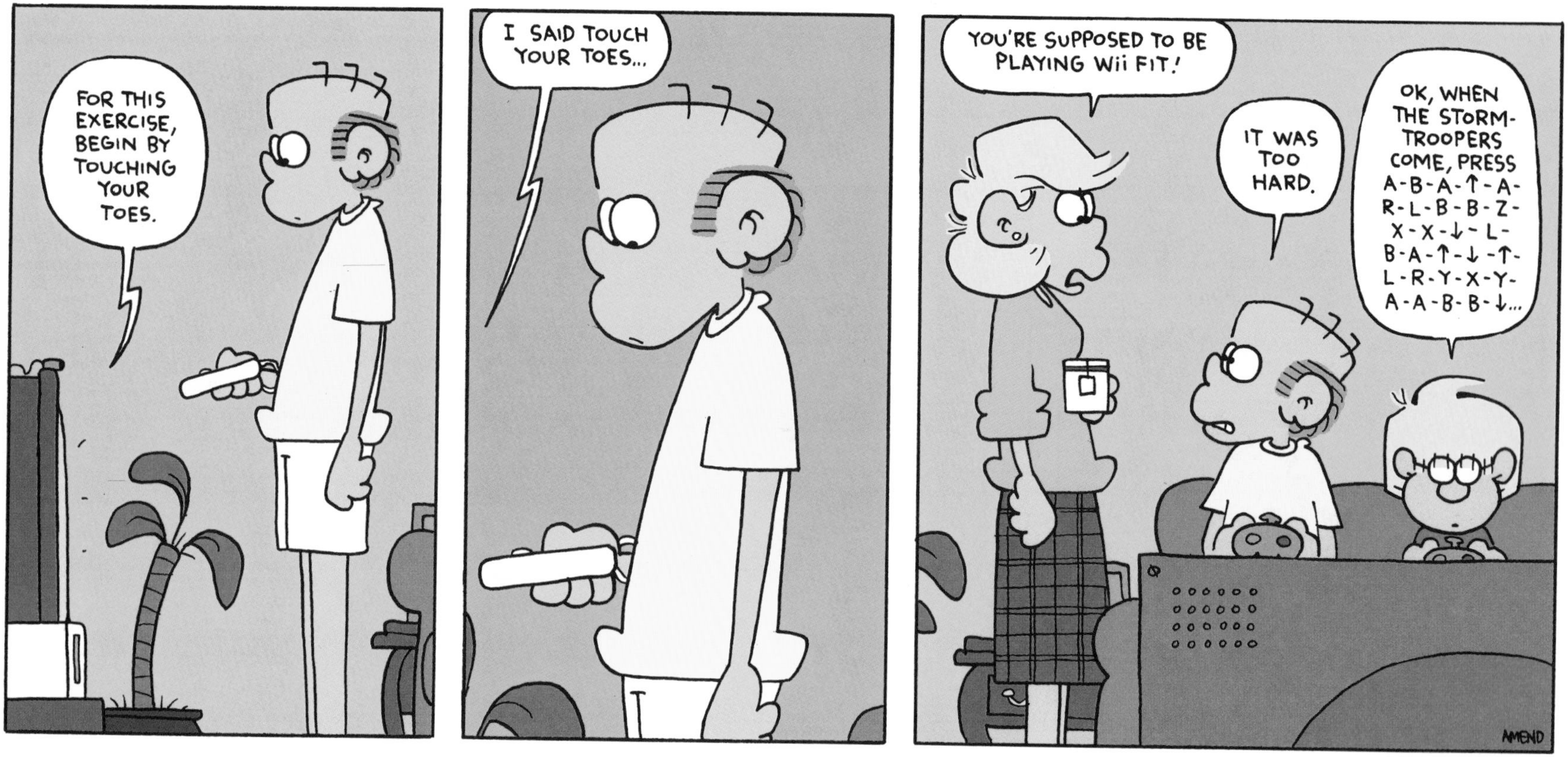
FOR THIS EXERCISE, BEGIN BY TOUCHING YOUR TOES.
I SAID TOUCH YOUR TOES...
YOU'RE SUPPOSED TO BE PLAYING Wii FIT!
IT WAS TOO HARD.
OK, WHEN THE STORM-TROOPERS COME, PRESS A-B-A-↑-A-R-L-B-B-Z-X-X-↓-L-B-A-↑-↓-↑-L-R-Y-X-Y-A-A-B-B-↓...
AMEND

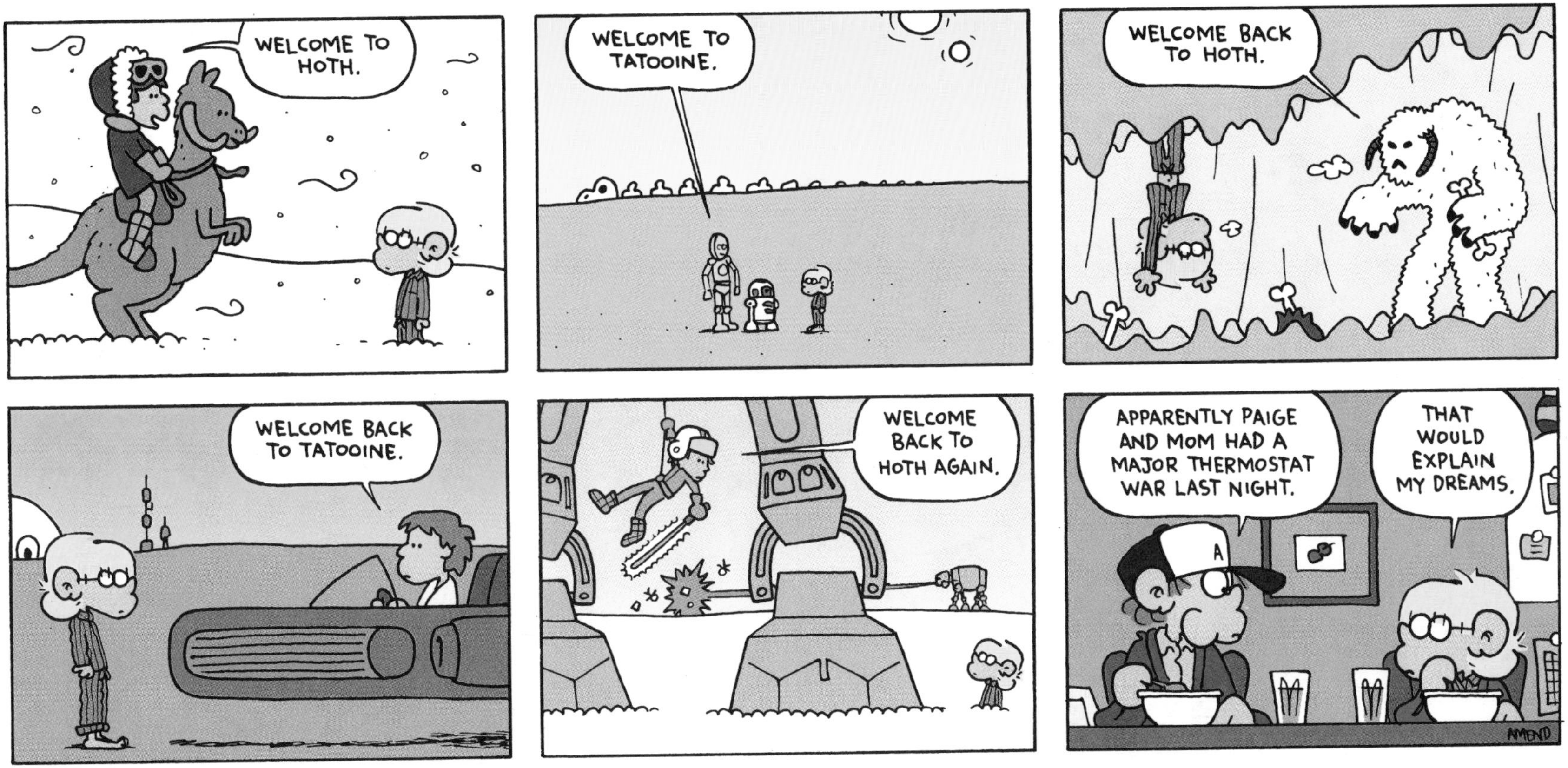
WELCOME TO HOTH.
WELCOME TO TATOOINE.
WELCOME BACK TO HOTH.
WELCOME BACK TO TATOOINE.
WELCOME BACK TO HOTH AGAIN.
APPARENTLY PAIGE AND MOM HAD A MAJOR THERMOSTAT WAR LAST NIGHT.
THAT WOULD EXPLAIN MY DREAMS.
AMEND

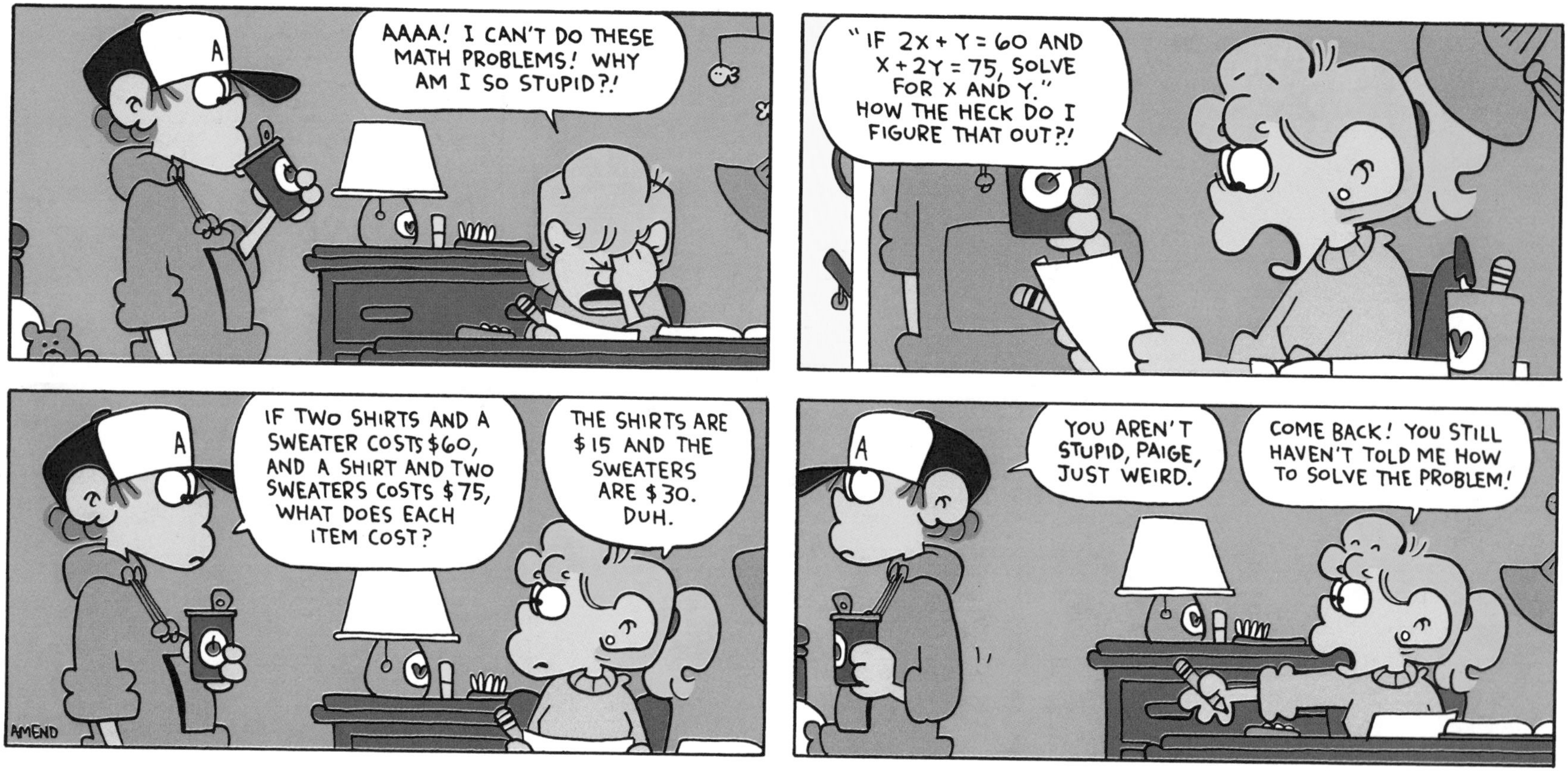
AAAA! I CAN'T DO THESE MATH PROBLEMS! WHY AM I SO STUPID?!
"IF 2X + Y = 60 AND X + 2Y = 75, SOLVE FOR X AND Y." HOW THE HECK DO I FIGURE THAT OUT?!
IF TWO SHIRTS AND A SWEATER COSTS $60, AND A SHIRT AND TWO SWEATERS COSTS $75, WHAT DOES EACH ITEM COST?
THE SHIRTS ARE $15 AND THE SWEATERS ARE $30. DUH.
AMEND
YOU AREN'T STUPID, PAIGE, JUST WEIRD.
COME BACK! YOU STILL HAVEN'T TOLD ME HOW TO SOLVE THE PROBLEM!

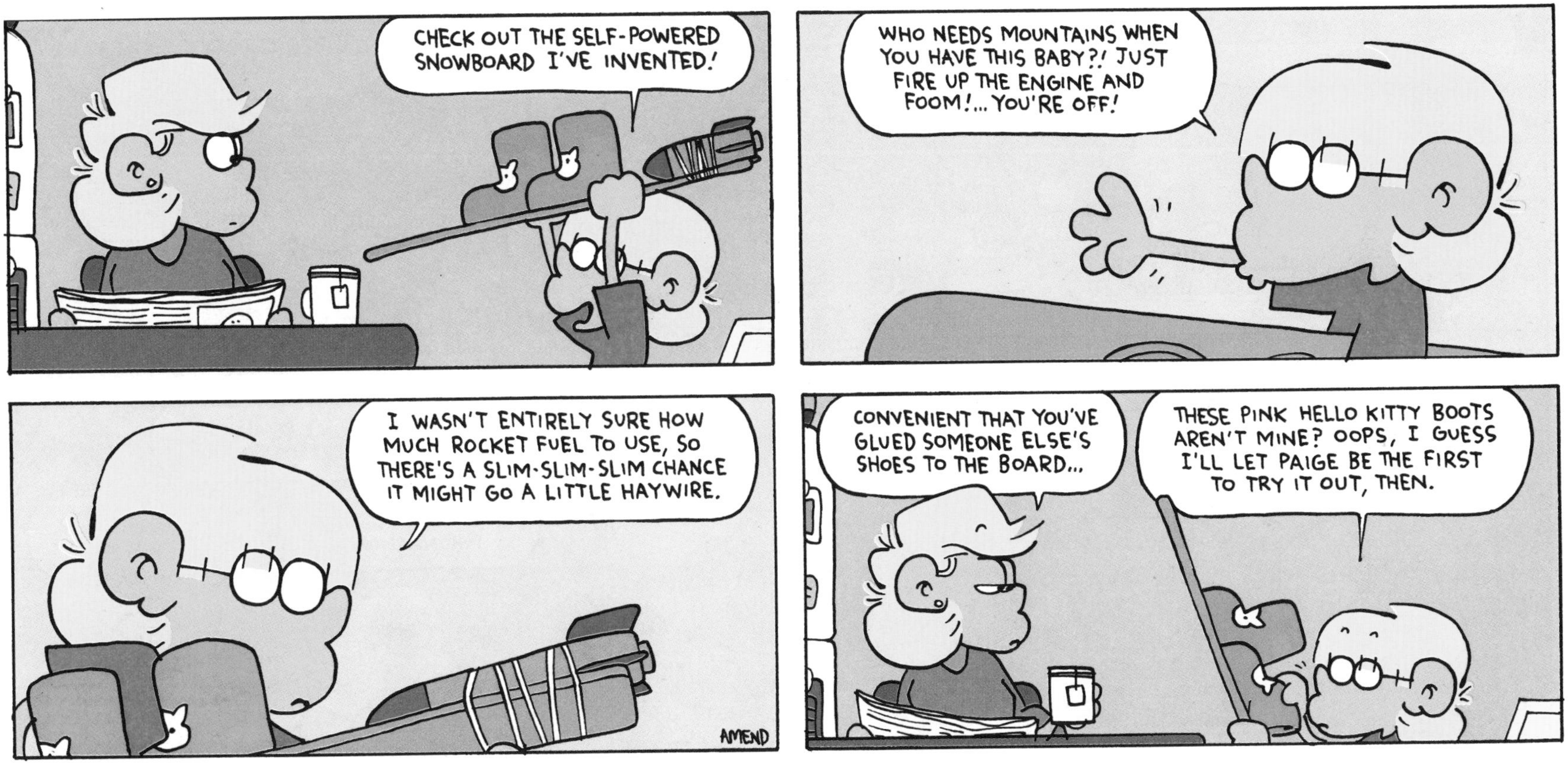
CHECK OUT THE SELF-POWERED SNOWBOARD I'VE INVENTED!
WHO NEEDS MOUNTAINS WHEN YOU HAVE THIS BABY?! JUST FIRE UP THE ENGINE AND FOOM!... YOU'RE OFF!
I WASN'T ENTIRELY SURE HOW MUCH ROCKET FUEL TO USE, SO THERE'S A SLIM-SLIM-SLIM CHANCE IT MIGHT GO A LITTLE HAYWIRE.
AMEND
CONVENIENT THAT YOU'VE GLUED SOMEONE ELSE'S SHOES TO THE BOARD...
THESE PINK HELLO KITTY BOOTS AREN'T MINE? OOPS, I GUESS I'LL LET PAIGE BE THE FIRST TO TRY IT OUT, THEN.

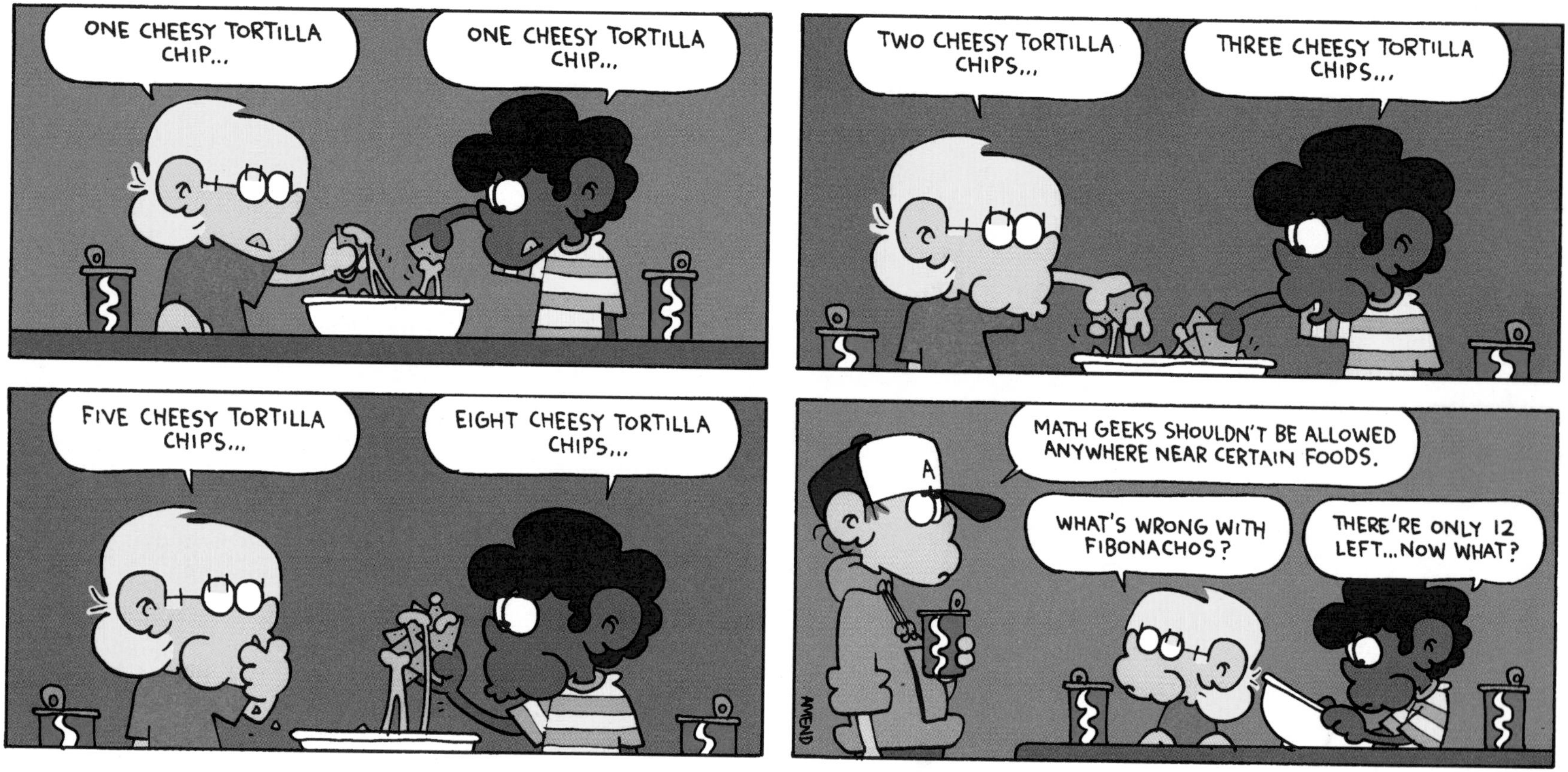
ONE CHEESY TORTILLA CHIP...
ONE CHEESY TORTILLA CHIP...
TWO CHEESY TORTILLA CHIPS...
THREE CHEESY TORTILLA CHIPS...
FIVE CHEESY TORTILLA CHIPS...
EIGHT CHEESY TORTILLA CHIPS...
MATH GEEKS SHOULDN'T BE ALLOWED ANYWHERE NEAR CERTAIN FOODS.
WHAT'S WRONG WITH FIBONACHOS?
THERE'RE ONLY 12 LEFT...NOW WHAT?
AMEND

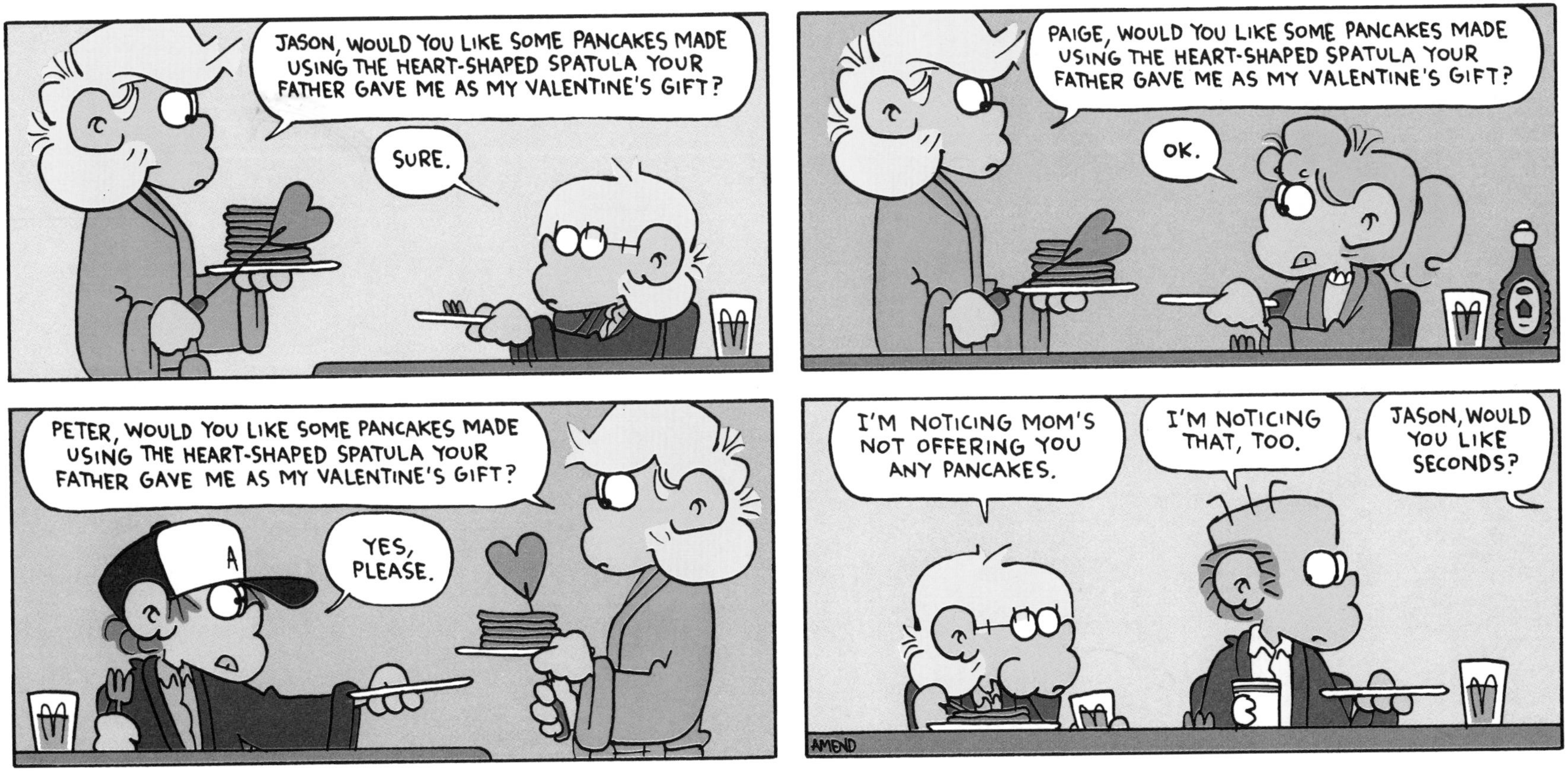
JASON, WOULD YOU LIKE SOME PANCAKES MADE USING THE HEART-SHAPED SPATULA YOUR FATHER GAVE ME AS MY VALENTINE'S GIFT?
SURE.
PAIGE, WOULD YOU LIKE SOME PANCAKES MADE USING THE HEART-SHAPED SPATULA YOUR FATHER GAVE ME AS MY VALENTINE'S GIFT?
OK.
PETER, WOULD YOU LIKE SOME PANCAKES MADE USING THE HEART-SHAPED SPATULA YOUR FATHER GAVE ME AS MY VALENTINE'S GIFT?
YES, PLEASE.
I'M NOTICING MOM'S NOT OFFERING YOU ANY PANCAKES.
I'M NOTICING THAT, TOO.
JASON, WOULD YOU LIKE SECONDS?
AMEND

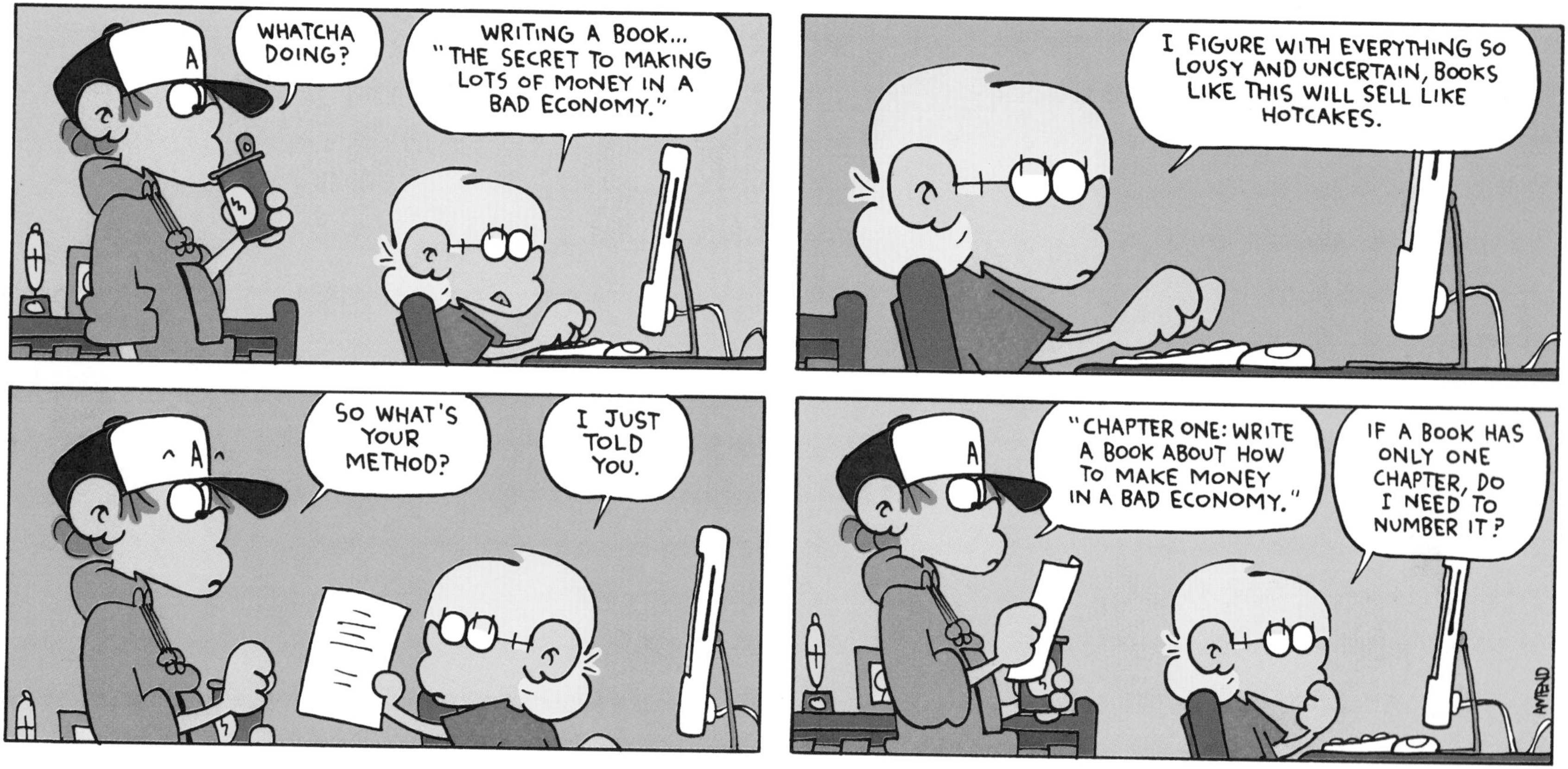
WHATCHA DOING?
WRITING A BOOK... "THE SECRET TO MAKING LOTS OF MONEY IN A BAD ECONOMY."
I FIGURE WITH EVERYTHING SO LOUSY AND UNCERTAIN, BOOKS LIKE THIS WILL SELL LIKE HOTCAKES.
SO WHAT'S YOUR METHOD?
I JUST TOLD YOU.
"CHAPTER ONE: WRITE A BOOK ABOUT HOW TO MAKE MONEY IN A BAD ECONOMY."
IF A BOOK HAS ONLY ONE CHAPTER, DO I NEED TO NUMBER IT?
AMEND

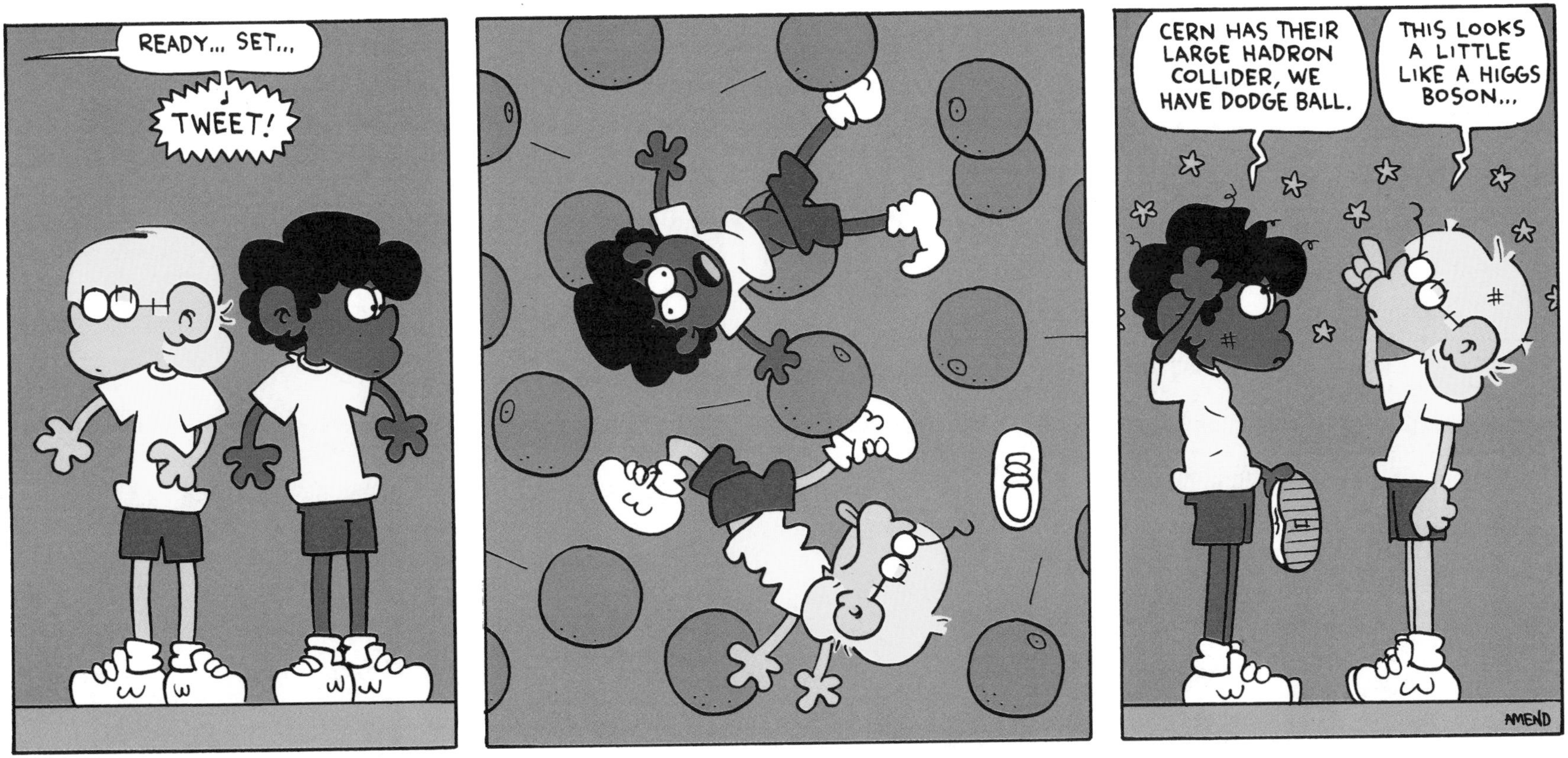
READY... SET...
TWEET!
CERN HAS THEIR LARGE HADRON COLLIDER, WE HAVE DODGE BALL.
THIS LOOKS A LITTLE LIKE A HIGGS BOSON...
AMEND

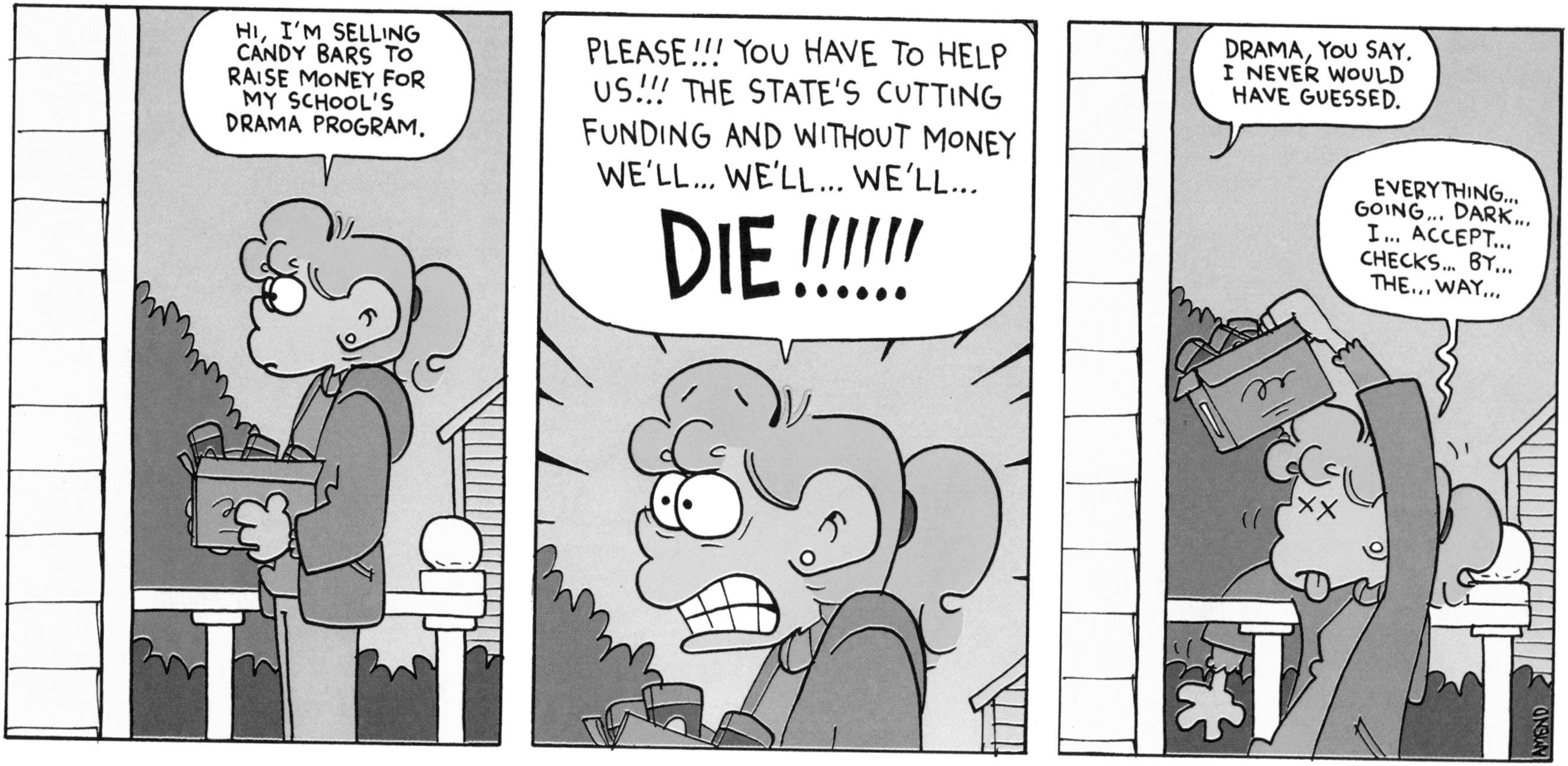
HI, I'M SELLING CANDY BARS TO RAISE MONEY FOR MY SCHOOL'S DRAMA PROGRAM.
PLEASE!!! YOU HAVE TO HELP US!!! THE STATE'S CUTTING FUNDING AND WITHOUT MONEY WE'LL... WE'LL... WE'LL...
DIE!!!!!!
DRAMA, YOU SAY. I NEVER WOULD HAVE GUESSED.
EVERYTHING... GOING... DARK... I... ACCEPT... CHECKS... BY... THE... WAY...
AMEND

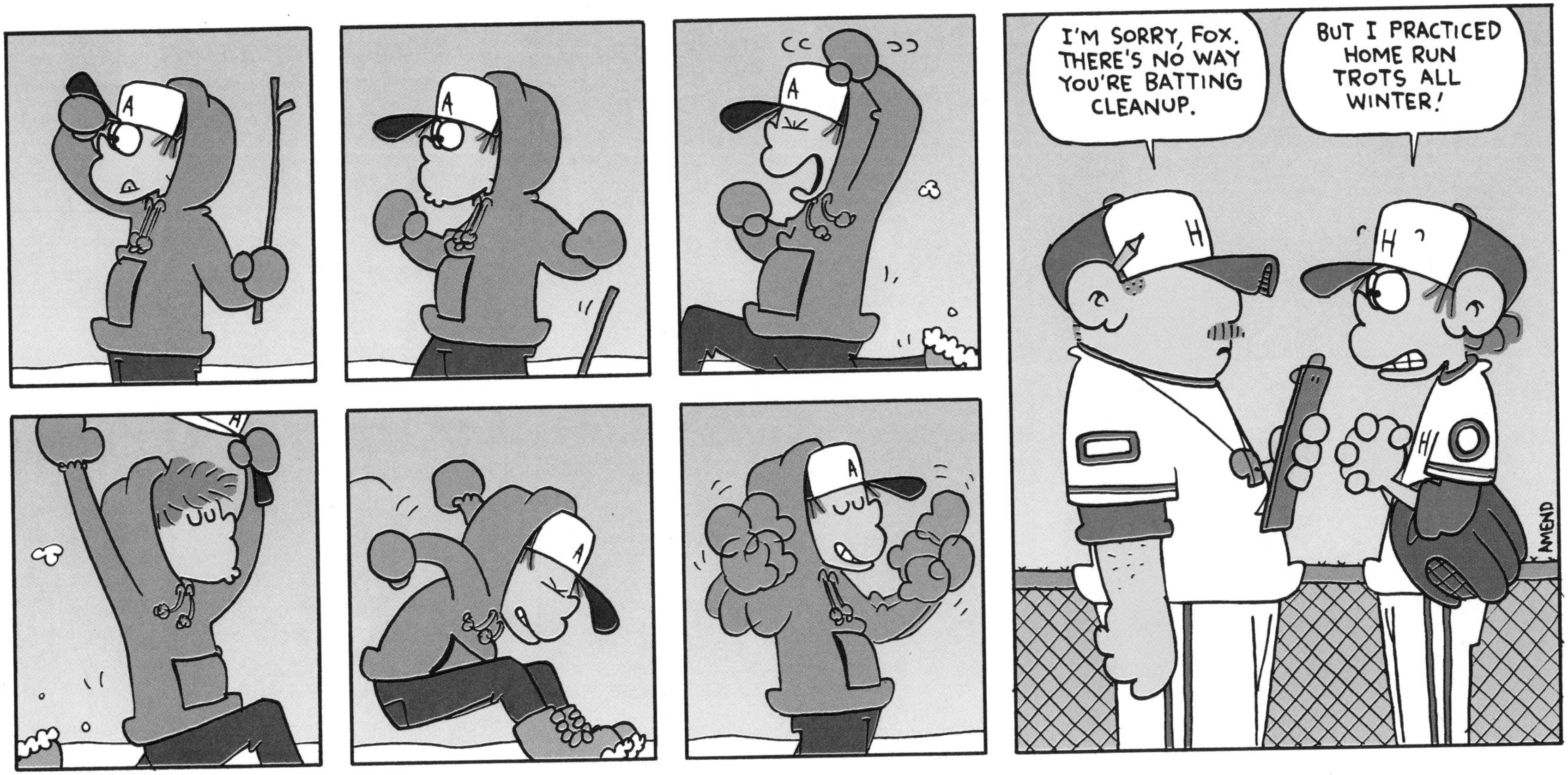
I'M SORRY, FOX. THERE'S NO WAY YOU'RE BATTING CLEANUP.
BUT I PRACTICED HOME RUN TROTS ALL WINTER!
AMEND

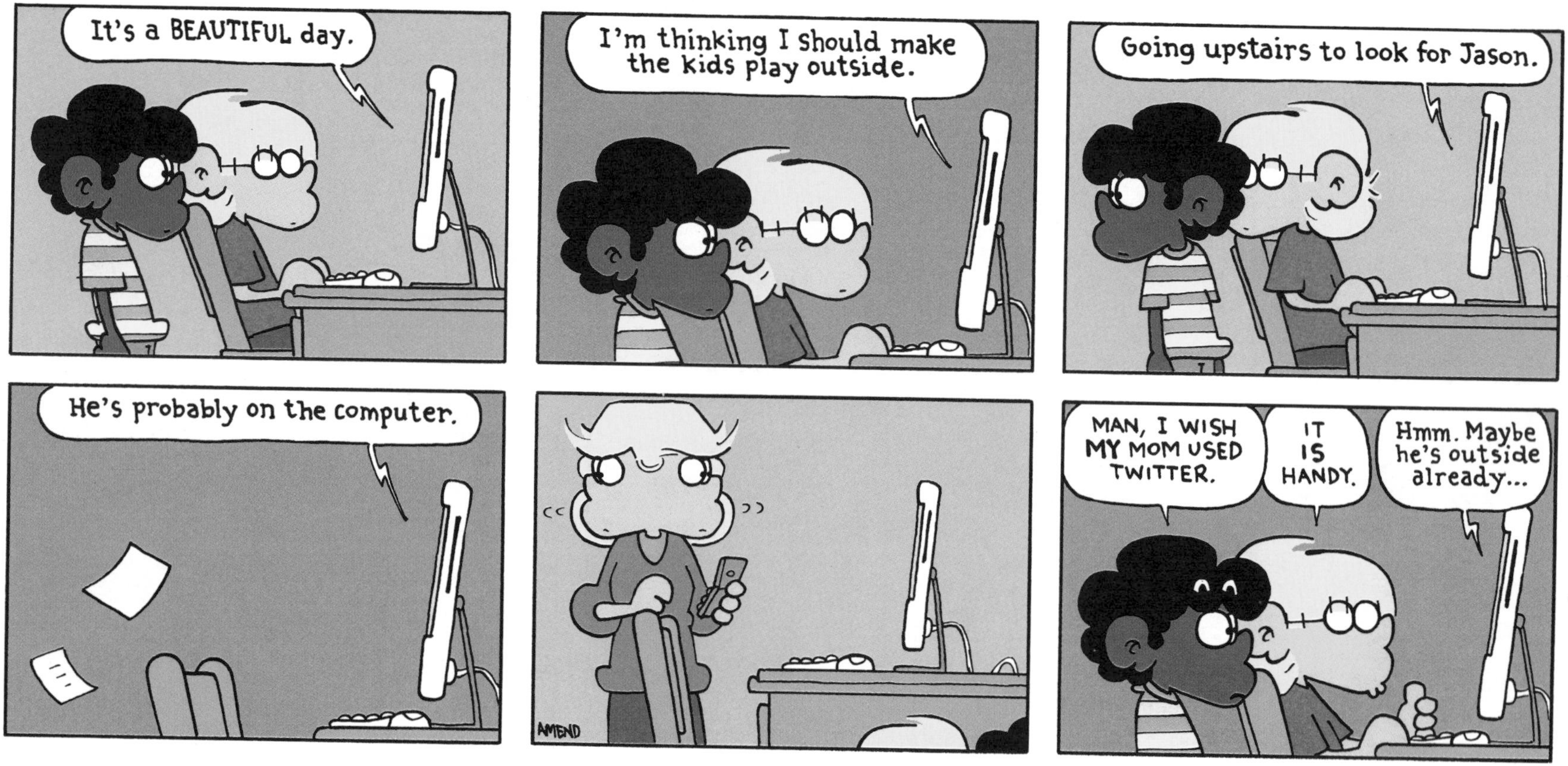
It's a BEAUTIFUL day.
I'm thinking I should make the kids play outside.
Going upstairs to look for Jason.
He's probably on the computer.
AMEND
MAN, I WISH MY MOM USED TWITTER.
IT IS HANDY.
Hmm. Maybe he's outside already...

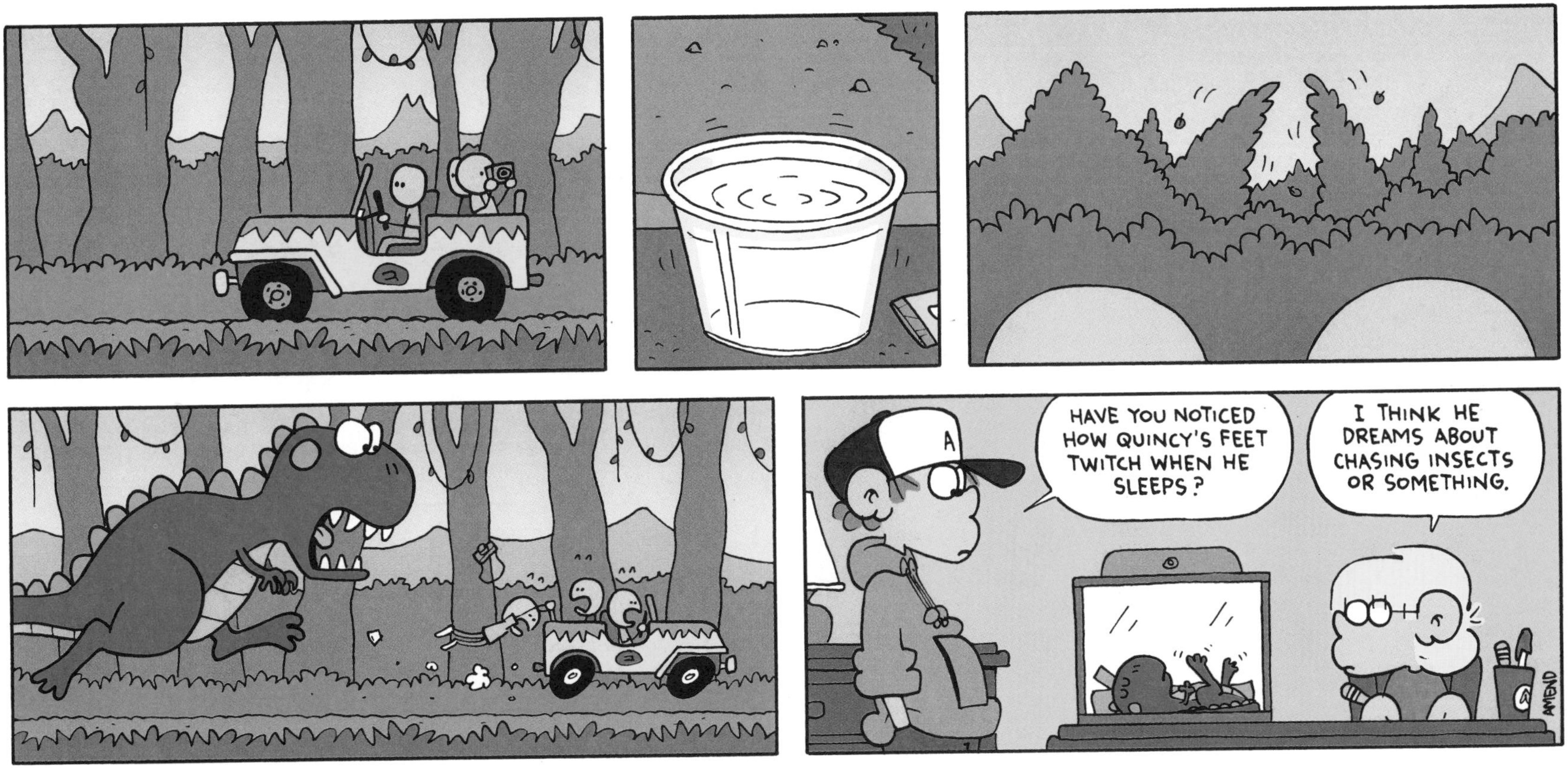
HAVE YOU NOTICED HOW QUINCY'S FEET TWITCH WHEN HE SLEEPS?
I THINK HE DREAMS ABOUT CHASING INSECTS OR SOMETHING.

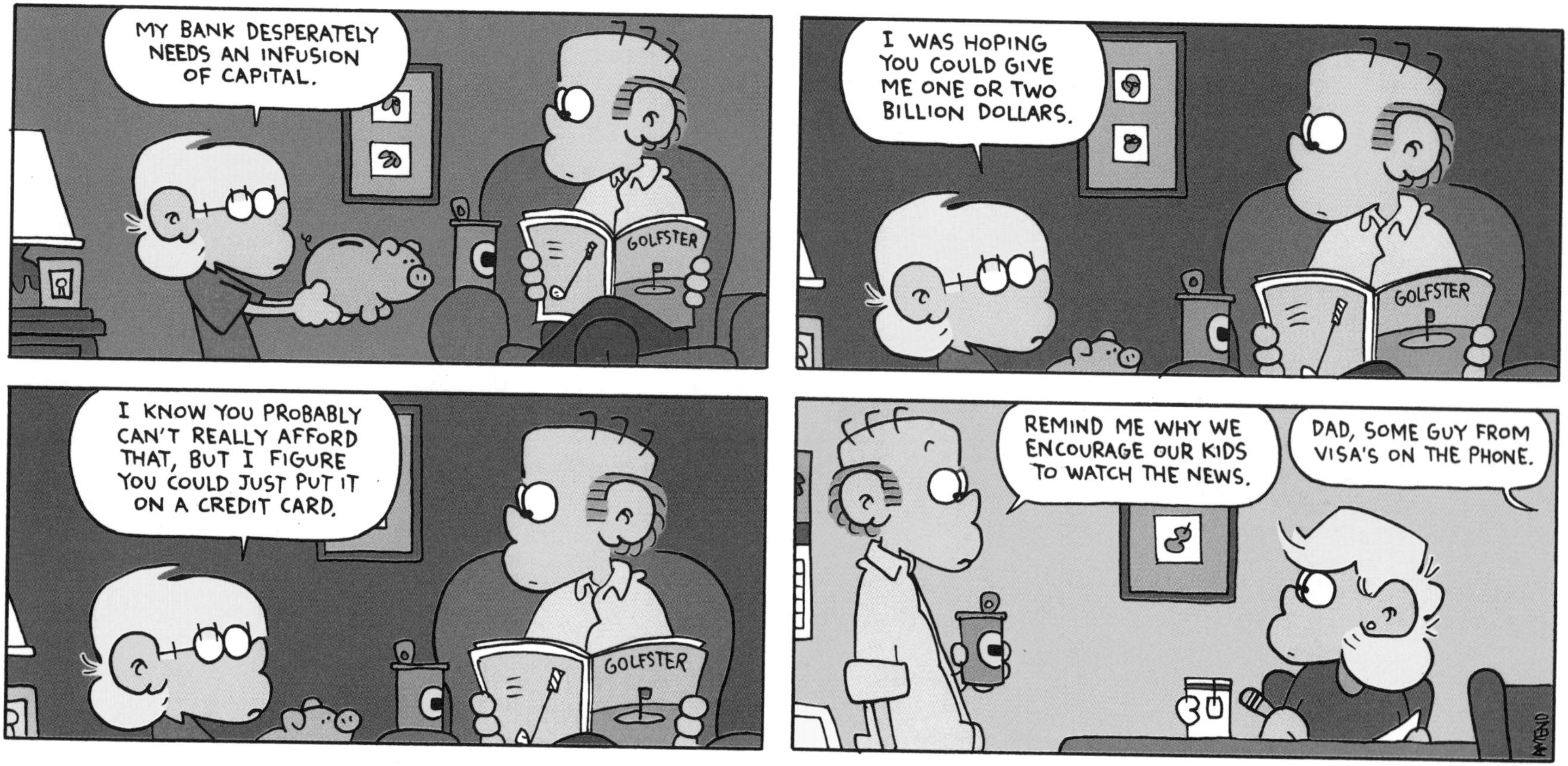
MY BANK DESPERATELY NEEDS AN INFUSION OF CAPITAL.
GOLFSTER
I WAS HOPING YOU COULD GIVE ME ONE OR TWO BILLION DOLLARS.
GOLFSTER
I KNOW YOU PROBABLY CAN'T REALLY AFFORD THAT, BUT I FIGURE YOU COULD JUST PUT IT ON A CREDIT CARD.
GOLFSTER
REMIND ME WHY WE ENCOURAGE OUR KIDS TO WATCH THE NEWS.
DAD, SOME GUY FROM VISA'S ON THE PHONE.

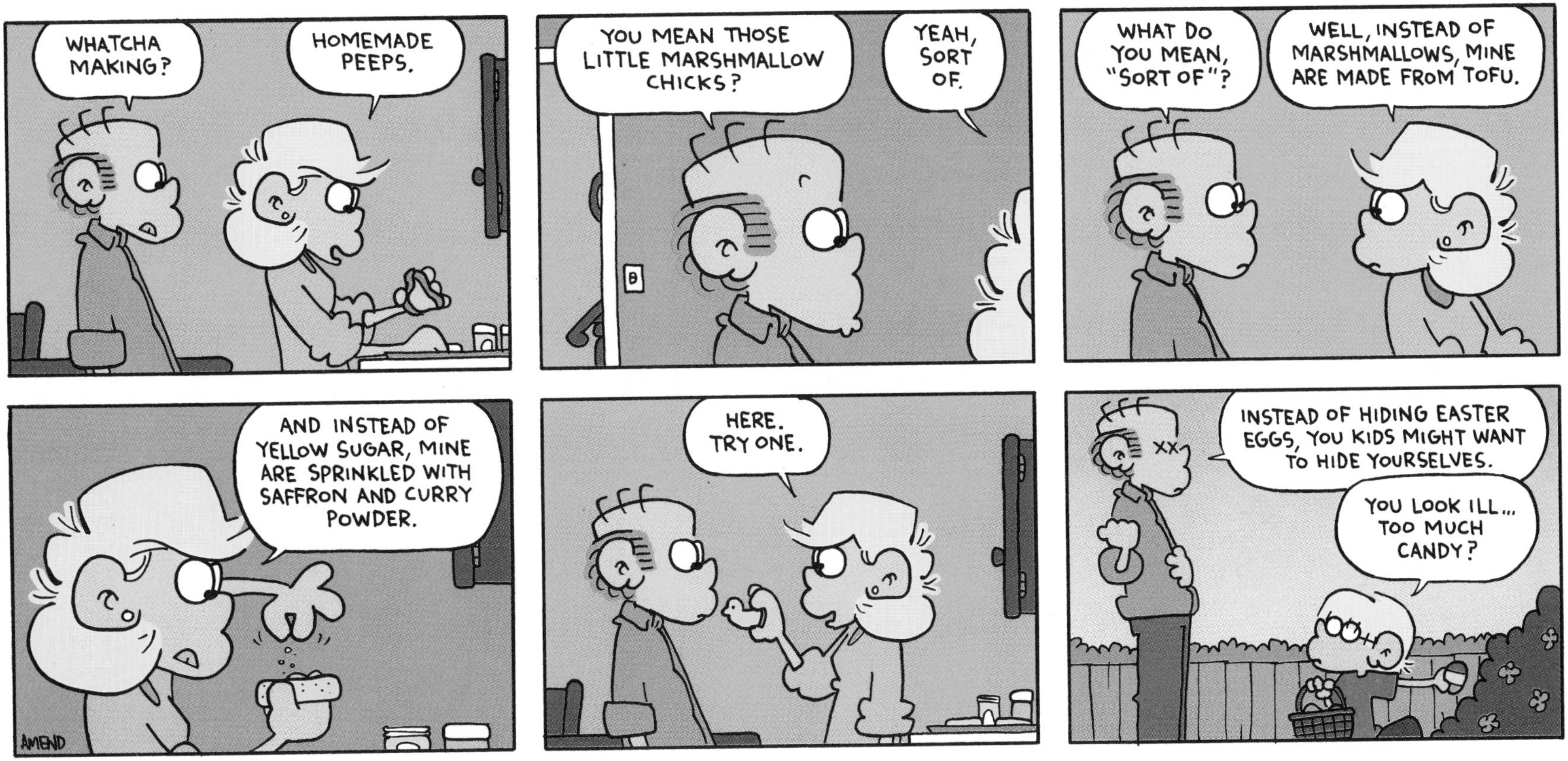
WHATCHA MAKING?
HOMEMADE PEEPS.
YOU MEAN THOSE LITTLE MARSHMALLOW CHICKS?
YEAH, SORT OF.
WHAT DO YOU MEAN, "SORT OF"?
WELL, INSTEAD OF MARSHMALLOWS, MINE ARE MADE FROM TOFU.
AND INSTEAD OF YELLOW SUGAR, MINE ARE SPRINKLED WITH SAFFRON AND CURRY POWDER.
AMEND
HERE. TRY ONE.
INSTEAD OF HIDING EASTER EGGS, YOU KIDS MIGHT WANT TO HIDE YOURSELVES.
YOU LOOK ILL... TOO MUCH CANDY?

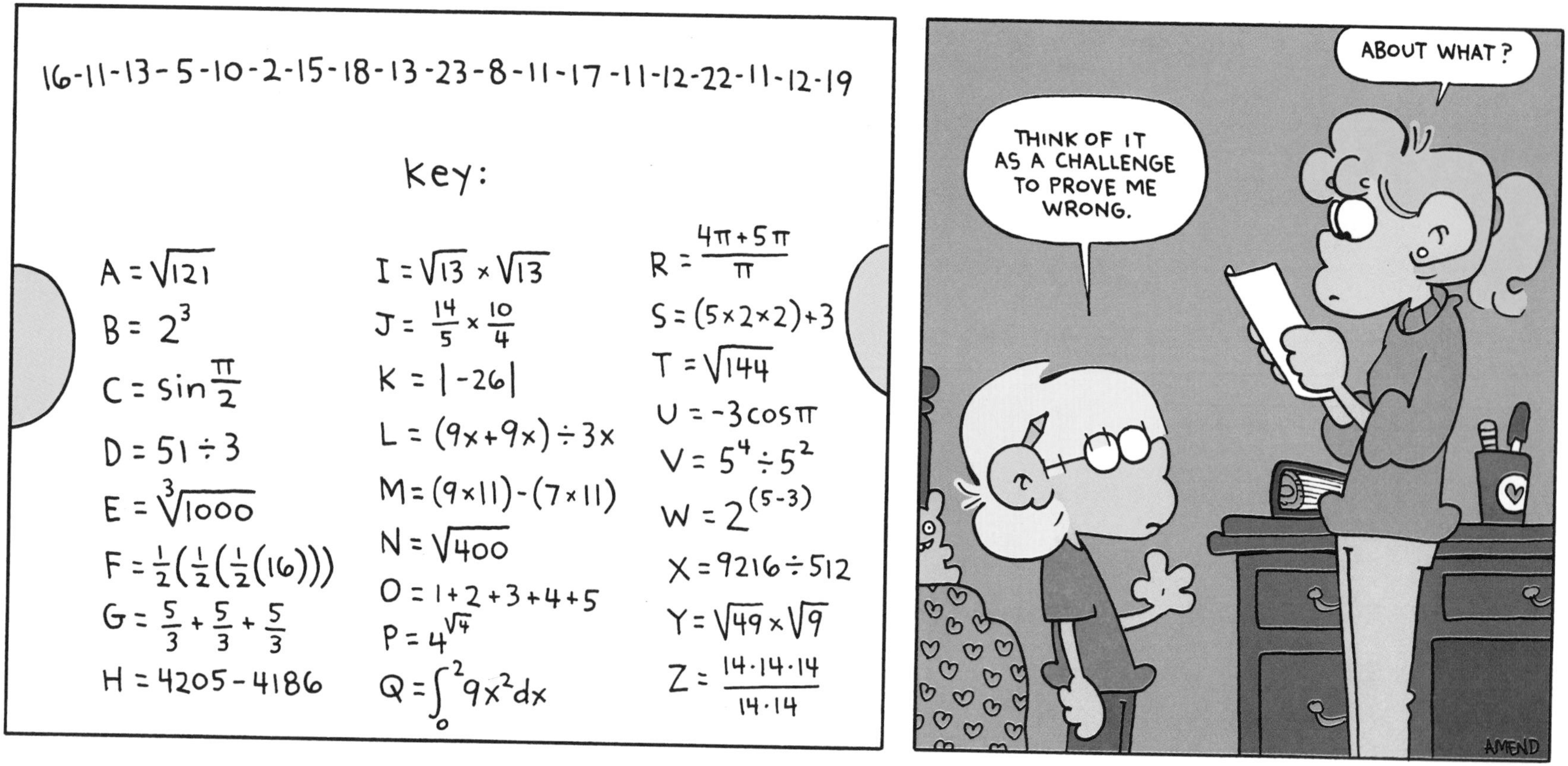
16-11-13-5-10-2-15-18-13-23-8-11-17-11-12-22-11-12-19
Key:
$A = \sqrt{121}$
$B = 2^3$
$C = \sin\frac{\pi}{2}$
$D = 51 \div 3$
$E = \sqrt[3]{1000}$
$F = \frac{1}{2}(\frac{1}{2}(\frac{1}{2}(16)))$
$G = \frac{5}{3} + \frac{5}{3} + \frac{5}{3}$
$H = 4205 - 4186$
$I = \sqrt{13} \times \sqrt{13}$
$J = \frac{14}{5} \times \frac{10}{4}$
$K = |-26|$
$L = (9x + 9x) \div 3x$
$M = (9 \times 11) - (7 \times 11)$
$N = \sqrt{400}$
$O = 1 + 2 + 3 + 4 + 5$
$P = 4^{\sqrt{4}}$
$Q = \int_0^2 9x^2 dx$
$R = \frac{4\pi + 5\pi}{\pi}$
$S = (5 \times 2 \times 2) + 3$
$T = \sqrt{144}$
$U = -3\cos\pi$
$V = 5^4 \div 5^2$
$W = 2^{(5-3)}$
$X = 9216 \div 512$
$Y = \sqrt{49} \times \sqrt{9}$
$Z = \frac{14 \cdot 14 \cdot 14}{14 \cdot 14}$
ABOUT WHAT?
THINK OF IT AS A CHALLENGE TO PROVE ME WRONG.
AMEND

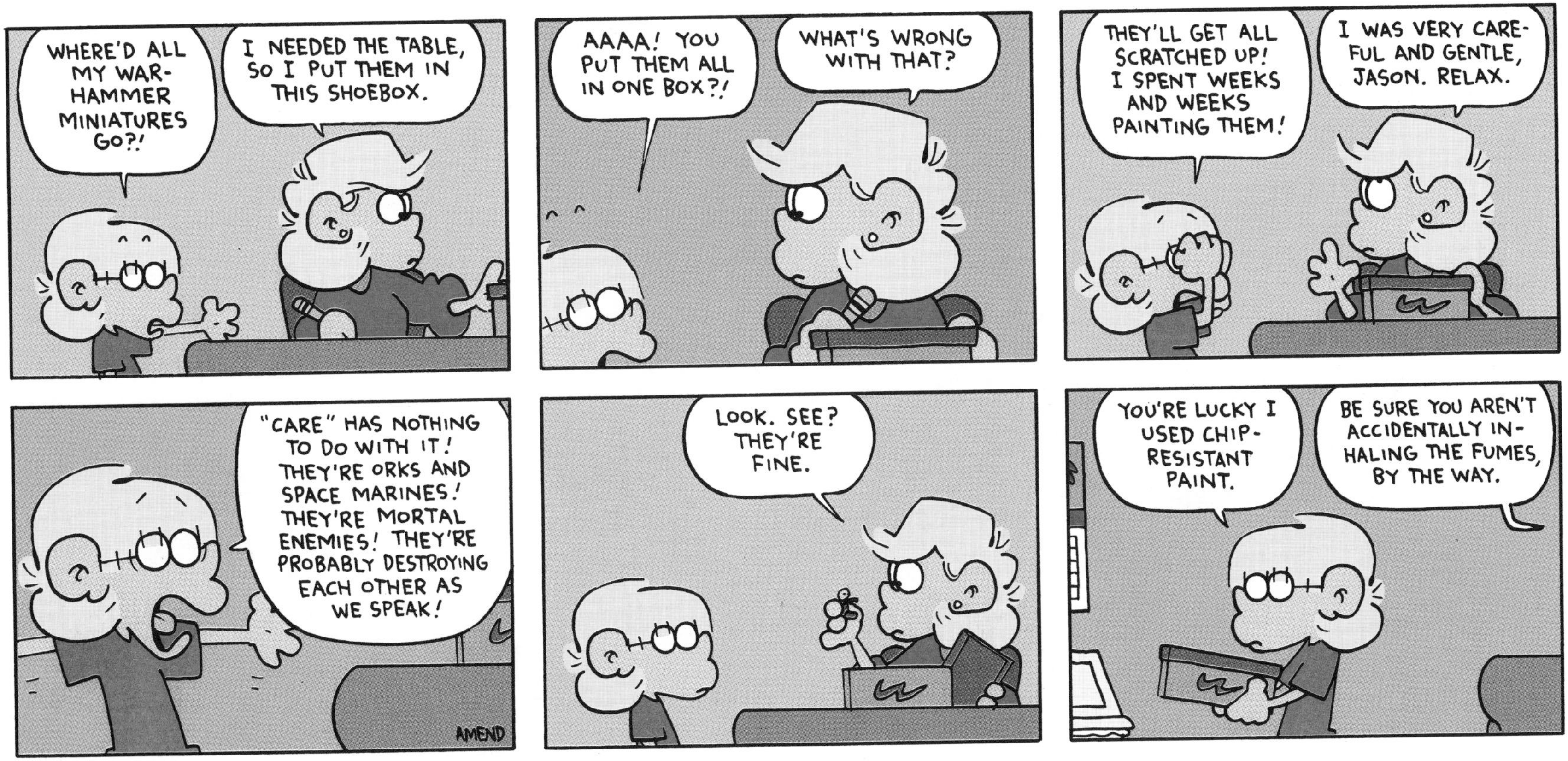
WHERE'D ALL MY WAR-HAMMER MINIATURES GO?!
I NEEDED THE TABLE, SO I PUT THEM IN THIS SHOEBOX.
AAAA! YOU PUT THEM ALL IN ONE BOX?!
WHAT'S WRONG WITH THAT?
THEY'LL GET ALL SCRATCHED UP! I SPENT WEEKS AND WEEKS PAINTING THEM!
I WAS VERY CARE-FUL AND GENTLE, JASON. RELAX.
"CARE" HAS NOTHING TO DO WITH IT! THEY'RE ORKS AND SPACE MARINES! THEY'RE MORTAL ENEMIES! THEY'RE PROBABLY DESTROYING EACH OTHER AS WE SPEAK!
AMEND
LOOK. SEE? THEY'RE FINE.
YOU'RE LUCKY I USED CHIP-RESISTANT PAINT.
BE SURE YOU AREN'T ACCIDENTALLY IN-HALING THE FUMES, BY THE WAY.

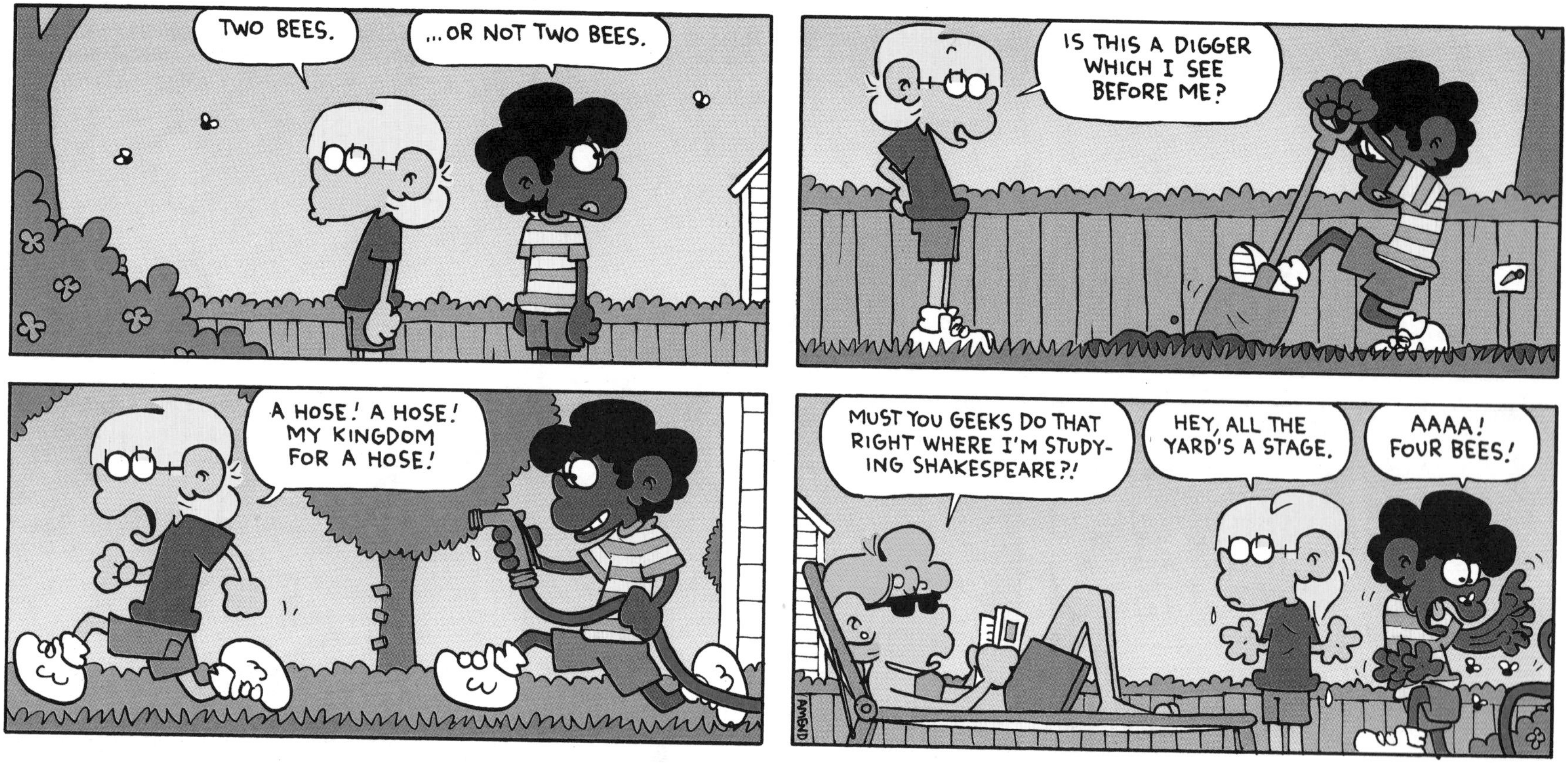
TWO BEES.
...OR NOT TWO BEES.
IS THIS A DIGGER WHICH I SEE BEFORE ME?
A HOSE! A HOSE! MY KINGDOM FOR A HOSE!
AMEND
MUST YOU GEEKS DO THAT RIGHT WHERE I'M STUDYING SHAKESPEARE?!
HEY, ALL THE YARD'S A STAGE.
AAAA! FOUR BEES!

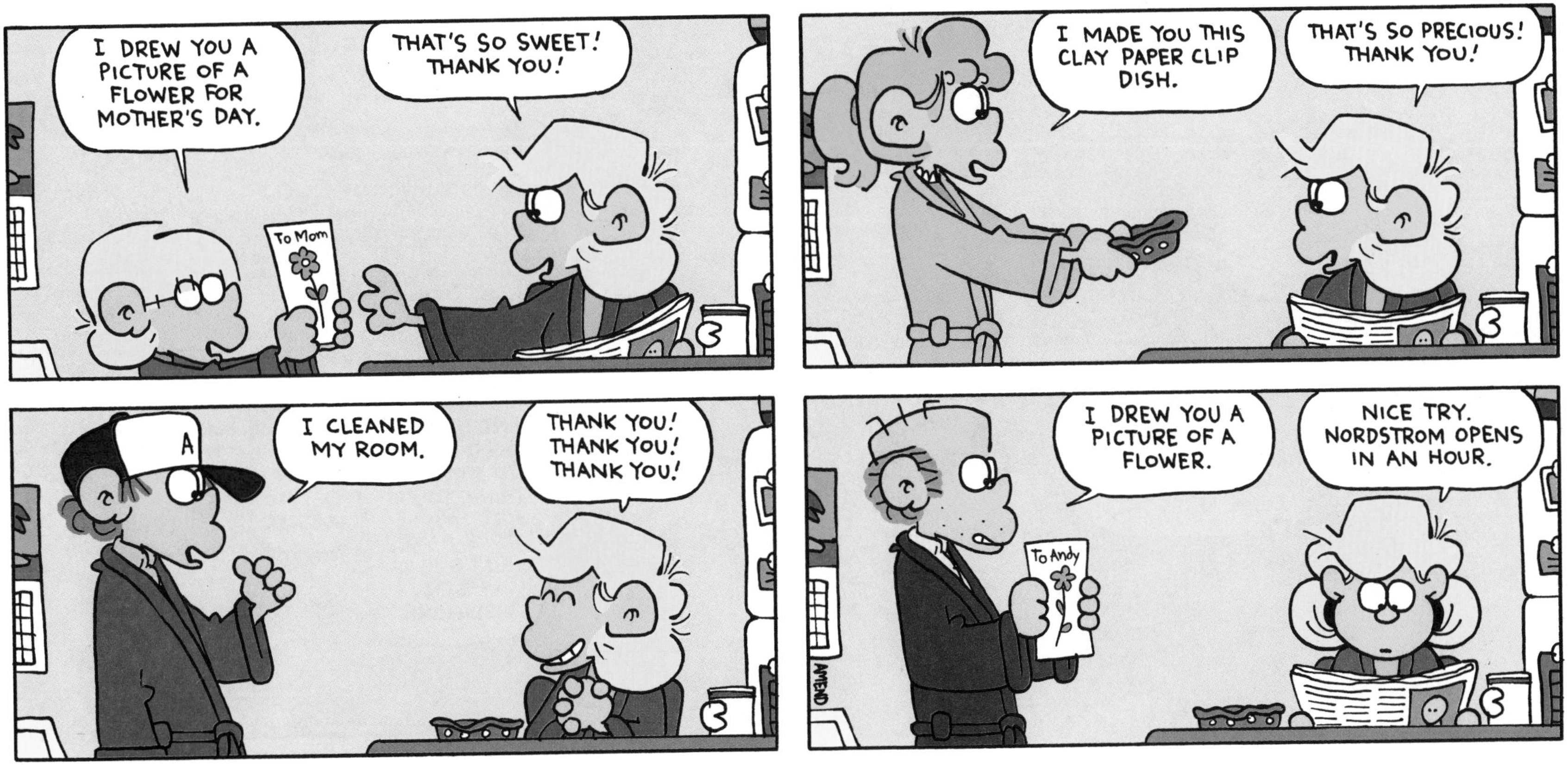
I DREW YOU A PICTURE OF A FLOWER FOR MOTHER'S DAY.
To Mom
THAT'S SO SWEET! THANK YOU!
I MADE YOU THIS CLAY PAPER CLIP DISH.
THAT'S SO PRECIOUS! THANK YOU!
A
I CLEANED MY ROOM.
THANK YOU! THANK YOU! THANK YOU!
I DREW YOU A PICTURE OF A FLOWER.
To Andy
NICE TRY. NORDSTROM OPENS IN AN HOUR.
AMEND

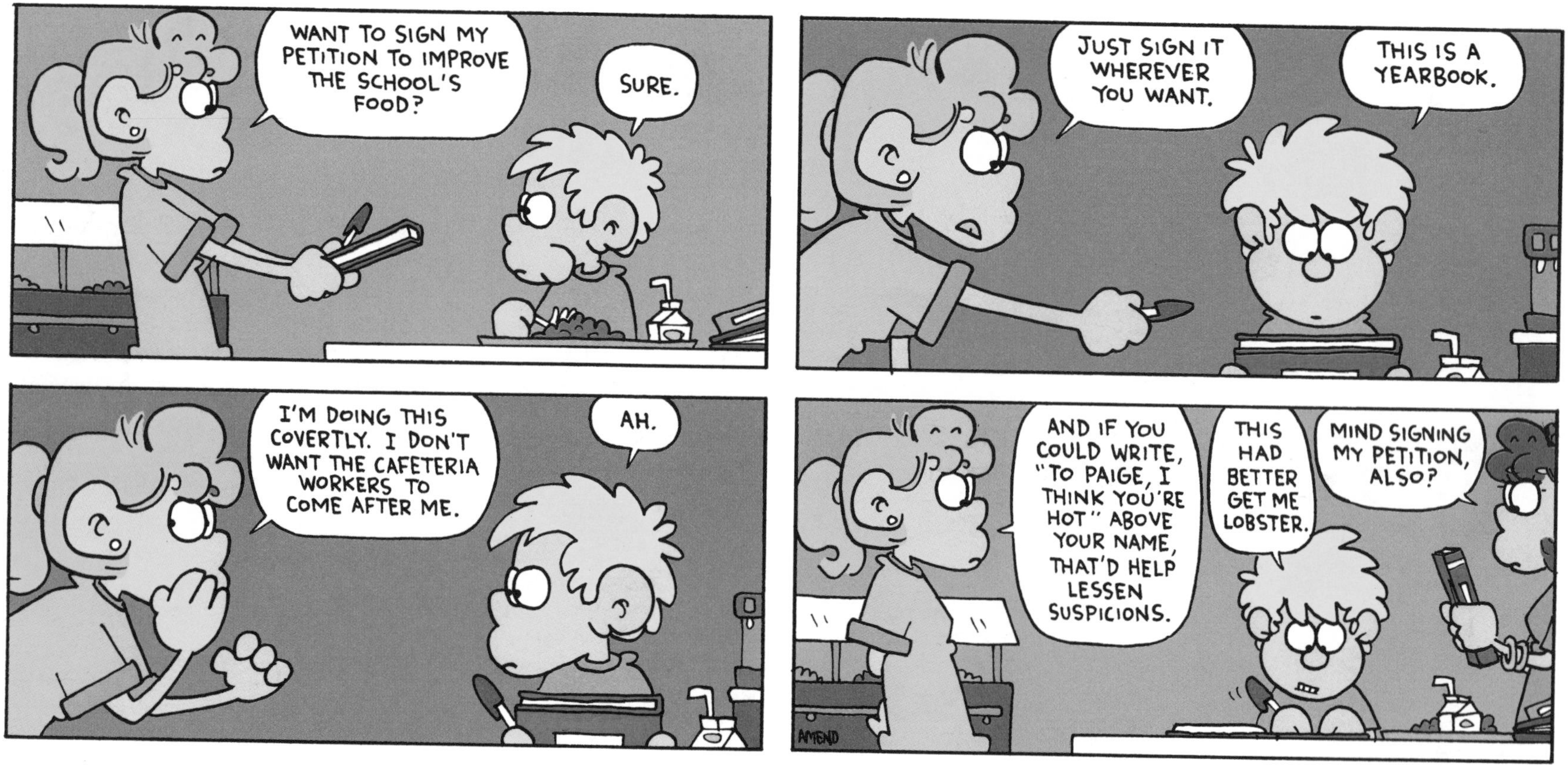
WANT TO SIGN MY PETITION TO IMPROVE THE SCHOOL'S FOOD?
SURE.
JUST SIGN IT WHEREVER YOU WANT.
THIS IS A YEARBOOK.
I'M DOING THIS COVERTLY. I DON'T WANT THE CAFETERIA WORKERS TO COME AFTER ME.
AH.
AND IF YOU COULD WRITE, "TO PAIGE, I THINK YOU'RE HOT" ABOVE YOUR NAME, THAT'D HELP LESSEN SUSPICIONS.
THIS HAD BETTER GET ME LOBSTER.
MIND SIGNING MY PETITION, ALSO?
AMEND

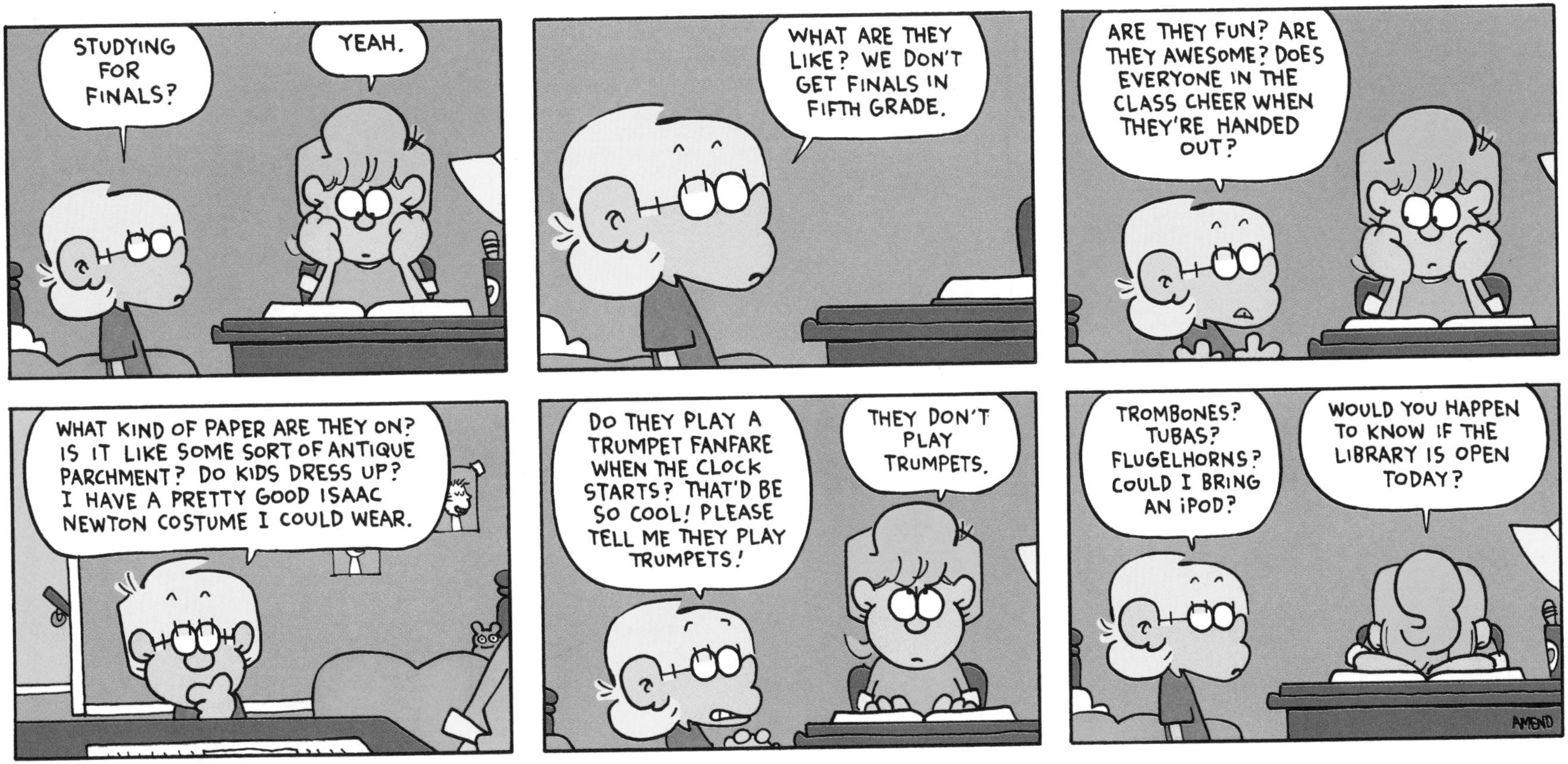

STUDYING FOR FINALS?
YEAH.
WHAT ARE THEY LIKE? WE DON'T GET FINALS IN FIFTH GRADE.
ARE THEY FUN? ARE THEY AWESOME? DOES EVERYONE IN THE CLASS CHEER WHEN THEY'RE HANDED OUT?
WHAT KIND OF PAPER ARE THEY ON? IS IT LIKE SOME SORT OF ANTIQUE PARCHMENT? DO KIDS DRESS UP? I HAVE A PRETTY GOOD ISAAC NEWTON COSTUME I COULD WEAR.
DO THEY PLAY A TRUMPET FANFARE WHEN THE CLOCK STARTS? THAT'D BE SO COOL! PLEASE TELL ME THEY PLAY TRUMPETS!
THEY DON'T PLAY TRUMPETS.
TROMBONES? TUBAS? FLUGELHORNS? COULD I BRING AN iPOD?
WOULD YOU HAPPEN TO KNOW IF THE LIBRARY IS OPEN TODAY?
AMEND

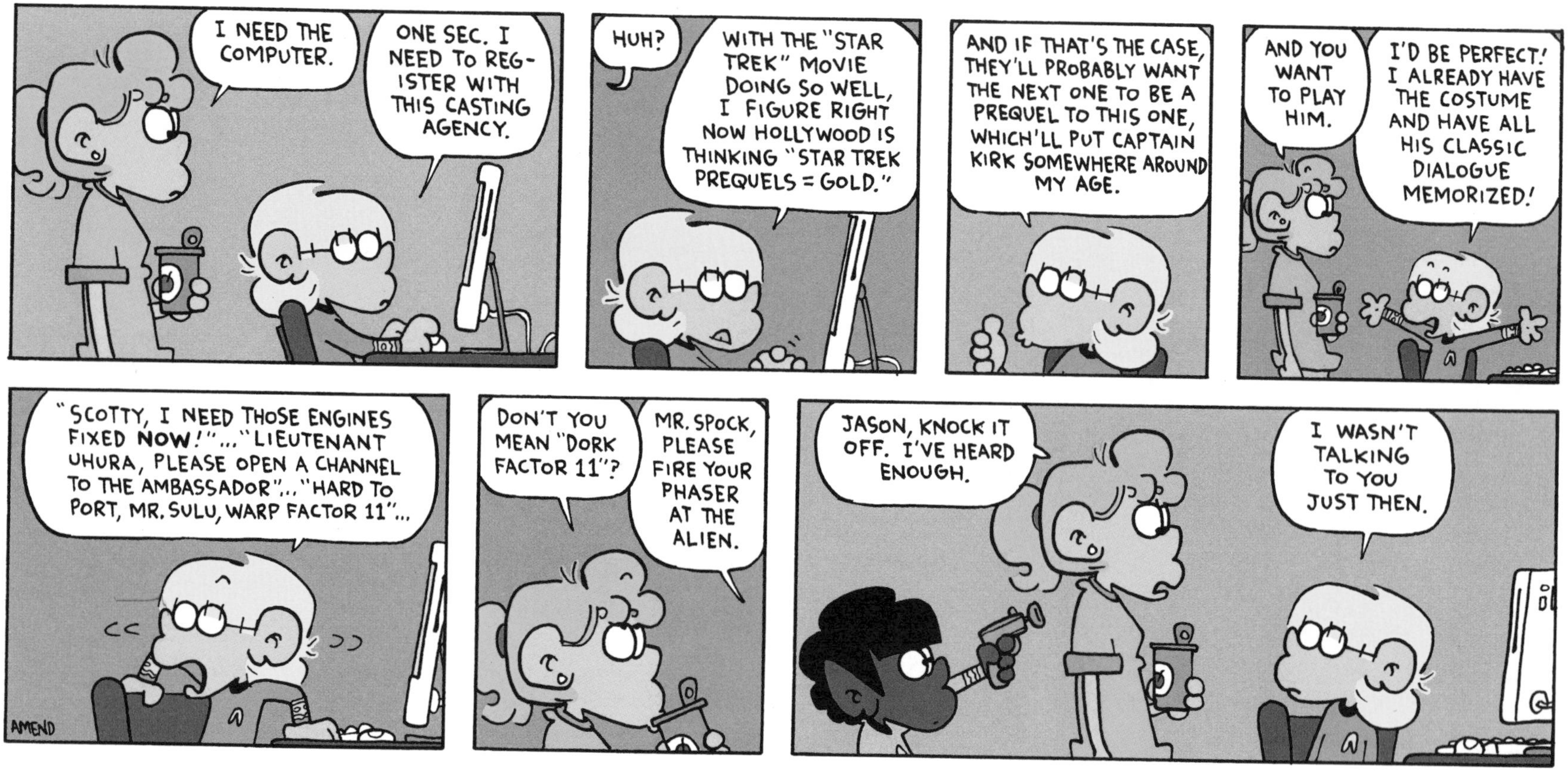
I NEED THE COMPUTER.
ONE SEC. I NEED TO REGISTER WITH THIS CASTING AGENCY.
HUH?
WITH THE "STAR TREK" MOVIE DOING SO WELL, I FIGURE RIGHT NOW HOLLYWOOD IS THINKING "STAR TREK PREQUELS = GOLD."
AND IF THAT'S THE CASE, THEY'LL PROBABLY WANT THE NEXT ONE TO BE A PREQUEL TO THIS ONE, WHICH'LL PUT CAPTAIN KIRK SOMEWHERE AROUND MY AGE.
AND YOU WANT TO PLAY HIM.
I'D BE PERFECT! I ALREADY HAVE THE COSTUME AND HAVE ALL HIS CLASSIC DIALOGUE MEMORIZED!
"SCOTTY, I NEED THOSE ENGINES FIXED **NOW**!"..."LIEUTENANT UHURA, PLEASE OPEN A CHANNEL TO THE AMBASSADOR"..."HARD TO PORT, MR. SULU, WARP FACTOR 11"...
AMEND
DON'T YOU MEAN "DORK FACTOR 11"?
MR. SPOCK, PLEASE FIRE YOUR PHASER AT THE ALIEN.
JASON, KNOCK IT OFF. I'VE HEARD ENOUGH.
I WASN'T TALKING TO YOU JUST THEN.

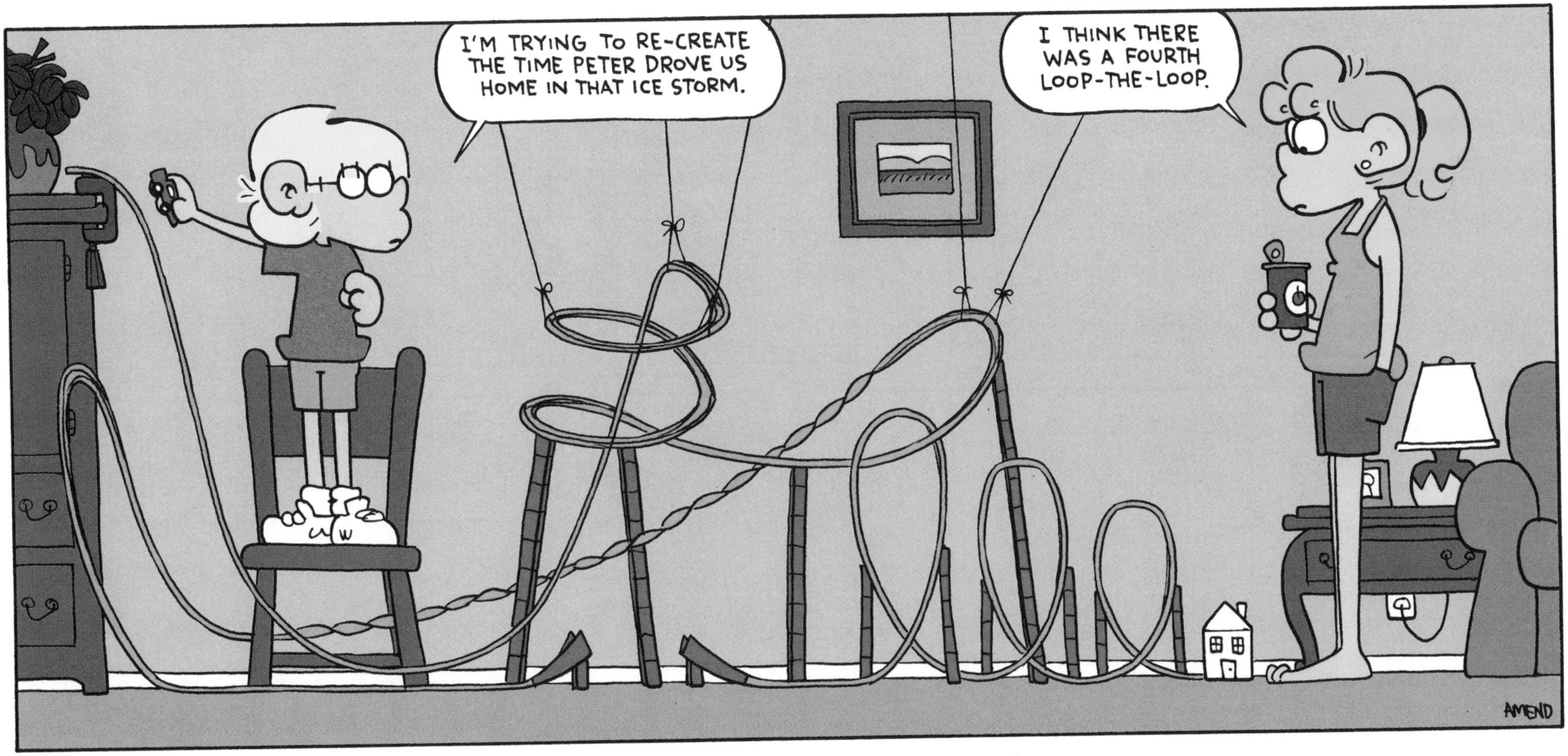
I'M TRYING TO RE-CREATE THE TIME PETER DROVE US HOME IN THAT ICE STORM.
I THINK THERE WAS A FOURTH LOOP-THE-LOOP.
AMEND

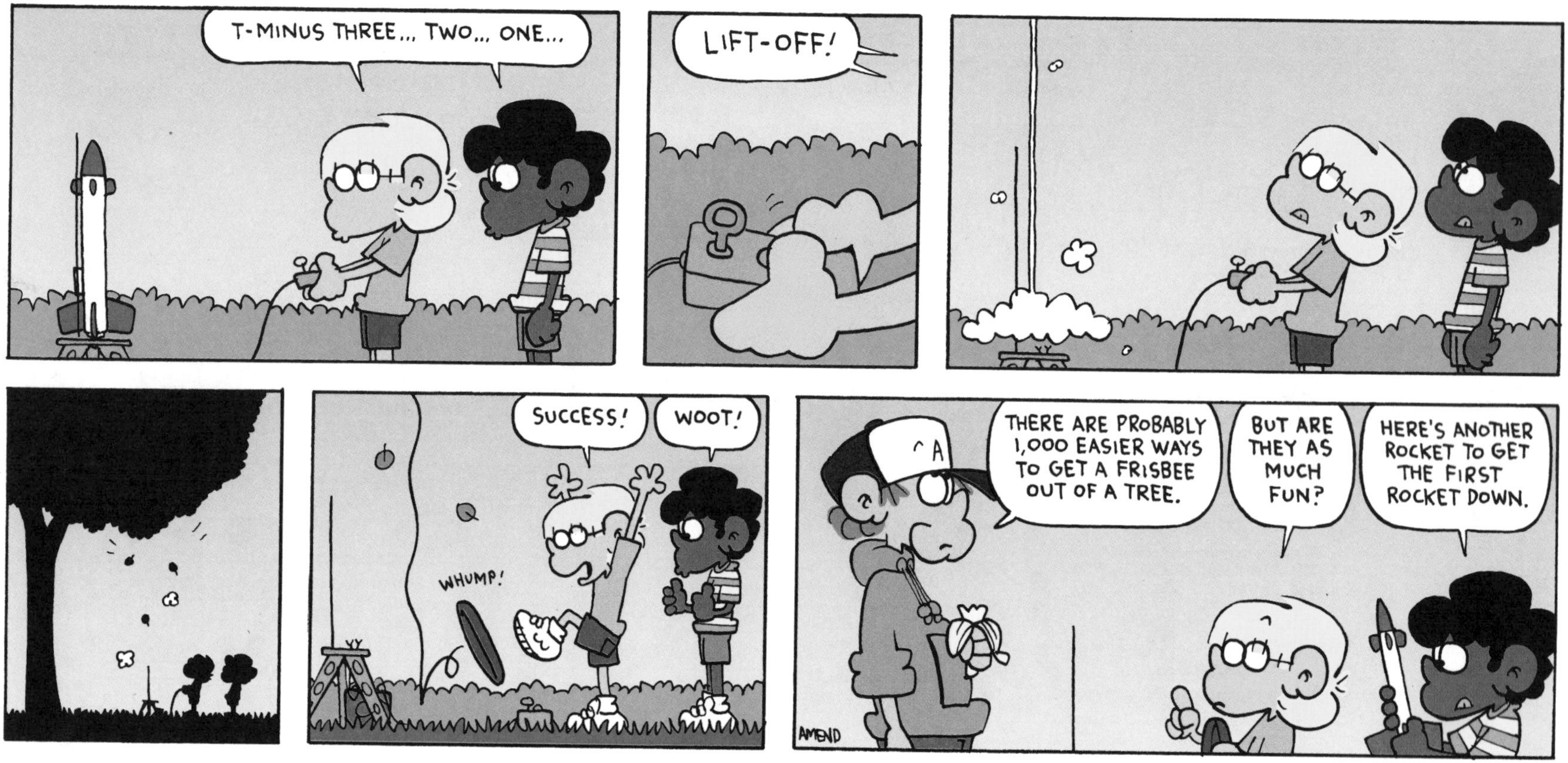

T-MINUS THREE... TWO... ONE...
LIFT-OFF!
SUCCESS!
WOOT!
WHUMP!
AMEND
THERE ARE PROBABLY 1,000 EASIER WAYS TO GET A FRISBEE OUT OF A TREE.
BUT ARE THEY AS MUCH FUN?
HERE'S ANOTHER ROCKET TO GET THE FIRST ROCKET DOWN.

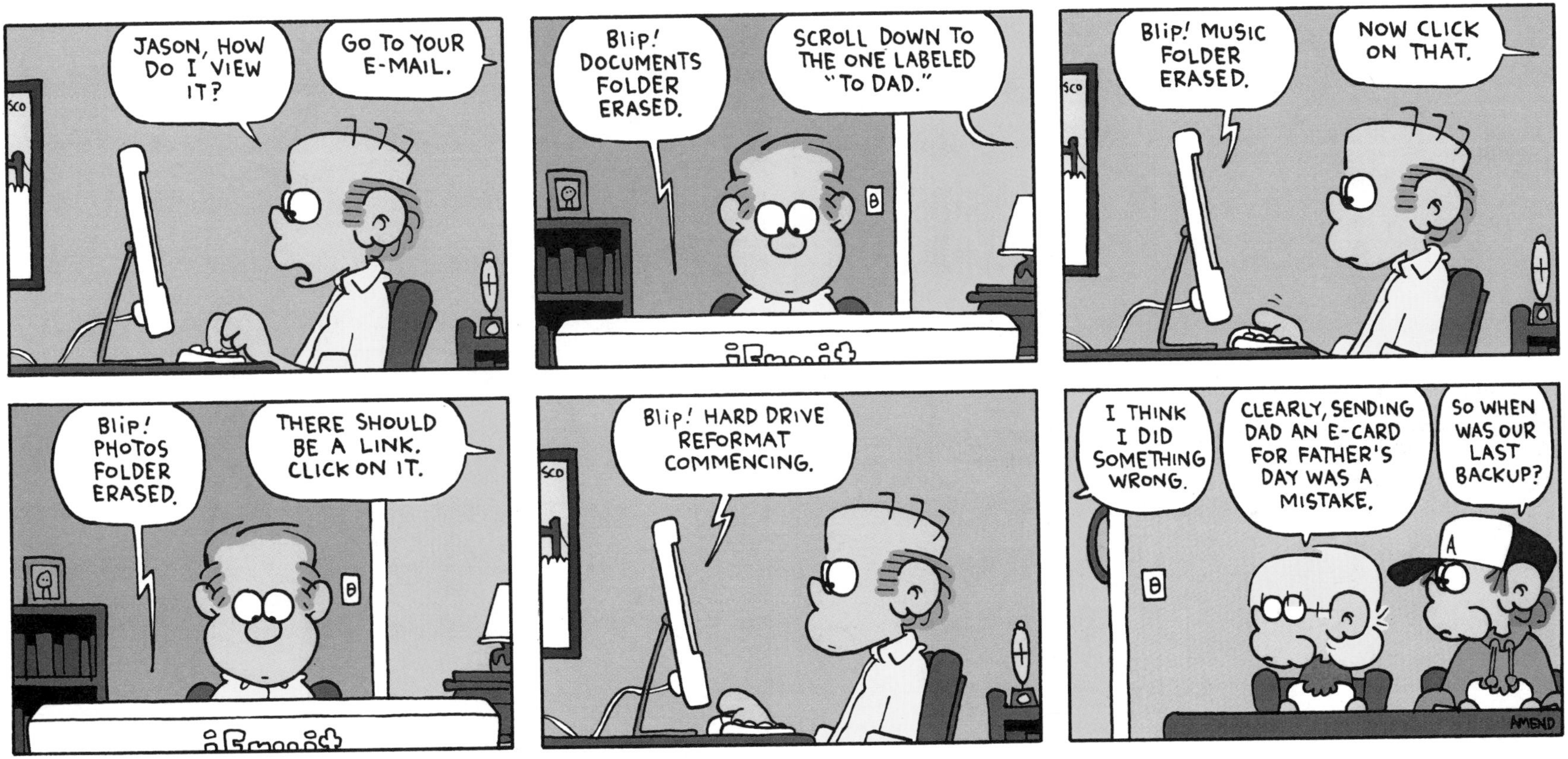
JASON, HOW DO I VIEW IT?
GO TO YOUR E-MAIL.
Blip! DOCUMENTS FOLDER ERASED.
SCROLL DOWN TO THE ONE LABELED "TO DAD."
Blip! MUSIC FOLDER ERASED.
NOW CLICK ON THAT.
Blip! PHOTOS FOLDER ERASED.
THERE SHOULD BE A LINK. CLICK ON IT.
Blip! HARD DRIVE REFORMAT COMMENCING.
I THINK I DID SOMETHING WRONG.
CLEARLY, SENDING DAD AN E-CARD FOR FATHER'S DAY WAS A MISTAKE.
SO WHEN WAS OUR LAST BACKUP?
AMEND

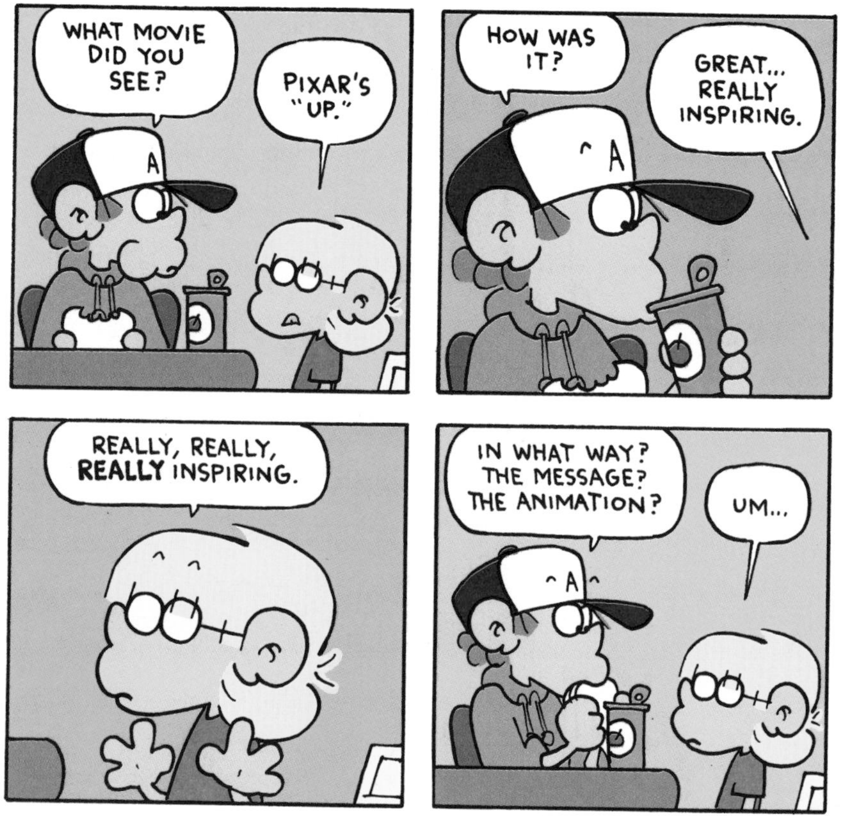
WHAT MOVIE DID YOU SEE?
PIXAR'S "UP."
HOW WAS IT?
GREAT... REALLY INSPIRING.
REALLY, REALLY, **REALLY** INSPIRING.
IN WHAT WAY? THE MESSAGE? THE ANIMATION?
UM...

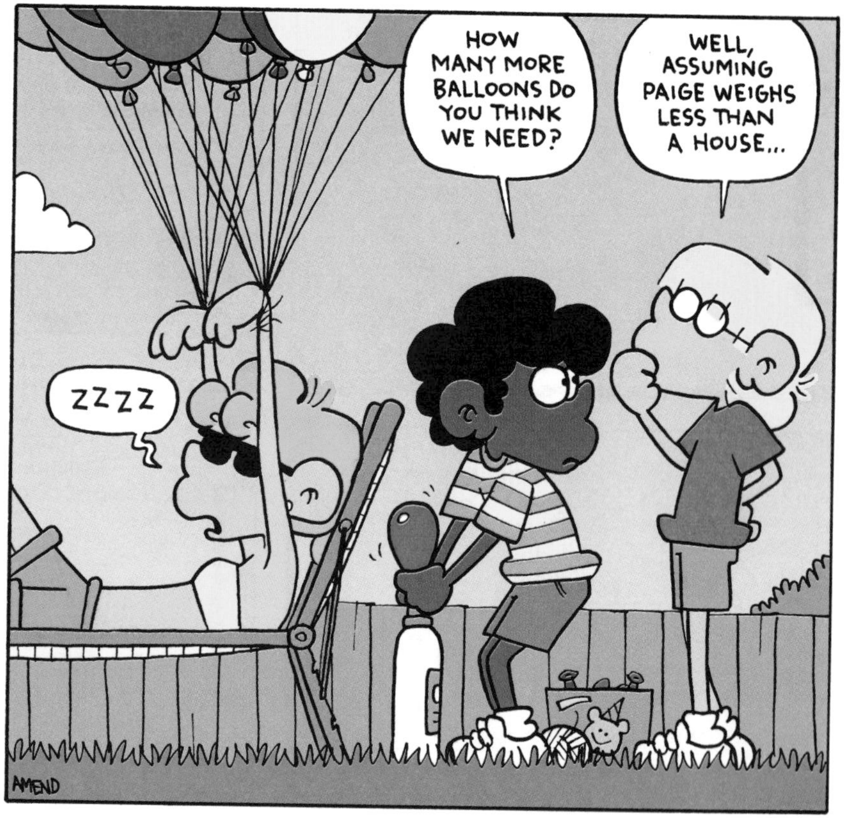
HOW MANY MORE BALLOONS DO YOU THINK WE NEED?
WELL, ASSUMING PAIGE WEIGHS LESS THAN A HOUSE...
ZZZZ
AMEND

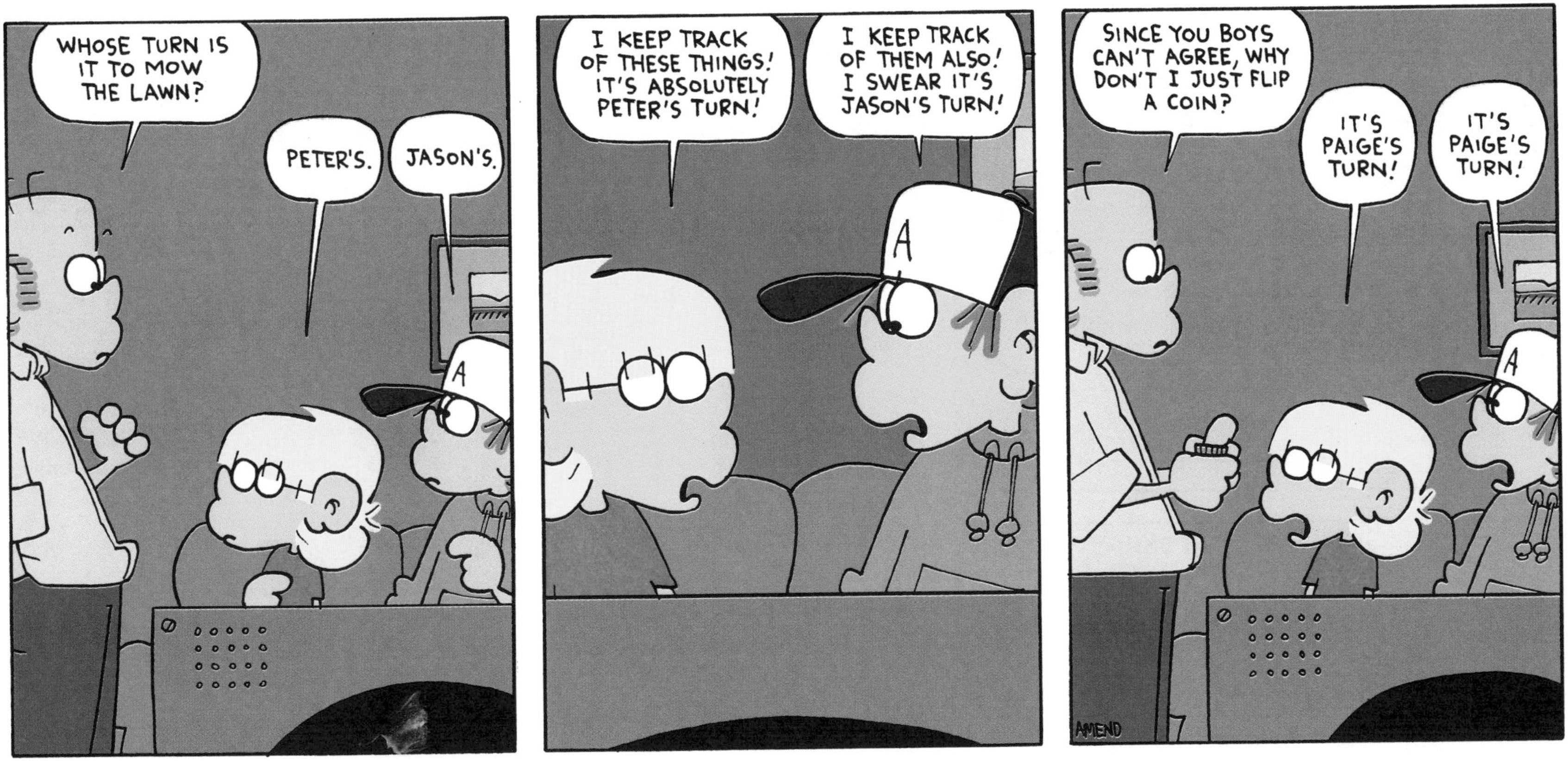
WHOSE TURN IS IT TO MOW THE LAWN?
PETER'S.
JASON'S.
I KEEP TRACK OF THESE THINGS! IT'S ABSOLUTELY PETER'S TURN!
I KEEP TRACK OF THEM ALSO! I SWEAR IT'S JASON'S TURN!
SINCE YOU BOYS CAN'T AGREE, WHY DON'T I JUST FLIP A COIN?
IT'S PAIGE'S TURN!
IT'S PAIGE'S TURN!
AMEND

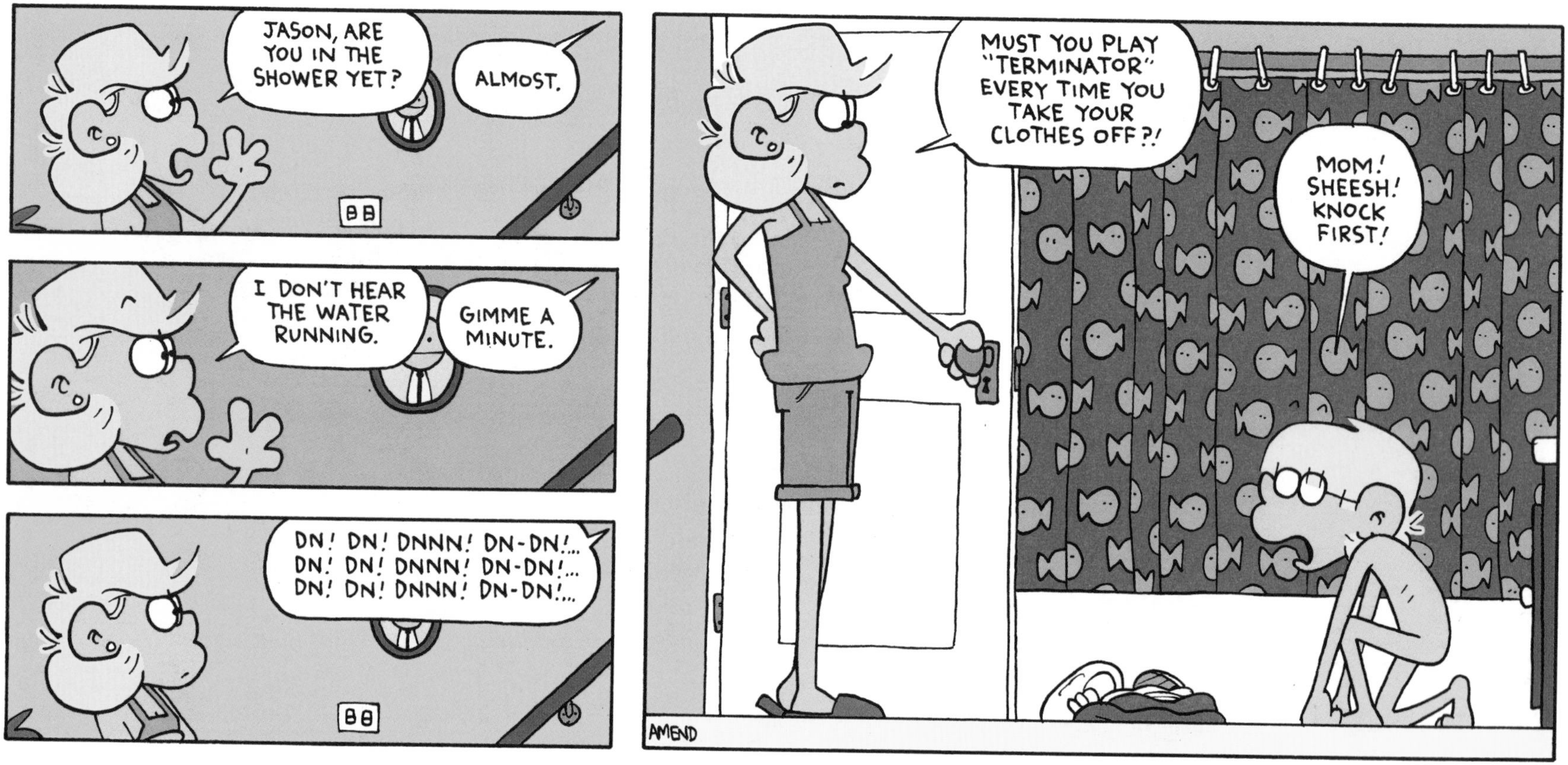
JASON, ARE YOU IN THE SHOWER YET?
ALMOST.
I DON'T HEAR THE WATER RUNNING.
GIMME A MINUTE.
DN! DN! DNNN! DN-DN!... DN! DN! DNNN! DN-DN!... DN! DN! DNNN! DN-DN!...
MUST YOU PLAY "TERMINATOR" EVERY TIME YOU TAKE YOUR CLOTHES OFF?!
MOM! SHEESH! KNOCK FIRST!
AMEND

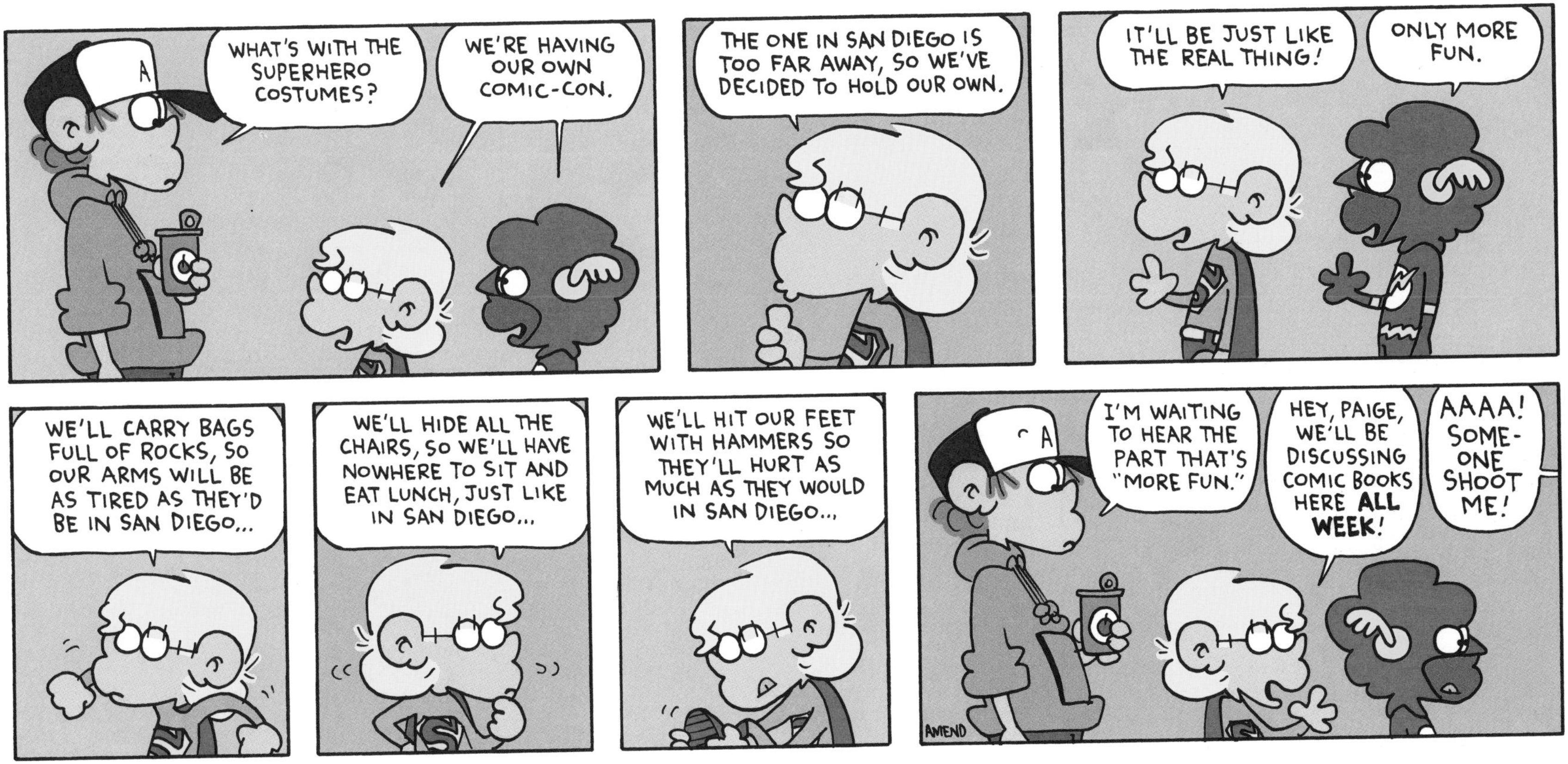
WHAT'S WITH THE SUPERHERO COSTUMES?
WE'RE HAVING OUR OWN COMIC-CON.
THE ONE IN SAN DIEGO IS TOO FAR AWAY, SO WE'VE DECIDED TO HOLD OUR OWN.
IT'LL BE JUST LIKE THE REAL THING!
ONLY MORE FUN.
WE'LL CARRY BAGS FULL OF ROCKS, SO OUR ARMS WILL BE AS TIRED AS THEY'D BE IN SAN DIEGO...
WE'LL HIDE ALL THE CHAIRS, SO WE'LL HAVE NOWHERE TO SIT AND EAT LUNCH, JUST LIKE IN SAN DIEGO...
WE'LL HIT OUR FEET WITH HAMMERS SO THEY'LL HURT AS MUCH AS THEY WOULD IN SAN DIEGO...
I'M WAITING TO HEAR THE PART THAT'S "MORE FUN."
HEY, PAIGE, WE'LL BE DISCUSSING COMIC BOOKS HERE **ALL WEEK**!
AAAA! SOME-ONE SHOOT ME!
AMEND

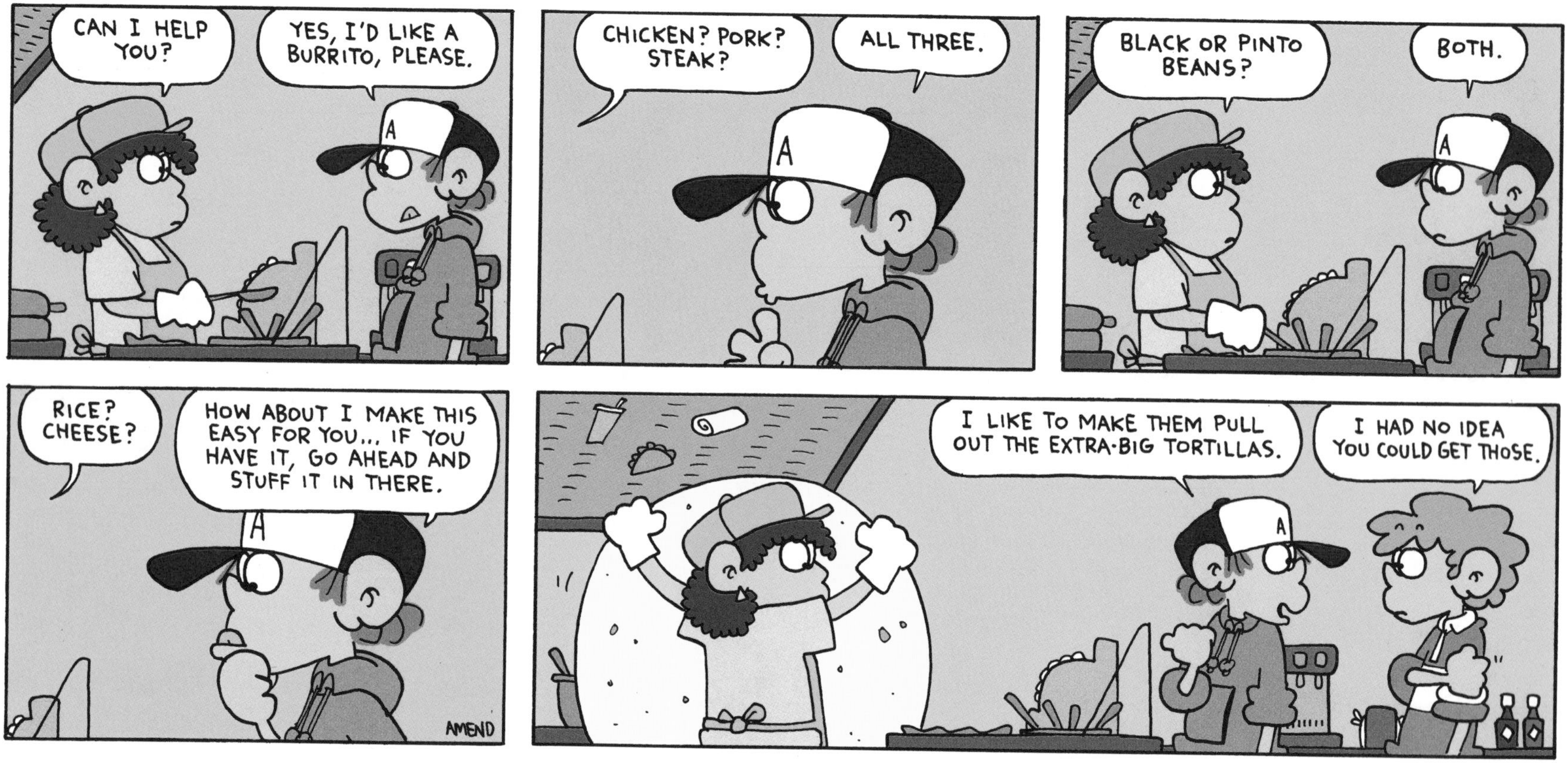
CAN I HELP YOU?
YES, I'D LIKE A BURRITO, PLEASE.
CHICKEN? PORK? STEAK?
ALL THREE.
BLACK OR PINTO BEANS?
BOTH.
RICE? CHEESE?
HOW ABOUT I MAKE THIS EASY FOR YOU... IF YOU HAVE IT, GO AHEAD AND STUFF IT IN THERE.
AMEND
I LIKE TO MAKE THEM PULL OUT THE EXTRA-BIG TORTILLAS.
I HAD NO IDEA YOU COULD GET THOSE.

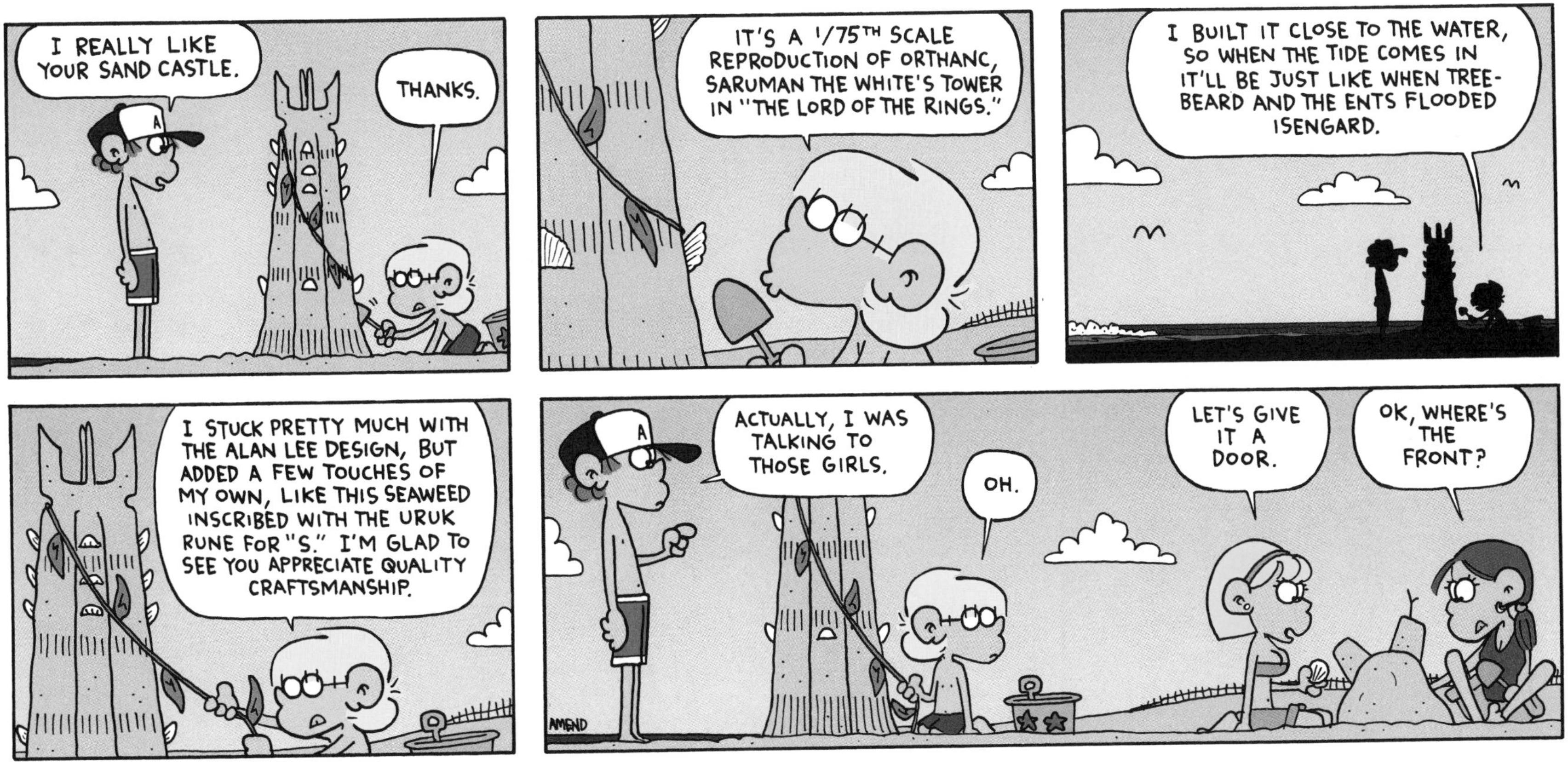
I REALLY LIKE YOUR SAND CASTLE.
THANKS.
IT'S A 1/75TH SCALE REPRODUCTION OF ORTHANC, SARUMAN THE WHITE'S TOWER IN "THE LORD OF THE RINGS."
I BUILT IT CLOSE TO THE WATER, SO WHEN THE TIDE COMES IN IT'LL BE JUST LIKE WHEN TREE-BEARD AND THE ENTS FLOODED ISENGARD.
I STUCK PRETTY MUCH WITH THE ALAN LEE DESIGN, BUT ADDED A FEW TOUCHES OF MY OWN, LIKE THIS SEAWEED INSCRIBED WITH THE URUK RUNE FOR "S." I'M GLAD TO SEE YOU APPRECIATE QUALITY CRAFTSMANSHIP.
ACTUALLY, I WAS TALKING TO THOSE GIRLS.
OH.
LET'S GIVE IT A DOOR.
OK, WHERE'S THE FRONT?
AMEND

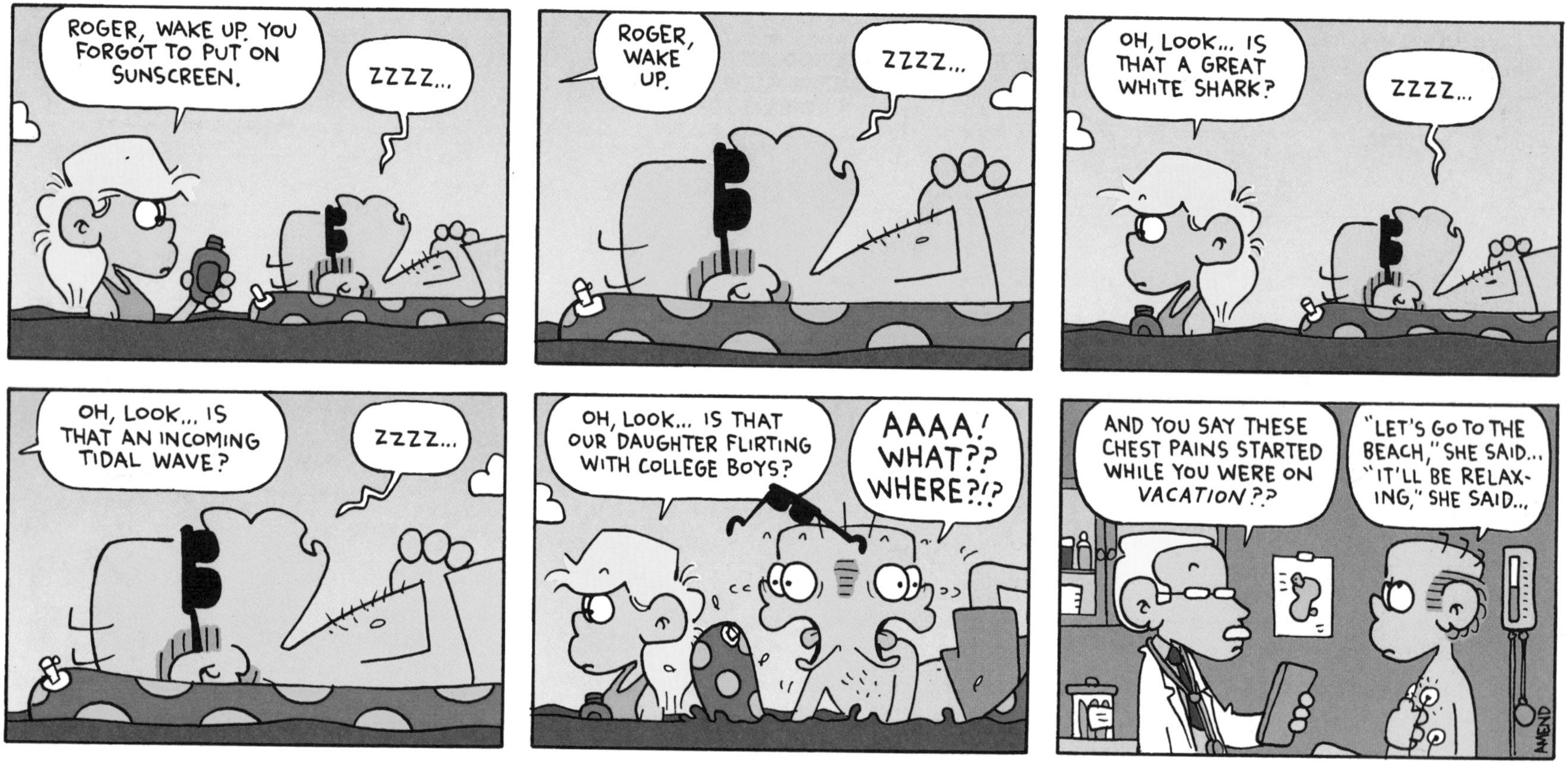
ROGER, WAKE UP. YOU FORGOT TO PUT ON SUNSCREEN.
ZZZZ...
ROGER, WAKE UP.
ZZZZ...
OH, LOOK... IS THAT A GREAT WHITE SHARK?
ZZZZ...
OH, LOOK... IS THAT AN INCOMING TIDAL WAVE?
ZZZZ...
OH, LOOK... IS THAT OUR DAUGHTER FLIRTING WITH COLLEGE BOYS?
AAAA! WHAT?? WHERE?!?
AND YOU SAY THESE CHEST PAINS STARTED WHILE YOU WERE ON *VACATION*??
"LET'S GO TO THE BEACH," SHE SAID... "IT'LL BE RELAXING," SHE SAID...
AMEND